SCHOLA LATINA

BOOK II

G͎H
GLOSSAHOUSE
WILMORE, KY
www.glossahouse.com

Schola Latina Book II

© GlossaHouse, 2023

All rights reserved. No part of this work may be reproduced or transmitted in any form or by any means, electronic or mechanical, including photocopying and recording, or by means of any information storage or retrieval system, except as may be expressly permitted by the 1976 Copyright Act or in writing from the publisher. Requests for permission should be addressed in writing to:

GlossaHouse, LLC
110 Callis Circle
Wilmore, KY 40390

Publisher's Cataloging-in-Publication Data

Stephenson, Ken (revised by Thomas Caucutt and Ruth Baldwin)
    Schola Latina Book II / Wilmore, KY: GlossaHouse, 2023

xvi, 230 pages ; 22 cm.– (LAETA— Latin Ancient Educational Tools & Aids)

ISBN: 978-1-63663-065-6 (paperback)

Library of Congress Control Number:

Corrected Version, June 2024

Cover Design by T. Michael W. Halcomb

Book Layout and volume editing by Thomas Caucutt and Ruth Baldwin

Original content by Ken Stephenson who grants GlossaHouse the rights to publish *Schola Latina I & II*.

Select maps used with permission from Ancient World Mapping Center at https://awmc.unc.edu/.

Schola Latina

Book II

By

Ken Stephenson

Revised by

Thomas Caucutt   Ruth Baldwin

GlossaHouse
Wilmore, KY
www.glossahouse.com

LAETA
Latin Ancient Educational Tools & Aids

SERIES EDITOR
T. Michael W. Halcomb

LAETA

The Latin term LAETA is an adjective that means "fertile" or "welcoming," especially when describing land. It is also a term that captures the link between this series and its Hebrew (HA'ARETS) and Greek (AGROS) counterparts also bearing land-related names and published by GlossaHouse. In keeping with those series, LAETA functions as an acronym: Latin Ancient Educational Tools & Aids. This series exists because, while there are many great resources on Latin, more can and always will need to be created. Thus, LAETA welcomes new and innovative works, those that make a contribution, however big or small, to the journey of learning Latin. The long-term aim is to create a tiered curriculum suite featuring innovative readers, grammars, specialized studies, and similar resources that will both encourage and foster the use of Latin. Additionally, the LAETA series endeavors to facilitate the creation and publication of innovative and inexpensive print and digital resources within the context of the global community.

Table of Contents

Preface ix
Pronunciation xi
At the Beginning of Class xii
Prayers, Creeds and Hymns xiii

Lectiōnēs

I   Review of 1ˢᵗ Declension and 1st Conjugation . . 2
II   Review of 2ⁿᵈ Declension and Adjectives; *ego*. . 8
III   Review of 2ⁿᵈ Conjugation; Direct Objects; *tū*. 14
IV   More Direct Objects; Numbers. 17
V   3ʳᵈ Declension. 23
VI   Adverbs; Infinitives; *is, ea, id* 29
VII   The Genitive, *ūnus* 37
VIII   Prepositions (+Acc.); *duo* 43
IX   The Dative Case; *trēs* 47
X   Prepositions (+Abl.); *hic, haec, hoc* 53
XI   2-Case Prepositions; *ille, illa, illud* 59
XII   Question Words 65
XIII   3rd Conjugation. 73
XIV   Imperfect Tense 79
XV   More Imperfect Tense 85
XVI   Vestīmenta 91
XVII   Tempora Annī. 97
XVIII Mensēs 103
XIX   Quod Erit Erit 109
XX   Perfect Tense 115
XXI   3rd Conjugation -iō Verbs 121
XXII   4 Conjugation 127
XXIII 3rd Declension Adjectives. 133
XXIV Commands 139

Glossary (Latin to English) 145
Glossary (English to Latin) 153
Numbers 160
Vocabulary by Lectiō 161
Paradigms 165
Dicta 171
Colloquia 173
Timeline 177
Map of the Roman Empire 179
Historia. 181

SCHOLA LATINA II

by Ken Stephenson

revised by Ruth Baldwin
& Thomas Caucutt

Preface

Where did my Latin education, starting so well as it did, go wrong? . . . I think it would have helped me very much if I had ever been got into the habit of speaking Latin, if only to say "Please" and "Thank you" and "Pass the mustard."

– Dorothy Sayers

The need for the present volume arises from my agreement with Dorothy Sayers' comments on learning Latin. In order for a language to become natural and spontaneous with a student, it must become a *language*, which means, as Latin scholars know, it must become a matter of the tongue, the *lingua*. It must be on the lips during the course of a normal day. In the first volume of this method, the student learned the names of familiar objects – animals, parts of the body, and household items – and everyday verbs, e.g., *to eat* rather than *to seize*. In this volume, the student will learn the Latin names of articles of clothing, foods, and fun activities, as well as some basic transitive verbs, e.g., *to know, to have, to hold*.

This book also continues with more useful conversational phrases that would put the language onto the tongue even before the mastery of grammar. Students will learn how to give the time and date, to talk about seasons, and to complain about a cold. And they'll learn how to say "Please pass the butter." Make these conversations a part of your routine at home, and soon Latin will become a living language for you, despite rumors you've heard to the contrary.

The history summaries correspond to stories from *Famous Men of Rome* by John H. Haaren and A. B. Poland and are meant for review only. The students should at least read the stories from the book or hear them read and should be encouraged, in order to reinforce the material and to make the learning more fun, to act the stories out or to illustrate them.

Make sure to do all the exercises: the tedious, the tough, and the fun. Above all, practice the forms – out loud. A list of all forms, by *lectiō*, is provided on pages 165-168. Practice saying them – out loud – at least twice a week. And have I mentioned that you should say them out loud? The student who faithfully rehearses the forms as if they were nonsense poetry will much more easily make his way down the road to mastery of Latin than will the student who thinks to himself that it all looks pretty straightforward. Take it from the voice of experience: say them out loud.

Eāmus!

Pronunciation

Several different methods of pronouncing Latin exist. The following notes correspond to what is known as "classical" pronunciation.

Vowels

If you were to say the word "no" very slowly, you would discover that your pronunciation of the vowel "o" probably started something like "uh" and ended something like "oo." Such glides do not occur in single vowels in Latin. There are six vowels in Latin, and these six vowels may be pronounced either long or short. A macron (a small horizontal mark above the vowel) indicates a long vowel. A short vowel has no macron. Below are each of the six Latin vowels, both short and long, with an English word to help guide your pronunciation:

Short vowels		**Long vowels**	
a	as in *a*lter	ā	as in f*a*ther (twice as long as short *a*)
e	as in p*e*t	ē	as in th*ey*
i	as in p*i*n	ī	as in sk*i*
o	as in *o*ff	ō	as in t*o*tal
u	as in p*u*t	ū	as in r*u*le
y	as in p*u*t	ȳ	as in r*u*le

Macrons

Macrons are small horizontal bars written above long vowels in Latin. Macrons indicate the proper pronunciation and length of vowels and give important clues to a word's use & meaning within a sentence.

Diphthongs

Diphthongs are vowel combinations. Below are some common to Latin:

ae	like *i* in k*i*te
au	like *ou* in l*ou*d
ei	like *e* in h*e*y
eu	like *eu* in f*eu*d
ui	like *uey* in gl*uey*

Consonants

The consonants are pronounced as in English with the following exceptions:

b	as in English (except before *s* and *t,* where it is pronounced *p)*
c	always like *c* in *c*ar
ch	always like *k* in *k*ite
g	always like *g* in *g*ap
i	like *y* in *y*et (only when it begins a word or precedes a vowel)
ph	like *ph* in *ph*one
r	trilled or rolled
s	always like *s* in *s*ing
th	like *t* in *t*ell
v	like *w* in *w*ine

Accents & Syllables

The Latin accent is a musical one: accented syllables are spoken with a higher pitch than are other syllables and not necessarily with any more force.

In two-syllable words, the first syllable is always accented. In longer words, the accent comes either on the next-to-last syllable (if that one is long) or on the third-to-last syllable (if the next-to-last isn't long). Latin words are never stressed or accented on the last syllable.

audēmus	au·´dē·mus
iūra	´iū·ra
nostra	´nos·tra
dēfendere	dē·´fen·de·re

A syllable is long if it contains a long vowel (with a macron) or if it contains a vowel is followed by two consonants.

At the Beginning of Class

Magister:	Salvēte, discipulī.	Hello, students.
Discipulī:	Salvē, magister.	Hello, teacher.
Magister:	Surgite. Ōrēmus.	Stand up. Let's pray.
Omnēs:	Domine Deus, adiūvā nōs	Lord God, help us
	linguam Latīnam discere. Amen.	to learn the Latin language. Amen.
Omnēs:	Pater noster, quī in caelī es,	Our Father, You who are in heaven,
	sanctificētur nōmen tuum;	may Your name be made holy;
	veniat rēgnum tuum;	may Your kingdom come;
	fiat voluntās tua	may Your will be done
	sicut in caelō et in terrā.	on earth just as in heaven.
	Pānem nostrum supersubstantiālem	Our daily bread
	dā nōbīs hodiē,	give us today,
	et dimitte nōbīs debita nostra	and forgive us our debts
	sicut et nōs dimissimus debitōribus nostrīs;	just as we also forgive our debtors;
	et nē indūcās nōs in temptātiōnem,	and lead us not into temptation,
	sed līberā nōs ā malō. Amen.	but deliver us from evil. Amen.
Magister:	Grātiās, discipulī. Sedēte.	Thank you, students. Sit down.

Prayers, Creeds, and Hymns

Christus Vincit

Glōria Patrī

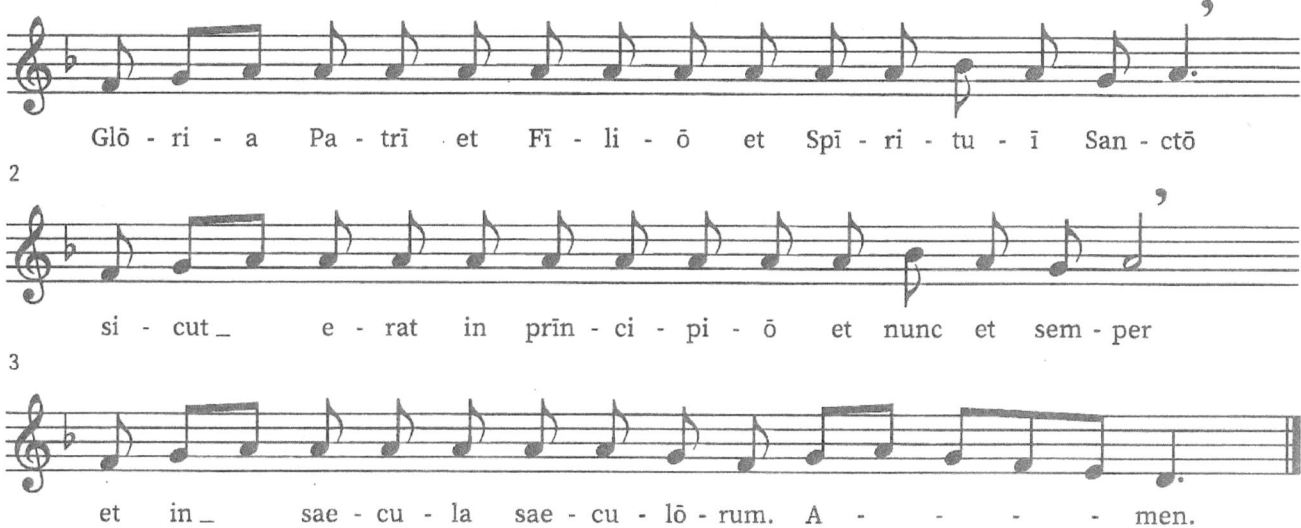

Sanctus and Benedictus

Symbolum Apostolicum (The Apostles' Creed)

Crēdō in Deum Patrem omnipotentem;	I believe in one God the Father almighty;
Creatōrem caelī et terrae.	Creator of the heaven and the earth,
Et in Iēsum Christum,	And in Jesus Christ
Fīlium euis ūnīcum, Dominum nostrum;	His only Son, our Lord;
quī conceptus est dē Spīritū Sanctō,	who was conceived of the Holy Spirit,
nātus ex Mariā virgine;	born of the virgin Mary;
passus sub Pontiō Pilatō,	He suffered under Pontius Pilate,
crucifixus, mortuus, et sepultus;	was crucified, dead, and buried;
descendit ad īnferna;	He descended into hell;
tertia diē resurrexit ā mortuīs;	on the third day He rose again from the dead;
ascendit ad caelōs;	He ascended to the heavens;
sedet ad dexteram	and is seated at the right hand
Deī Patris omnipotentis;	of God the Father almighty;
inde ventūrus est iūdicāre	from thence He shall come to judge
vīvōs et mortuōs	both the quick and the dead.
Crēdō in Spīritum Sanctum;	I believe in the Holy Spirit;
sanctam ecclēsiam catholicam;	the holy catholic church;
sanctōrum commūniōnem;	the communion of the saints;
remissiōnem peccatōrum;	the forgiveness of sins;
carnis resurrectiōnem;	the resurrection of the body;
vītam aeternam. Amen.	and the life everlasting. Amen.

Tē Deum

Tē Deum laudāmus;	We praise you, O God;
Tē Dominum cōnfitēmur.	We acclaim you, O Lord.
Tē aeternum Patrem	You, eternal Father,
omnis terra venerātur.	all the world worships.
Tibi omnēs angelī,	To you all angels,
Tibi caelī et ūniversae potestātēs,	To you the powers of heaven and the universe,
Tibi cherubim et seraphim	To you cherubim and seraphim
incessābilī vōce proclamant:	proclaim with unceasing voice:

Sanctus Sanctus Sanctus
    Dominus Deus sabaoth.
Plenī sunt caelī et terra
    māiestātis glōriae tuae.

Holy, holy, holy,
    Lord, God of Hosts,
heaven and earth are full
    of the majesty of your glory.

Tē gloriōsus apostolōrum chorus,
Tē prophetārum laudābilis numerus,
Tē martyrum candidātus laudat exercitus.
Tē per orbem terrārum
    sancta cōnfitētur ecclēsia,
Patrem immensae maiestātis.
Venerandum
tuum vērum et ūnicum Fīlium;
Sanctum quoque Paraclītum Spiritum.

You the glorious chorus of apostles,
You the noble fellowship of prophets,
You the white-robed army of martyrs praise.
You through the world
    the holy Church acclaims,
Father, of majesty unbounded.
Worthy of worship
is your true and only Son,
and the Holy Spirit, Comforter.

Tū Rēx glōriae Christe.
Tū Patris sempiternus es Fīlius.
Tū ad liberandum susceptūrus hominem,
nōn horruistī virginis ūterum.
Tū dēvictō mortis aculeō,
aperuistī crēdentibus rēgna caelōrum.
Tū ad dexteram Deī sedēs,
in glōria Patris.
Iūdex crēderis esse ventūrus.
Tē ergō quaesimus,
tuīs famulīs subvenī,
quōs pretiōsō sanguine rēdemistī.
Aeternā fac cum sanctīs tuīs
    in glōriā numerārī.

You, Christ, are the King of glory.
You are the eternal Son of the Father.
You when undertaking man's deliverance,
did not spurn the virgin's womb.
You, having overcome the sting of death,
opened the kingdom of heaven to believers.
You sit at God's right hand
in the glory of the Father.
You are believed to be coming as Judge.
We ask you then,
come down to your servants,
whom you have redeemed by your precious blood.
Make us to be numbered with your saints in
    eternal glory

I – Prīma   Nōmen: _____

I – Prīma lectiō (1 – First lesson)   **REVIEW**

I. Dictum

Audēmus iūra nostra dēfendere.   _____
(Alabama state motto)

II. Colloquium   *Latīnē*   *Anglicē*

Sextus:	Salvē! Quōmodō aestās erat?	Hi! How was the summer?
Iūlia:	Optimē! Et quōmodō tē habēs?	Great! And how are you?
Sextus:	Bene mē habeō.	I'm well.
		(see page 173 for other answers)

III. Verba renovanda (Vocabulary for review) – 1st Conjugation and 1st Declension

Latīnē	*Anglicē*	*Latīnē*	*Anglicē*	*Latīnē*	*Anglicē*
ambulō, ambulāre	to walk	agricola, -ae, m.	farmer	nauta, -ae, m.	sailor
amō, amāre	to love, to like	aqua, -ae, f.	water	patella, -ae, f.	plate
arō, arāre	to plow	aquila, -ae, f.	eagle	patria, -ae, f.	fatherland, country
cantō, cantāre	to sing	charta, -ae, f.	paper		
cēnō, cēnāre	to dine, to eat	culīna, -ae, f.	kitchen	pecūnia, -ae, f.	money
cōgitō, cōgitāre	to think	corōna, -ae, f.	crown	puella, -ae, f.	girl
dubitō, dubitāre	to doubt, to be uncertain	culpa, -ae, f.	fault	rēgīna, -ae, f.	queen
		discipula, -ae, f.	student	Rōma, -ae, f.	Rome
dūrō, dūrāre	to endure	ecclēsia, -ae, f.	church	sella, -ae, f.	chair
errō, errāre	to err, to wander, to be mistaken	fēmina, -ae, f.	woman	silva, -ae, f.	forest
		fenestra, -ae, f.	window	stella, -ae, f.	star
festīnō, festīnāre	to hurry	fīlia, -ae, f.	daughter	terra, -ae, f.	land, earth
imperō, imperāre	to rule, to order	furca, -ae, f.	fork	ursa, -ae, f.	bear
intrō, intrāre	to enter	Gallia, -ae, f.	Gaul	via, -ae, f.	road, way
iūdicō, iūdicāre	to judge	gallīna, -ae, f.	chicken	victōria, -ae, f.	victory
labōrō, labōrāre	to work	glōria, -ae, f.	glory	vīta, -ae, f.	life
nāvigō, nāvigāre	to sail	herba, -ae, f.	plant, herb		
ōrō, ōrāre	to pray, to speak	Hispania, -ae, f.	Spain		
peccō, peccāre	to sin	hōra, -ae, f.	hour		
pugnō, pugnāre	to fight	iānua, -ae, f.	door		
recitō, recitāre	to recite	īnsula, -ae, f.	island		
rēgnō, rēgnāre	to reign	Ītalia, -ae, f.	Italy		
stō, stāre	to stand	lingua, -ae, f.	language, tongue		
superō, superāre	to overcome, to conquer	lūna, -ae, f.	moon		
		magistra, -ae, f.	teacher		
tardō, tardāre	to be slow	Maria, -ae, f.	Mary		
volō, volāre	to fly	mēnsa, -ae, f.	table		

1. What detail distinguishes 1st conjugation? _____

2. What detail distinguishes 1st declension? _____

I – Prīma   Nōmen:

IV. Grammatica

Here are the forms you learned for present tense of 1ˢᵗ-conjugation verbs in Book I.

	Singular	Plural		Personal Endings Singular	Plural
1ˢᵗ person	amō	amāmus		-ō	-mus
2ⁿᵈ person	amās	amātis		-s	-tis
3ʳᵈ person	amat	amant		-t	-nt

A <u>verb</u> is a word that expresses action or state of being. The <u>subject</u> of a sentence tells who or what is acting or being. In Latin, <u>pronouns</u> (words that replace nouns) are built into the ends of verbs as <u>personal endings</u>. Pronouns are distinguished by <u>person</u> (1ˢᵗ, 2ⁿᵈ, or 3ʳᵈ) and <u>number</u> (singular or plural). <u>Conjugating a verb</u> means adding personal endings to a <u>stem</u> to indicate the person and number of the pronoun.

The second principal part of a verb is its infinitive, translated *to +* ____, e.g., *amāre = to love*.

Amāre is a 1ˢᵗ-conjugation verb. To find the stem of a 1ˢᵗ-conjugation verb, drop the *–re* from the <u>infinitive</u>. For example, the stem of *amō, amāre* is *amā-*. To conjugate a verb in present tense, add the personal endings to the stem. For 1ˢᵗ conjugation, remember that the first-person singular form drops the final *ā* of the stem, e.g.: *amō*, not *amāō*.

Here are the forms you learned for 1ˢᵗ declension in Book I.

	Singular	Plural		Case Endings Singular	Plural
nominative	ursa	ursae		-a	-ae
genitive	ursae	ursārum		-ae	-ārum
dative	ursae	ursīs		-ae	-īs
accusative	ursam	ursās		-am	-ās
ablative	ursā	ursīs		-ā	-īs

A <u>noun</u> is a word that names a person, place, thing, or idea. <u>Declining a noun</u> means adding <u>case endings</u> to a <u>stem</u>. *Ursa, -ae, f.* is a 1ˢᵗ-declension noun. To find the stem of any Latin noun, drop the <u>genitive singular case ending</u> (the second form in the <u>declension</u>). For example, the stem of **ursa, -ae, f.** above, would be **urs-**. To decline a noun, write the <u>nominative singular form</u>; then add the rest of the case endings to the stem, column by column, top to bottom.

A <u>sentence</u> must have a subject and a verb. In Latin, a complete sentence may have only one word since a pronoun is built into every conjugated verb form. Latin also uses two-word sentences: one <u>subject noun</u> and one verb. The subject noun must be in the nominative case; the noun and the verb must agree in person and number. In a sentence that has a subject noun, the verb will *always* be 3ʳᵈ person whether singular or plural, to agree with its subject noun, e.g. *Ursa stat. Ursae stant.* It is most common in Latin for the verb to be the last word in the sentence. A linking verb, however, may stand at the beginning or in the middle of a sentence, e.g.: *Est puella. Puella est rēgīna.*

I – Prīma   Nōmen:

V. Historia (*Famous Men of Rome*, Chapter XIV)

Between 264-241 BC, Rome begins the first of three wars with Carthage. These are known as the Punic Wars since the founders of Carthage were Phoenicians, a people the Romans called *Punicī*. The Roman general, Marcus Atilius Regulus, defeats a large Carthaginian navy, but he is then defeated in Africa and is captured by an army led by Xanthippus. He recommends that the Roman Senate reject peace terms, even though doing so means he must remain a prisoner.

VI. Dēlēgāta

A. *Scrībe* the conjugation of <u>amō, amāre</u> in present tense two times.

1. _____ _____   2. _____ _____

   _____ _____   _____ _____

   _____ _____   _____ _____

B. *Scrībe* the personal endings for present tense two times.

1. _____ _____   2. _____ _____

   _____ _____   _____ _____

   _____ _____   _____ _____

C. *Scrībe* the declension of <u>ursa, -ae, f.</u> two times.

1. _____ _____   2. _____ _____

   _____ _____   _____ _____

   _____ _____   _____ _____

   _____ _____   _____ _____

   _____ _____   _____ _____

D. *Variātiōnēs* (Variations): *Recitā* these sentences. Notice changes that make each one plural.

    a. Ursa stat.   Ursae stant.   (The bear stands. The bears stand.)
    b. Agricola stat.   Agricolae stant.   (The farmer stands. The farmers stand.)
    c. Ecclēsia stat.   Ecclēsiae stant.   (The church stands. The churches stand.)
    d. Discipula stat.   Discipulae stant.   (The student stands. The students stand.)
    e. Iānua stat.   Iānuae stant.   (The door stands. The doors stand.)
    f. Mēnsa stat.   Mēnsae stant.   (The table stands. The tables stand.)

I – **Prīma**   **Nōmen:** _____

E. Translate these sentences (from Latin to English or from English to Latin).

1. Puella ambulat. _____

2. Aquila cēnat. _____

3. Fīliae cōgitant. _____

4. Rēgīna rēgnat. _____

5. Discipulae recitant. _____

6. Agricola arat. _____

7. Chickens fight. _____

8. The hours are slow. _____

9. The country conquers. _____

10. The church speaks. _____

11. Eagles are flying. _____

12. Rome endures. _____

F. Fill in the blanks.

1. Personal endings indicate the _____ and _____ of the subject of a verb.

2. To find the stem of 1st-conjugation verbs, drop the _____ of the _____.

3. Adding personal endings to the stem of a verb is called _____.

4. Adding case endings to the stem of a noun is called _____.

5. To find the stem of any noun, drop the _____ _____ case ending.

6. The subject and verb of a sentence must agree in _____ and _____.

G. Translate these *verba* and phrases.

1. prīma lectiō _____ 2. variātiōnēs _____

3. verba renovanda _____

I – Prīma   Nōmen:

4. Audēmus iūra nostra dēfendere. _____

H. *Scribe* **these sentences** *Latine.*

1. We are loving. _____   6. You all are doubting. _____

2. You enter. _____   7. They do judge. _____

3. We hurry. _____   8. The road wanders. _____

4. The girl speaks. _____ 9. Mary works. _____

5. They are slow. _____   10. The sailors sail. _____

I. Conjugate these verbs in present tense. *Scribe* **the meaning of each in the blank by it.**

1. arō, arāre _____   2. rēgnō, rēgnāre _____

_____ _____   _____ _____

_____ _____   _____ _____

_____ _____   _____ _____

3. dūrō, dūrāre _____   4. peccō, peccāre _____

_____ _____   _____ _____

_____ _____   _____ _____

_____ _____   _____ _____

I – Prīma   Nōmen: _____

J. Crossword Puzzle. When you complete this puzzle, the shaded letters, when read row by row from top to bottom, will tell you for what you should aim: _____

RĒCTĒ

1. forests
4. you (sing.) eat
6. plates
7. land
8. crown
10. table
12. language
13. they sail
15. I err
16. we love

DEORSUM

2. I rule
3. life
4. papers
5. chairs
8. kitchens
9. sailor
11. you all plow
14. road

K. Historia. Review the history and fill in the blanks.

1. What are the three wars with Carthage called? _____

2. Why do they have this name? _____
   _____

3. What are the dates of the first of these wars? _____

4. What Roman general lands in Africa to attack the Carthaginians? _____

5. How does he show bravery after being taken prisoner? _____
   _____

6

II – Secunda   Nōmen: _____

II – Secunda lectiō (2 – Second lesson)   **MORE REVIEW**

I. Dictum

Hannibal ad portās! _____

II. Colloquium   *Latīnē*   *Anglicē*

Līvia:	Ubi habitās?	Where do you live?
Gāius:	In Alabāmā.	In Alabama.
		(See p. 173 for more states)

III. Verba nova

Latīnē	*Anglicē*	*Scrībe tōtum verbum Latīnum.*	*Dērīvātī*
angelus, -ī, m.	angel	_____	_____
thronus, -ī, m.	throne	_____	_____

Verba renovanda – 2nd Declension and Adjectives

Latine	*Anglice*	*Latine*	*Anglice*	*Latine*	*Anglice*
agnus, -ī, m.	lamb	mendācium, -ī, n.	lie	verbum, -ī, n.	word
amīcus, -ī, m.	friend	mundus, -ī, m.	world	vīnum, -ī, n.	wine
annus, -ī, m.	year	mūrus, -ī, m.	wall		
bellum, -ī, n.	war	nāsus, -ī, m.	nose	**Adjectives**	
brācchium, -ī, n.	arm	nimbus, -ī, m.	cloud	aeternus, -a, -um	eternal
caelum, -ī, n.	sky, heaven	nuntius, -ī, m.	message, messenger	altus, -a, -um	high, deep
calamus, -ī, m.	pen			angustus, -a, -um	narrow
capillus, -ī, m.	hair	oculus, -ī. m.	eye	antīquus, -a, -um	old, ancient
Christus, -ī, m.	Christ	oppidum, -ī, n.	town	bellus, -a, -um	pretty
cubiculum, -ī, n.	bedroom	peccātum, -ī, n.	sin	bonus, -a, -um	good
culter, cultrī, m.	knife	pōculum, -ī, n.	cup	lātus, -a, -um	wide
Deus, -ī, m.	God	porcus, -ī, m.	pig	magnus, -a, -um	large, great
digitus, -ī, m.	finger, toe	praemium, -ī, n.	reward	malus, -a, -um	bad
discipulus, -ī, m.	student	puer, puerī, m.	boy	meus, -a, um	my
dominus, -ī, m.	lord, master	puteus, -ī, m.	well	multus, -a, -um	much, many
dōnum, -ī, n.	gift	rēgnum, -ī, n.	kingdom	novus, -a, -um	new
equus, -ī, m.	horse	servus, -ī, m.	slave	optimus, -a, -um	best
exedrium, -ī. n.	living room	signum, -ī, n.	sign, standard	parvus, -a, -um	small
fīlius, -ī, m.	son	solum, -ī, n.	floor	prīmus, -a, -um	first
focus, -ī, m.	fireplace, family	speculum, -ī, n.	mirror	sanctus, -a, -um	holy
gaudium, -ī, n.	joy	stīlus, -ī, m.	pencil	secundus, -a, um	second
gladius, -ī, m.	sword	stomachus, -ī, m.	stomach	tōtus, -a, -um	whole
lectus, -ī, m.	bed, couch	taurus, -ī, m.	bull	tūtus, -a, -um	safe
liber, librī, m.	book	tēlum, -ī, n.	weapon	tuus, -a, -um	your
magister, magistrī, m.	teacher	vallum, -ī, n.	wall, rampart		

II – Secunda   Nōmen:

IV. Grammatica

Here are the forms for 2nd-declension nouns from Book I:

Masculine	Singular	Plural
nominative	nimb**us**	nimb**ī**
genitive	nimb**ī**	nimb**ōrum**
dative	nimb**ō**	nimb**īs**
accusative	nimb**um**	nimb**ōs**
ablative	nimb**ō**	nimb**īs**

Case Endings

	Singular	Plural
	-us	-ī
	-ī	-ōrum
	-ō	-īs
	-um	-ōs
	-ō	-īs

Neuter	Singular	Plural
nominative	dōn**um**	dōn**a**
genitive	dōn**ī**	dōn**ōrum**
dative	dōn**ō**	dōn**īs**
accusative	dōnum	dōn**a**
ablative	dōn**ō**	dōn**īs**

	Singular	Plural
	-um	-a
	-ī	-ōrum
	-ō	-īs
	-um	-a
	-ō	-īs

Latin nouns are distinguished by <u>gender</u>, <u>number</u>, and <u>case</u>. Most 1st-declension nouns are feminine. (Exceptions such as *agricola* and *nauta* are masculine.) Latin nouns ending in *–us* and *–er* in the nominative singular are <u>2nd-declension masculine</u>. Latin nouns ending in *–um* in the nominative singular are <u>2nd-declension neuter</u>.

<u>Adjectives</u> modify or describe nouns, pronouns, or other adjectives. A Latin adjective *must* agree with the noun it modifies in gender, number, and case. Use 1st-declension case endings for feminine adjectives. Use 2nd-declension masculine or neuter case endings for masculine or neuter adjectives. Adjectives indicating size or quantity (number) usually come *before* the noun; other adjectives usually *follow* the noun.

So far, pronouns have been built into verbs, but the Romans also had separate pronouns. Here's the <u>form for *I*</u>.

	Singular	Plural	Translation	
nominative	ego	nōs	I	we
genitive	meī	nostrī	of me	of us
dative	mihi	nōbīs	to/for me	to/for us
accusative	mē	nōs	me	us
ablative	mē	nōbīs	by/with/from me	by/with/from us

II – Secunda   Nōmen: _____

And here's one more form for you to review, present tense of *sum, esse*:

	Singular	Plural		Translation:	
1st person	sum	sumus		I am	we are
2nd person	es	estis		you are	you all are
3rd person	est	sunt		he/she/it is	they are

V. Historia (*Famous Men of Rome*, Chapter XV, Parts I-II)

In the 2nd Punic War, 218-202 BC, Hannibal attacks Italy with an army and elephants. Quintus Fabius attempts a policy of delay, now known as a Fabian policy. The Romans lose 70,000 soldiers at the battle of Cannae. Publius Cornelius Africanus decides Rome has been too cautious, and he leads an army to Africa.

VI. Dēlēgāta

A. *Scrībe* the new Latin *verba* and their meanings.

Latīnē   *Anglicē*

1. _____   1. _____

2. _____   2. _____

B. *Scrībe* the declensions of <u>nimbus, -ī, m.</u> (1) and <u>dōnum, -ī, n.</u> (2).

1. _____ _____   2. _____ _____

   _____ _____   _____ _____

   _____ _____   _____ _____

   _____ _____   _____ _____

   _____ _____   _____ _____

   _____ _____   _____ _____

C. *Scrībe* the present-tense conjugation of <u>sum, esse</u> two times.

1. _____ _____   2. _____ _____

   _____ _____   _____ _____

   _____ _____   _____ _____

II – Secunda   Nōmen:

D. *Variātiōnēs.* *Recita* these sentences several times, sometimes row by row and sometimes column by column. Pay close attention to the changes involved in making the adjective agree with its noun in gender, number, and case.

   1. Furca est nova.   Furcae sunt novae.   (The fork is new. The forks are new.)
   2. Furca est parva.   Furcae sunt parvae.   (The fork is small. The forks are small.)
   3. Calamus est novus.   Calamī sunt novī.   (The pen is new. The pens are new.)
   4. Calamus est parvus.   Calamī sunt parvī.   (The pen is small. The pens are small.)
   5. Speculum est novum.   Specula sunt nova.   (The mirror is new. The mirrors are new.)
   6. Speculum est parvum.   Specula sunt parva.   (The mirror is small. The mirrors are small.)
   7. Nauta est bonus.   Nautae sunt bonī.   (The sailor is good. The sailors are good.)
   8. Nauta bonus nāvigat.   Nautae bonī nāvigant.   (A good sailor sails. Good sailors sail.)

E. **Translate these sentences (from Latin to English or from English to Latin).**

   1. Mūrus est altus. _____

   2. Oppidum est tūtum. _____

   3. Nimbī sunt magnī. _____

   4. Nāsus meus est angustus. _____

   5. Multa verba sunt antīqua. _____

   6. The best gifts are small. _____

   7. Prīma mēnsa est magna. _____

   8. Prīma mēnsa magna est. _____

   9. Joy is a gift. _____

   10. Many angels are singing. _____

   11. My sons are praying. _____

F. **Fill in the blanks.**

   1. Nouns with a nominative ending in ____ and ____ are 2nd-declension masculine nouns.

   2. Nouns with a nominative ending in _____ are 2nd-declension neuter nouns.

   3. An adjective must agree with the noun it modifies in _____, _____,

      and _____ .

II – Secunda   Nōmen: _____

G. Translate these Latin sentences (from Latin to English or from English to Latin).

1. Amīcī sumus. _____

2. Tūta es. _____

3. Bonī estis. _____

4. I am small. _____

5. We are holy. _____

6. Your kingdom is wide. _____

Ex Scriptūrīs (from the Bible):

7. Dominus rēgnat. (Ps. 97:1, alt.) _____

8. Caelum thronus meus est. (Is. 66:1, alt.) _____

9. Rēgnat Deus tuus. (Is. 52:7, alt.) _____

10. Ego sum Dominus Deus tuus. (Ex. 20:5) _____

H. *Scrībe* the declensions of <u>annus, -ī, m.</u> (1) and <u>signum, -ī, n.</u> (2).

1. _____ _____   2. _____ _____

   _____ _____   _____ _____

   _____ _____   _____ _____

   _____ _____   _____ _____

   _____ _____   _____ _____

   _____ _____   _____ _____

I. Translate these *verba* and phrases.

1. secunda lectiō _____   2. ex Scriptūrīs _____

3. Ubi habitās? _____

4. prīma _____   5. variātiōnēs _____

II – Secunda   Nōmen: _____

J. Crossword Puzzle. All adjectives are in the nominative case, but watch carefully for gender and number. Unscramble the shaded letters to spell a two-word Latin sentence *and* its two-word English translation, an important name for God.

RECTĒ
1. good (f. pl.)
3. small (f. sing.)
5. great (f. pl.)
6. wide (m. pl.)
7. second (n. pl.)
8. whole (m. pl.)
10. much (m. sing.)
12. high (n. sing.)

DEORSUM
1. pretty (m. sing.)
2. ancient (n. sing.)
4. narrow (m. sing.)
5. bad (f. sing.)
9. safe (n. sing.)
11. your (n. pl.)

Hidden sentences:
   Latin: __ __ __ __ __ __ .   English: __ __ __ .

K. Historia. Review the history and fill in the blanks.

1. What are the dates of the 2nd Punic War? _____

2. What Carthaginian general attacks Italy? _____

3. What special feature does his army have? _____

4. What is the name of Rome's first strategy in this war? _____

5. In what battle do the Romans suffer great losses? _____

6. What Roman general leads an army to Africa? _____

III – Tertia   Nōmen: _____

III – Tertia lectiō (3 – Third lesson)   **DIRECT OBJECTS**

I. Dictum

ē plūribus ūnum

II. Colloquium   *Latīnē*   *Anglicē*

Minister:	Salvē. Possumne tibi ministrāre?	Hello. Can I help you?
Marcus:	Velim mālum.	I'd like an apple.

III. Verba nova

Latīnē	*Anglicē*	*Scrībe tōtum verbum Latīnum.*	*Dērīvātī*
argentum, -ī, n.	silver		
aurum, -ī, n.	gold		
mālum, -ī, n.	apple		
sapientia, -ae, f.	wisdom		
dō, dare, dedī, datum	to give		
laudō, laudāre, laudāvī, laudātum	to praise		
habeō, habēre, habuī, habitum	to have, to possess		
videō, vidēre, vīdī, vīsum	to see		

IV. Verba renovanda – 2nd Conjugation

doceō, docēre	to teach	moveō, movēre	to move	timeō, timēre	to fear, be afraid
doleō, dolēre	to ache	pateō, patēre	to be open	valeō, valēre	to be strong
fleō, flēre	to weep, to cry	placeō, placēre	to please	**Other**	
gaudeō, gaudēre	to rejoice	rīdeō, rīdēre	to laugh		
lūceō, lūcēre	to shine	salveō, salvēre	to be well	et	and
maneō, manēre	to stay, to remain	sedeō, sedēre	to sit	nōn	not
misereō, miserēre	to be sorry	sileō, silēre	to be silent	spīritus, -ūs, m.	spirit

III – Tertia   Nōmen: _____

IV. Grammatica

Here is the form you learned in Book I for present tense of 2nd-conjugation verbs:

	Singular	Plural		**Personal Endings** Singular	Plural
1st person	maneō	manēmus		-ō	-mus
2nd person	manēs	manētis		-s	-tis
3rd person	manet	manent		-t	-nt

Second-conjugation verbs are recognizable because the inifinitive ends in *-ēre*. To find the stem of a 2nd conjugation verb, simply drop the *–re* of the infinitive. (E.g., the stem of *maneō, manēre* is *manē-*.) To conjugate the verb, add the personal endings to the stem.

Here is a new form to learn. It is for the Latin pronoun *you*:

	Singular	Plural	Translation	
nominative	tū	vōs	you	you all
genitive	tuī	vestrī	of you	of you all
dative	tibi	vōbīs	to/for you	to/for you all
accusative	tē	vōs	you	you all
ablative	tē	vōbīs	by/with/from you	b/w/f you all

Grammatica Nova

Until now, we have used only the nominative case in sentences, but now we will learn to use the other cases. Nominative case indicates the subject of a sentence. It reveals who or what the sentence is about, and may indicate who or what is doing the action of the verb. But there are other uses for nouns. For example, in Latin, the accusative case indicates the direct object of an action verb. A direct object receives the action of the verb. Consider this sentence:

"Mary sees the horse."

What is the verb in the sentence above? _____. Who or what is doing the action? _____.
Therefore, _____ is the subject of the sentence. Who or what is being seen? _____.
Therefore, _____ is the direct object of the sentence.

In English, the use of a noun is often indicated by word order: "The horse sees Mary" means something quite different from "Mary sees the horse"! Cases, rather than order, indicate the use of a noun in Latin. For instance,

*Maria **equum** videt.*
*Videt Maria **equum**.* } All mean the same thing: "Mary sees the **horse**."
***Equum** videt Maria.*

Word order in Latin can change a lot, but the *usual* order is **subject – direct object – adverb – verb.**

III – Tertia   Nōmen: _____

V. Historia (*Famous Men of Rome,* Chapter XV, Parts III and IV)

The Romans under Scipio defeat the Carthaginian army under Hasdrubal Gisco and invade Africa. Carthage calls Hannibal back from Italy, but at the battle of Zama, even the great Hannibal suffers defeat at the hands of Scipio, who is given the title "Africanus."

VI. Dēlēgāta

A. *Scrībe* the new Latin *verba* and their meanings.

Latīnē	*Anglicē*
1. _____	1. _____
2. _____	2. _____
3. _____	3. _____
4. _____	4. _____
5. _____	5. _____
6. _____	6. _____
7. _____	7. _____
8. _____	8. _____

B. *Variātiōnēs. Recita* these sentence patterns several times. Pay close attention to the form used for the direct object of the sentence. Hint: The accusative case always ends in –*m,* just as in hi<u>m</u> and the<u>m</u> in English. *Recitā* the whole Latin line, including the nominative form before the sentence.

1. Pecūnia.   Maria pecūniam videt.   (Money. Mary sees the money.)
2. Stella.   Maria stellam videt.   (Star. Mary sees the star.)
3. Gladius.   Maria gladium videt.   (Sword. Mary sees the sword.)
4. Nimbus.   Maria nimbum videt.   (Cloud. Mary sees the cloud.)
5. Aurum.   Maria aurum videt.   (Gold. Mary sees the gold.)
6. Signum.   Maria signum videt.   (Sign. Mary sees the sign.)
7. Magna herba. Maria magnam herbam videt. (Large plant. Mary sees the large plant.)
8. Agnus bellus. Maria agnum bellum videt.   (Pretty lamb. Mary sees the pretty lamb.)
9. Dōnum tuum.   Maria dōnum tuum videt.   (Your gift. Mary sees your gift.)

III – Tertia   Nōmen: _____

C. Translate these sentences.

1. Maria culīnam videt. _____

2. Nautae terram vident. _____

3. Agricola porcum videt. _____

4. Puer puellam amat. _____

5. Puella puerum nōn amat. _____

6. Deus mē amat. _____

7. Magister librum habet. _____

8. Servus pōculum habet. _____

9. Gallia silvam habet. _____

10. Rēgīna tē laudat. _____

11. Puellae Deum laudant. _____

12. Deum laudāmus. _____

13. Magister dōnum dat. _____

D. Fill in the blanks.

1. A direct object tells who or what _____ the _____ of the _____.

2. In Latin, the _____ case is used for direct objects.

3. The usual word order in a Latin sentence is _____ - _____ - _____ - _____.

4. The subject of 1st- and 2nd-person verbs is *always* the _____ built into them.

5. All Latin sentences with subject nouns *must* have _____-person verbs.

6. Accusative case endings are: 1st declension: _____ (S) _____ (P)

   2nd declension (M):   _____ (S) _____ (P)

   2nd declension (N):   _____ (S) _____ (P)

III – Tertia   Nōmen: _____

E. Translate these Latin sentences.

1. Maria magnum mālum videt. _____

2. Tōta ecclēsia Deum laudat. _____

3. Tē multī magistrī laudant. _____

4. Tē laudant multī magistrī. _____

5. Multī magistrī tē laudant. _____

6. Rēgīna multum argentum habet. _____

7. Agricola parvam mēnsam habet. _____

Ex Scriptūrīs:

8. Fīlius meus es tū. (Ps. 2:7) _____

9. Dominus dat sapientiam. (Pv. 2:6) _____

10. Spīritus vītam dat. (II Cor. 3:6)) _____

11. Argentum et aurum nōn habeō. _____
    (Acts 3:6)

F. Conjugate fleō, flēre (1) and moveō, movēre (2) in present tense.

1. _____ _____   2. _____ _____

   _____ _____   _____ _____

   _____ _____   _____ _____

G. Derivati. Complete each sentence with an English *verbum* chosen from the following *verba* The italicized *verbum* in the sentence should help you think of the Latin root.

            applause   data   vision   argentine

1. I have excellent _____; I can *see* very well. Latin root: _____

2. _____ are *given* facts about something. Latin root: _____

3. The _____ color of the relic gave it a *silvery* hue. Latin root: _____

III – Tertia   Nōmen:

4. The audience showed great *praise* with loud _____. Latin root:_____

H. Crossword Puzzle. Be sure to use the correct ending for the grammar indicated. Unscramble the shaded letters to find some good news (*Latīnē*).

RECTĒ
1. silver (acc. s.)
4. you (s.) laugh
6. chair (acc. s.)
8. apple (acc. s.)
11. I see
13. me (acc.)
15. wisdom (acc. s.)
17. and
19. land (acc. s.)

DEORSUM
1. gold (acc. s.)
2. nose (acc. s.)
3. bear (acc. s.)
5. we ache
7. you (pl.) praise
9. I give
10. son (acc. s.)
12. she has
14. you (s.) love
16. not
18. you (acc. s.)

Hidden message: ___ ___ ___ ___ ___ ___ ___ ___ ___ ___ .

I. Historia. Review the history and fill in the blanks.

1. What general first defends Carthage against Scipio? _____

2. In what battle does Scipio defeat Hannibal? _____

3. What title is given to Scipio after his victory? _____

IV – Quarta lectiō (4 – Fourth lesson) MORE DIRECT OBJECTS

I. Dictum

Carthāgō dēlenda est !
— Cato the Censor

II. Colloquium

Latīnē   *Anglicē*

Claudia:	Velīsne lūdum facere?	Would you like to play a game?
Marcus:	Certē volō lūdum facere!	Sure, I want to play a game!

N.B.: *-ne* is a particle added to the end of the first word of a sentence. It asks a "yes or no" question.

III. Verba nova

Latīnē	*Anglicē*	*Scrībe tōtum verbum Latīnum.*	*Dērīvātī*
abacus, -ī, m.	gameboard		
ālea, -ae, f.	(game) die		
calculus, -ī, m.	stone, game piece		
dextera, -ae, f.	right hand		
lūdus, -ī, m.	game, school		
spatium, -ī, n.	space		
teneō, tenēre, tenuī, tentum to hold			

Verba renovanda – Numbers

Latine	Anglice				
		octō	eight	septendecim	seventeen
		novem	nine	duodēvīgintī	eighteen
ūnus	one	decem	ten	ūndēvīgintī	nineteen
duo	two	ūndecim	eleven	vīgintī	twenty
trēs	three	duodecim	twelve	vīgintī ūnus	twenty-one
quattuor	four	tredecim	thirteen	vīgintī duo	twenty-two (etc.)
quīnque	five	quattuordecim	fourteen	centum	one hundred
sex	six	quīndecim	fifteen	mīlle	one thousand
septem	seven	sēdecim	sixteen		

IV – Quarta   Nōmen: _____

IV. Grammatica

Here are the personal endings for future tense you learned in Book I.

	Singular	Plural	
1st person _____	-bō	-bimus	_____
2nd person _____	-bis	-bitis	_____
3rd person _____	-bit	-bunt	_____

To conjugate 1st- and 2nd-conjugation verbs in future tense, add the appropriate ending to the stem of the verb. Here are the forms for *amō, amāre* and *maneō, manēre* in future tense.

amābō	amābimus
amābis	amābitis
amābit	amābunt

manēbō	manēbimus
manēbis	manēbitis
manēbit	manēbunt

Here is the present tense of *possum, posse* to review.

	Singular	Plural	
1st person _____	possum	possumus	_____
2nd person _____	potes	potestis	_____
3rd person _____	potest	possunt	_____

Remember that a present-tense Latin verb can usually be translated three ways. Besides the *simple* present, there is the *progressive* (using the helping verbs *is, am,* or *are* and a form of the verb ending in *–ing*) and the *emphatic* (using the helping verbs verbs *does* or *do*).

Ursa mē terret.	The bear frightens me.	(simple)
	The bear is frightening me.	(progressive)
	The bear does frighten me.	(emphatic)
Lūdōs spectō.	I watch games.	(simple)
	I am watching games.	(progressive)
	I do watch games.	(emphatic)

Grammatica Nova

In this lesson, we'll use plural nouns as direct objects. Watch for *–ās* (1st declension), *-ōs* (2nd-declension masculine), and *–a* (2nd-declension neuter) at the end of these plural direct objects.

IV – Quarta   Nōmen: _____

V. Historia (*Famous Men of Rome,* Chapter XVI)

Plebeian farmers return after decades of war to farms ruined by neglect. The patricians, on the other hand, become richer and more decadent. Marcus Porcius Cato, the Censor, taxes luxuries to stop the moral decline, and he urges Rome to utterly destroy Carthage, which happens at the end of the third Punic War, in 146 BC.

VI. Dēlēgāta

A. *Scrībe* the new Latin *verba* and their meanings.

Latīnē	*Anglicē*
1. _____	1. _____
2. _____	2. _____
3. _____	3. _____
4. _____	4. _____
5. _____	5. _____
6. _____	6. _____
7. _____	7. _____

B. *Variātiōnēs.* *Recitā* these sentence patterns several times. Pay close attention to the form used for the direct object of the sentence. Be sure to read the whole Latin line aloud, including the nominative form before the sentence.

1. Patella.   Marcus patellās tenet.   (Plate. Mark holds the plates.)
2. Ālea.   Marcus āleās tenet.   (Die. Mark holds the dice.)
3. Lūdus.   Marcus lūdōs tenet.   (Game. Mark holds the games.)
4. Calculus.   Marcus calculōs tenet.   (Stone. Mark holds the stones.)
5. Dōnum.   Marcus dōna tenet.   (Gift. Mark holds the gifts.)
6. Pōculum.   Marcus pōcula tenet.   (Cup. Mark holds the cups.)
7. Parva furca.   Marcus parvās furcās tenet.   (Small fork. Mark holds the small forks.)
8. Stilus bonus.   Marcus stilōs bonōs tenet.   (Good pencil. Mark holds the good pencils.)
9. Mālum bellum.   Marcus māla bella tenet.   (Pretty apple. Mark holds the pretty apples.)

C. Translate these sentences (from Latin to English or English to Latin).

1. Maria lūdōs habet.   _____

2. Puellae lūdum habent.   _____

IV – Quarta   Nōmen: _____

3. Marcus calculum movet. _____

4. Dextera tua āleās tenet. _____

5. Puerī abacōs movent. _____

6. Deus vōs amat. _____

7. Nautae tē vident. _____

8. Nautae nōs vident. _____

9. Servants are moving mirrors. _____

10. The queen praises you all. _____

11. I see ramparts. _____

12. You all see bears. _____

13. The teacher is giving rewards. _____

D. Fill in the blanks.

1. *Scrībe* the accusative case endings for 1st- and 2nd-declension nouns.

   1st declension: _____ (S) _____ (P)

   2nd declension (M):   _____ (S) _____ (P)

   2nd declension (N):   _____ (S) _____ (P)

E. Translate these Latin sentences.

1. Iulia quattuor lūdōs habet. _____

2. Abacus vīgintī spatia habet. _____

3. Magistrī nōs docēbunt. _____

4. Rēgīnās bonās laudābō. _____

5. Nautās bonōs vidēbis. _____

6. Calculus meus calculum tuum superābit. _____

IV – Quarta   Nōmen: _____

7. Multa praemia dabimus. _____

Ex Scriptūrīs:

8. Dextera tua mē tenēbit. (Ps. 139:10, alt.) _____

9. Angelōs iūdicābimus. (I Cor. 6:3, alt.) _____

F. Conjugate <u>teneō, tenēre</u> (1) and <u>laudō, laudāre</u> (2) in future tense.

1. _____ _____   2. _____ _____

   _____ _____   _____ _____

   _____ _____   _____ _____

G. Translate these *verba* and phrases.

1. quarta _____   2. second _____

3. first _____   4. variātiōnēs _____

5. Carthāgō dēlenda est. _____

6. How was the summer? _____

7. Velīsne lūdum facere? _____

8. Velīsne mālum? _____

H. Dērīvātī. Complete each sentence with an English *verbum* chosen from the following *verba*. The italicized *verbum* in the sentence should help you think of the Latin root.

   ludicrous   dexterity   calculate   tenacity   spatial

1. *Stones* were used to _____ the total. Latin root: _____

2. _____ relationships define things in *space*. Latin root: _____

3. The athlete's _____ helped her to *hold* on in pain. Latin root: _____

4. A _____ move quickly ended the *game*. Latin root: _____

5. Manual _____ requires careful *hand* movement. Latin root: _____

IV – Quarta   Nōmen:

I. Crossword Puzzle. Be sure to use the correct ending for the grammar indicated.

RĒCTĒ
1. novem + quattuor =
4. you all (acc. pl)
6. gamboards (acc.)
9. they will move
11. games (acc.)
12. right hand (nom.)
14. us
15. sēdecim - decem =

DEORSUM
1. we will hold
2. me (acc. s)
3. trēs x sex =
5. spaces (acc.)
7. game pieces (acc.)
8. you (nom. s)
10. dice (acc.)
11. quīndecim ÷ quīnque =
13. I give

J. Historia. Review the history and fill in the blanks.

1. Why do the plebians lose their farms? _____

2. What problem does Cato see in Roman society? _____

3. About what other great enemy does Cato warn Rome repeatedly? _____

4. In what year does the third and last Punic War end? _____

5. How long do the Punic Wars last altogether? _____

_____

_____

V – Quīnta   Nōmen: _____

V – Quīnta lectiō (5 – Fifth lesson)   3ʳᵈ DECLENSION

I. Dictum

Senātus Populusque Rōmānus (_____) _____

II. Colloquium   *Latīnē*   *Anglicē*

| Magistra: | Silentium, quaesō. Aperīte librōs ad lectiōnem quīntam. | Silence, please. Open (your) books to lesson five. |

III. Verba nova

Latīnē	*Anglicē*	*Scrībe tōtum verbum Latīnum.*	*Dērīvātī*
cāritās, cāritātis, f.	love		
dīves, dīvitis, m./f.	rich person		
humilitās, humilitātis, f.	humility		
pedāle, pedālis, n. (nom. pl. – pedāl<u>i</u>a)	sock		
portiō, portiōnis, f.	portion, snack		
resurrectiō, resurrectiōnis, f.	resurrection		

Verba renovanda – 3ʳᵈ declension

Latīnē	*Anglicē*
auris, auris, f.	ear
avis, avis, f.	bird
bōs, bovis, m./f.	ox, cow
Caesar, -is, m.	Caesar
canis, canis, m./f.	dog
caput, capitis, n.	head
cochleāre, cochleāris, n.	spoon
collis, collis, m.	hill
corpus, corporis, n.	body
crūs, crūris, n.	leg
crux, crucis, f.	cross
dēns, dentis, m.	tooth
fēles, fēlis, f.	cat
flūmen, flūminis, n.	river
frāter, frātris, m.	brother
homō, hominis, m.	person, human
hostis, hostis, m./f.	enemy
ignis, ignis, m.	fire
imperātor, -is, m.	commander
lacūnar, -is, n.	ceiling
legiō, legiōnis, f.	legion
lēx, lēgis, f.	law
lūx, lūcis, f.	light
māter, mātris, f.	mother
mīles, mīlitis, m.	soldier
mōns, montis, m.	mountain
mors, mortis, f.	death
nāvis, nāvis, f.	ship
nōmen, nōminis, n.	name
nox, noctis, f.	night
ōs, ōris, n.	mouth
pars, partis, f.	part
pāstor, pāstōris, m.	shepherd
pater, patris, m.	father
pax, pācis, f.	peace
pēs, pedis, m.	foot
rēx, rēgis, m.	king
serpēns, serpentis, m./f.	snake
soror, sorōris, f.	sister
tempus, temporis, n.	time
urbs, urbis, f.	city
vēritās, vēritātis, f.	truth
virtūs, virtūtis, f.	courage, virtue
vōx, vōcis, f.	voice

V – Quīnta   Nōmen:

IV. Grammatica

Here are the forms for 3rd-declension nouns from Book I. The first two are an example of a noun declension and the case endings for most masculine and feminine nouns of 3rd declension.

	Singular	Plural	Singular	Plural
nominative	pater	patrēs	(varies)	-ēs
genitive	patris	patrum	-is	-um
dative	patrī	patribus	-ī	-ibus
accusative	patrem	patrēs	-em	-ēs
ablative	patre	patribus	-e	-ibus

And here is an example of a neuter of 3rd declension noun and its case endings.

	Singular	Plural	Singular	Plural
nominative	flūmen	flūmina	(varies)	-a
genitive	flūminis	flūminum	-is	-um
dative	flūminī	flūminibus	-ī	-ibus
accusative	flūmen	flūmina	(varies)	-a
ablative	flūmine	flūminibus	-e	-ibus

Here is a model declension and case endings for masculine and faminine *i-stem nouns of 3rd declension*. These nouns have either (1) a nominative and genitive singular of two syllables (e.g., *fēles, fēlis, f.*) or they have (2) stems ending with two consonants (e.g., *pars, pa<u>rt</u>-*).

	Singular	Plural	Singular	Plural
nominative	fēles	fēlēs	(varies)	-ēs
genitive	fēlis	fēlium	-is	-ium
dative	fēlī	fēlibus	-ī	-ibus
accusative	fēlem	fēl<u>ēs</u>	-em	-īs
ablative	fēle	fēlibus	-e	-ibus

V – Quīnta   Nōmen:

V. Historia (*Famous Men of Rome*, Chapter XVII)

Cornelia, daughter of Scipio Africanus, has two sons, Tiberius Gracchus and Caius Gracchus, whom she calls her jewels. In 133 BC, Tiberius Gracchus is elected tribune, but jealous nobles kill him during a riot. In 123 BC, Caius Gracchus is elected tribune, but he has himself killed to avoid a second riot.

VI. Dēlēgāta

A. *Scrībe* the new Latin *verba* and their meanings.

      Latīnē   *Anglicē*

1. _____ 1. _____

2. _____ 2. _____

3. _____ 3. _____

4. _____ 4. _____

5. _____ 5. _____

6. _____ 6. _____

B. *Variātiōnēs.* *Recitā* these sentence patterns several times. Pay close attention to the form used for the direct object of the sentence. Be sure to read the whole line aloud, including the nominative form before the sentence.

1. Ego.	Deus mē amat.	(I. God loves me.)
2. Nōs.	Deus nōs amat.	(We. God loves us.)
3. Tū.	Deus tē amat.	(You. God loves you.)
4. Vōs.	Deus vōs amat.	(You all. God loves you all.)

C. Translate these sentences (from Latin to English or from English to Latin).

1. Avis volat. _____

2. Avēs volant. _____

3. Ōra silent. _____

4. Mīlitēs hostīs vident. _____

5. Pastor agnōs videt. _____

V – Quīnta   **Nōmen:**

6. Mōns altus est. _____

7. Lacūnar est altum. _____

8. Large cities are safe. _____

9. Death is an enemy. _____

10. My father is king. _____

11. I move chairs. _____

12. We see stars. _____

13. My teacher is giving gifts. _____

D. Fill in the blanks.

1. What are the accusative endings for 3rd-declension nouns?

     Masculine or feminine: sing.: _____ pl.: _____

     Neuter: sing.: _____ pl.: _____

E. Translate these sentences (from Latin to English or from English to Latin).

1. Humilitās est virtus. _____

2. Dīves frātrem habet. _____

3. Octō pedālia teneō. _____

4. Canis serpentēs videt. _____

5. My sister has a pretty voice. _____

6. The sailor will sail a ship. _____

7. A good man loves truth. _____

Ex Scriptūrīs:

8. Ego sum resurrectiō et vīta. (Jn. 11:25) _____

9. Lingua ignis est. (James 3:6) _____

V – Quīnta   Nōmen: _____

10. Deus lūx est. (I Jn. 1:5) _____

11. Deus cāritas est. (I Jn. 4:8) _____

12. Cāritās nōn cōgitat malum. (I Cor. 13:5) _____

F. Decline lēx, lēgis, f. (1), caput, capitis, n. (2), fēles, fēlis, m./f (3), and ōs, ōris, n. (4)

1. _____ _____   2. _____ _____

   _____ _____   _____ _____

   _____ _____   _____ _____

   _____ _____   _____ _____

   _____ _____   _____ _____

   _____ _____   _____ _____

3. _____ _____   4. _____ _____

   _____ _____   _____ _____

   _____ _____   _____ _____

   _____ _____   _____ _____

   _____ _____   _____ _____

   _____ _____   _____ _____

G. Translate these *verba* and phrases.

1. quīnta _____   2. fourth _____

3. Senātus Populusque Rōmānus _____

4. Hannibal at the gates! _____

5. Where do you live? _____

H. Dērīvātī. Complete each sentence with an English *verbum* chosen from the following *verba*. The italicized *verbum* in the sentence should help you think of the Latin root.

proportionate   humiliation   charity

1. *Humility* is not the same as _____. Latin root: _____

2. _____ is a sign of *love* in a Christian. Latin root: _____

V – Quīnta   **Nōmen:**

3. The meal *portions* were _____ to his size. Latin root: _____

I. Crossword Puzzle. Be sure to use the correct ending for the grammar indicated. Unscramble the shaded letters to find the name of a Roman *dīves*: _____

RECTĒ
1. bodies (acc. pl)
6. name (acc.)
9. hills (nom.)
10. mother (acc.s)
12. snacks (acc.)
13. humility (acc.)

DEORSUM
1. love (acc.)
2. resurrection (acc.s)
3. mouths (nom.)
4. night (nom.)
5. sock (nom.)
7. peace (acc.)
8. rivers (nom.)
11. foot (nom.)

J. Historia. Review the history story and fill in the blanks.

1. Who is Cornelia's father? _____

2. What are Cornelia's jewels? _____

3. What power did Roman tribunes have? _____

4. If the Gracchi both died so young, why do you think they are still remembered?

VI – Sexta   Nōmen: _____

VI – Sexta lectiō (6 – Sixth lesson) ADVERBS and INFINITIVES

I. Dictum
sine quā nōn

II. Colloquium   *Latīnē*   *Anglicē*

| Aemīlia: | Quid amās facere? | What do you like to do? |
| Publius: | Lūdōs facere amō. | I like to play games. |

III. Verba nova

Latīnē	*Anglicē*	Scrībe tōtum verbum Latīnum.	*Dērīvātī*
dīgnus, -a, -um	worthy		
faba, -ae, f.	bean		
holus, holeris, n.	vegetable		
nummus, -ī, m.	coin		
pōmum, -ī, n.	fruit		
spectāculum, -ī, n.	sight, show		
spectō, spectāre, spectāvī, spectātum	to look at, to watch		
terreō, terrēre, terruī, territum	to frighten		

1. Label each *verbum* as noun (N), verb (V), or adjective (Adj) to its left (in the margin).

2. Which nouns are from 1st declension? Which are from 2nd? Which are from 3rd?

3. Which verb is from 1st conjugation? Which is from 2nd?

Verba renovanda – Adverbs

Latīnē	*Anglicē*						
bene	well	male	badly	nunc	now		
hīc	here	multum	a lot	parum	a little		
ibi	there	nōn	not	saepe	often		
		numquam	never	semper	always		

VI – Sexta   Nōmen: _____

IV. Grammatica

An adverb is a word that modifies a _____, an _____, or another _____.
An adverb is normally placed before the word it modifies. Best of all, because adverbs never change their endings, they cannot be _____ or _____.

| Spectācula numquam spectō. | I never watch shows. |
| Spectācula saepe spectō. | I often watch shows. |

Here is a new form to learn – It is the <u>Latin demonstrative pronoun that means *he, she, it, they*</u>. Memorize this paradigm horizontally rather than vertically. (NB: b/w/f = by/with/from)

singular

	is (he)	ea (she)	id (it)		Translation		
nominative	is	ea	id		he	she	it
genitive	eius	eius	eius		of him/his	of her/her	of it/its
dative	eī	eī	eī		to/for him	to/for her	to/for it
accusative	eum	eam	id		him	her/her	it
ablative	eō	eā	eō		b/w/f him	b/w/f her	b/w/f it

plural

					Translation		
nominative	eī	eae	ea		they	they	they
genitive	eōrum	eārum	eōrum		of them/their	of them/their	of them/their
dative	eīs	eīs	eīs		to/for them	to/for them	to/for them
accusative	eōs	eās	ea		them	them	them
ablative	eīs	eīs	eīs		by/w/f them	b/w/f them	b/w/f them

The second principal part of a verb is its _____. It is translated "*to* _____."
E.g., *amāre* = _____; *ambulāre* = _____; *rīdēre* = _____.
The infinitive can also be used to complete the meaning of verbs like *amō, possum,* and *velisne*.

Amō ambulāre.	I like to walk.
Possum ambulāre.	I am able to walk. (I can walk.)
Velisne ambulāre?	Would you like to walk?

VI – Sexta   Nōmen: _____

V. Historia (*Famous Men of Rome,* Chapter XVIII, Parts I and II)

Caius Marius defeats the Teutones and Cimbri in 102 BC. He takes the side of the plebeians in the civil debates, but the patricians dare not harm him because of his great military skill.

VI. Dēlēgāta

A. *Scrībe* the new Latin *verba* and their meanings.

Latīnē	*Anglicē*
1. _____	1. _____
2. _____	2. _____
3. _____	3. _____
4. _____	4. _____
5. _____	5. _____
6. _____	6. _____
7. _____	7. _____
8. _____	8. _____

B. *Variātiōnēs.* *Recita* these sentence patterns several times.

1. Velīsne holera?   (Would you like vegetables?)
2. Velīsne cēnāre?   (Would you like to eat?)
3. Velīsne holera cēnāre?   (Would you like to eat vegetables?)
4. Velīsne sedēre?   (Would you like to sit?)
5. Velīsne cantāre?   (Would you like to sing?)
7. Cantāre amāmus.   (We like to sing.)
8. Cantāre possum.   (I am able to sing. / I can sing.)
9. Cantāre possumus.   (We are able to sing. / We can sing.)

C. Translate these sentences (from Latin to English or from English to Latin).

1. Faba est holus.   _____

2. The apple is fruit.   _____

3. The Lamb is worthy.   _____

VI – Sexta   Nōmen: _____

4. Nummus est parvus. _____

5. Now he is holding coins. _____

6. Is multōs nummōs tenet. _____

7. Ea nummōs novōs dabit. _____

8. Eī spectāculum spectant. _____

9. Eae spectācula spectābunt. _____

10. Spectācula placēbunt. _____

11. An eagle frightens the snake. _____

12. The eagle is not frightening the snake. _____

D. Fill in the blanks.

1. An adverb modifies a _____, an _____, or another _____.

2. The infinitive of a verb is its _____ principal part; it is translated ____ + (verb).

3. There are no *verba Latina* for _____ or _____.

E. Translate these sentences (from Latin to English or from English to Latin).

1. Angelī cantāre amant. _____

2. Dīves cantāre nōn amat. _____

3. Velisne portiōnem cēnāre? _____

4. Calculōs movēre nunc potest. _____

5. Nautae vidēre terram possunt. _____

6. She is looking at a coin. _____

7. She is able to look at coins here. _____

8. He likes to look at coins. _____

VI – Sexta   Nōmen: _____

Ex Scriptūrīs:

9. Quī (= he who) habet Fīlium habet vītam; quī nōn habet Fīlium vītam nōn habet.
(I Jn. 5:12, alt)

_____

F. Decline <u>faba, -ae, f.</u> (1) and <u>holus, holeris, n.</u> (2).

1. _____ _____   2. _____ _____

   _____ _____   _____ _____

   _____ _____   _____ _____

   _____ _____   _____ _____

   _____ _____   _____ _____

G. Translate these *verba* and phrases.

1. sexta _____   2. fifth _____

3. sine quā nōn _____   4. Out of many, one _____

5. Certē! _____   6. please _____

7. I would like an apple. _____

8. Quid amās facere? _____

9. Velīsne spectāre? _____

10. We are not able to laugh. _____

11. She loves to pray. _____

H. Dērīvātī. Complete each sentence with an English *verbum* chosen from the following *verba*. The italicized *verbum* in the sentence should help you think of the Latin root.

spectacles   spectacle   terrified   dignity

1. Someone with _____ is *worthy* of respect. Latin root: _____

2. The _____ was a *sight* to behold. Latin root: _____

VI – Sexta   Nōmen: _____

4. _____ are lenses through which one *looks*. Latin root: _____

4. People don't like to be *frightened* or _____. Latin root: _____

I. *Verbum* Search. *Verba* listed below can be found in the nominative or accusative form (singular or plural), reading forward, backward, up, down, or diagonally. Unused letters in the box spell pairs of opposites when read left to right, top to bottom.

In the grid to the right of the list, circle the letter corresponding to the form found in the word search. The circled letters in the grid will spell good news.

Opposites: _____ and _____, _____ and _____, _____ and _____

H	N	A	M	O	P	O	R	T	I	O
U	E	U	M	Q	P	N	U	M	M	I
M	A	I	T	N	E	I	P	A	S	T
I	E	U	A	M	D	S	C	A	P	C
L	L	E	M	A	A	P	U	A	E	
I	A	E	B	E	L	R	H	R	T	R
T	I	A	G	C	I	C	I	U	I	R
A	F	I	U	N	A	T	B	M	A	U
T	I	L	B	E	A	B	A	C	O	S
E	U	N	E	S	O	D	U	L	M	E
M	E	T	I	V	I	D	A	L	E	R

		nom		acc	
	s	pl	s	pl
ABACUS	R	E	L	A
ALEA	S	D	H	P
ANGELUS	D	V	M	K
AURUM	E	G	E	J
CALCULUS	P	O	R	X
CARITAS	B	N	U	Q
DIVES	A	C	S	T
FABA	D	F	Y	N
HUMILITAS	A	O	O	I
LUDUS	I	L	M	N
NUMMUS	X	T	F	R
PEDALE	E	C	E	C
POMUM	R	H	R	H
PORTIO	A	S	N	B
RESURRECTIO	N	D	E	R
SAPIENTIA	L	O	G	H
SPATIUM	D	E	D	E

Good news: _____

J. Historia. Review the history and fill in the blanks.

1. What tribes does Marius defeat? _____

2. In what year does he defeat them? _____

3. Whose side does he take in the civil unrest? _____

VII – Septima   Nōmen: _____

VII – Septima lectiō (7 – Seventh lesson)   **THE GENITIVE**

I. Dictum

       id est (_____)   _____

II. Colloquium   *Latīnē*   *Anglicē*

Lūcius:	Salvē, Claudia.	Hello, Claudia.
	Quid est tibi?	What's the matter?
Claudia:	Mē male habeō.	I feel poorly.

(For more names, see p. 174)

III. Verba

Latīnē	*Anglicē*	*Scrībe tōtum verbum Latīnum.*	*Dērīvātī*
cerasum, -ī, n.	cherry	_____	_____
clāvis, clāvis, f.	key	_____	_____
fīnis, fīnis, m.	end, border	_____	_____
infernus, -ī, m.	hell, underworld	_____	_____
lampas, lampadis, f.	lamp, torch	_____	_____
principium, -ī, n.	beginning	_____	_____
scientia, -ae, f.	knowledge	_____	_____
timor, timōris, m.	fear	_____	_____

1. What kind of *verba* are these? _____

2. *Scrībe* the declension (1, 2, or 3) of each *verbum* to its left.

3. How do you know the declension of each noun? _____

_____

4. We must _____ the gender of each noun.

5. _____ and _____ are *i*-stem nouns of 3rd declension.

VII – Septima   Nōmen:

IV. Grammatica

In this *lectiō*, we'll begin using the <u>genitive case</u> as a possessive form, and in other phrases which use the preposition *of* in English.

patria rēg<u>is</u>	the country *of* the king **or** the king's country
lūdus puell<u>ae</u>	the game *of* the girl **or** the girl's game
lūdus puell<u>ārum</u>	the game *of* the girls **or** the girls' game
librī discipul<u>ōrum</u>	the books *of* the students **or** the students' books
dentēs serpent<u>is</u>	the teeth *of* the snake **or** the snake's teeth
timor De<u>ī</u>	the fear *of* God

The genitive case is the possessive form of a noun. It modifies another noun, and it usually comes *after* the word it modifies. Notice that the genitive need not agree with the noun it modifies in gender, number, case, or declension.

<u>Numbers</u> can be adjectives, too. Most numbers are not declined (They behave themselves – like adverbs!), but *ūnus, duō,* and *trēs* must be declined. Here's the form for *ūnus, -a, um*.

	masculine	feminine	neuter
nominative	ūnus	ūna	ūnum
genitive	ūnīus	ūnīus	ūnīus
dative	ūnī	ūnī	ūnī
accusative	ūnum	ūnam	ūnum
ablative	ūnō	ūnā	ūnō

1. What two cases have different endings from those you already know? _____

2. Why are there no plural forms in this declension? _____

3. Numbers express quantity and should therefore _____ the nouns they modify.

V. Historia (*Famous Men of Rome,* Chapter XVIII, Part II)

General Sulla achieves great victories during the Social War between 91-89 BC. The patricians, believing they no longer need Marius, elect Sulla to be consul in 88 BC, and send Marius into exile. While Sulla goes off to war against Mithridates, Marius returns to Rome and slaughters many nobles.

VII – Septima   Nōmen: _____

VI. Dēlēgāta

A. *Scrībe* the new Latin *verba* and their meanings.

     Latīnē   *Anglicē*

1. _____ 1. _____

2. _____ 2. _____

3. _____ 3. _____

4. _____ 4. _____

5. _____ 5. _____

6. _____ 6. _____

7. _____ 7. _____

8. _____ 8. _____

B. *Variātiōnēs*. *Recita* these sentence patterns several times.

1. Librōs puellae teneō. (I am holding the books of the girl / the girl's books.)
2. Librōs puellārum teneō. (I am holding the books of the girls / the girls' books.)
3. Librōs magistrī teneō. (I am holding the books of the teacher / the teacher's books.)
4. Librōs magistrōrum teneō. (I am holding the books of the teachers / the teachers' books.)
5. Librōs puerī teneō. (I am holding the books of the boy / the boy's books.)
6. Librōs puerōrum teneō. (I am holding the books of the boys / the boys' books.)
7. Librōs mīlitis teneō. (I am holding the books of the soldier / the soldier's books.)
8. Librōs mīlitum teneō. (I am holding the books of the soldiers / the soldiers' books.)

C. Translate these Latin sentences.

1. Ūna rēgīna sedet. _____

2. Ūnus equus stat. _____

3. Ūnum dōnum patet. _____

4. Principium librī est bonum. _____

5. Fīnis librī est mala. _____

6. Fīnēs patriae sunt tūtae. _____

VII – Septima   Nōmen: _____

7. Scientia rēgis magna est. _____
8. Crūra sellārum sunt alta. _____
9. Oculī aquilae valent. _____
10. Ignis infernī est aeternus. _____
11. Vōcēs puerōrum numquam silent. _____
12. Pars flūminis est angusta. _____
13. Gladiī hostium sunt magnī. _____
14. Nummī dīvitum sunt multī. _____

D. Fill in the blanks.

1. The genitive case in Latin corresponds to the _____ (case) in English.
2. Genitive forms can be translated by placing the word _____ in front of the noun.
3. A noun in the genitive case usually _____ the noun it modifies.
5. Genitive case endings are: 1st: _____ (S) _____ (P) 2nd: _____ (S) _____ (P)

    3rd: _____ (S) _____ (P) 3rd i-stem: _____ (S) _____ (P).

5. The _____ case is used for direct objects.

E. Translate these sentences (from Latin to English or from English to Latin).

1. Cerasum est pōmum. _____
2. Cerasa cēnāre amō. _____
3. Ūnam lampadem habēmus. _____
4. Ūnam clāvem habēbimus. _____
5. The slave will hold one coin. _____
6. Mary is the mother of Christ. _____
7. Timōrem serpentium habeō. _____

VII – Septima   Nōmen: _____

8. Lūx ūnīus lampadis est magnus. _____

9. I have the teacher's key. _____

10. You have the teachers' keys. _____

11. Love is the end of fear. _____

Ex Scriptūrīs:

12. Habeō clāvīs mortis et infernī. (Rev. 1:18) _____
_____

13. Magna [est] glōria Dominī. (Ps. 138:5) _____

14. Tū es Christus, Fīlius Deī. (Matt. 16:16) _____

15. Timor Dominī est principium scientiae. (Prov. 1:7, alt.) _____
_____

F. Decline <u>cerasum, -ī, n.</u> (1) and <u>clāvis, clāvis, f.</u> (2).

1. _____ _____   2. _____ _____

   _____ _____   _____ _____

   _____ _____   _____ _____

   _____ _____   _____ _____

   _____ _____   _____ _____

   _____ _____   _____ _____

G. Translate these *verba* and phrases.

1. septima _____   2. sixth _____

3. id est _____   4. third _____

5. Carthage must be destroyed. _____

6. Ubi habitās? _____

7. Quid est tibi? _____

VII – Septima   Nōmen: _____

H. Dērīvātī. Complete each sentence with an English *verbum* chosen from the following *verba*. The italicized *verbum* in the sentence should help you think of the Latin root.

finite   principle   clavier   timidity   scientist

1. A _____ is a *beginning* assumption. Latin root: _____

2. _____ and *fear* are synonyms. Latin root: _____

3. People are _____; they have an *end*. Latin root: _____

4. A _____ seeks *knowledge*. Latin root: _____

5. A _____ was an early *keyboard* instrument. Latin root: _____

I. Alphabet Code. *Scrībe* the genitive singular of each *verba Latīna* in the spaces. A code letter is under each blank. Use the code to fill in the blanks in the shaded box.

FINIS   _ _ _ _ _
         y k f k u

CERASUM _ _ _ _ _ _
         x m d q u k

TIMOR   _ _ _ _ _ _
         h k b g d k u

INFERNUS _ _ _ _ _ _
         k f y m d f k

CLAVIS   _ _ _ _ _ _
         x w q e k u

SCIENTIA _ _ _ _ _ _ _ _
         u x k m f h k q m

LAMPAS   _ _ _ _ _ _ _
         w q b z q j k u

PRINCIPIUM _ _ _ _ _ _ _ _
           z d k f x k z k k

Now you know how to use the _ _ _ _ _ _ _ _ _ In Latin!
                             z g u u m u u k e m

J. Historia. Review the history story and fill in the blanks.

1. In what year is Sulla elected consul? _____

2. Which side does he take in the civil unrest? _____

3. What happens while he fights Mithridates? _____

VIII – Octāva   Nōmen: _____

VIII – Octāva lectiō (8 – Eighth lesson)   PREPOSITIONS (+ Ac)

I. Dictum

    ad nauseam   _____   (lit.: _____)

II. Colloquium   *Latīnē*   *Anglicē*

Claudia:	Multum sternuō et caput mihi dolet.	I am sneezing a lot and my head hurts.
Lūcius:	Gravēdine labōrās! Vīse medicum.	You have a cold! Go see a doctor.
		(See p. 174 for more illnesses)

III. Verba

Latīnē	*Anglicē*	*Scrībe tōtum verbum Latīnum.*	*Dērīvātī*
ad (+ Acc.)	to, toward, near, at	_____	_____
ante (+ Acc.)	before, in front of	_____	_____
circum (+ Acc.)	around, about	_____	_____
per (+ Acc.)	through	_____	_____
secundum (+ Acc.)	beside, according to	_____	_____
super (+ Acc.)	above, over	_____	_____
trāns (+ Acc.)	across	_____	_____
evangelium, -ī, n.	gospel	_____	_____
natō, natāre, natāvī, natātum to swim			_____

_____ _____ _____ _____

1. Which *verbum* is a verb? _____ Which conjugation? _____

2. What kind of *verbum* are most of the *verba*? _____

VIII – Octāva   Nōmen: _____

IV. Grammatica

Most of the new *verba* in this *lectiō* are prepositions. A preposition is followed by a noun (the object of the preposition) and tells the relationship in space or time between that noun and another noun, verb, or adjective in the sentence.

In Latin, prepositions are very particular about the case of the nouns that follow them. All prepositions take either the accusative (Acc.) and/or the ablative (Abl.) case. In this *lectiō*, all the prepositions are followed by nouns in the accusative case. We normally say that these prepositions *take the accusative*. When we memorize prepositions and their meanings, we must also memorize the case(s) that each preposition takes.

Note that prepositions that take the accusative case don't necessarily have anything to do with direct objects. The accusative case simply has two uses.

The prepositions themselves have no endings, but their objects *must* be written in either the accusative (Acc.) or the ablative (Abl.) case, depending upon which case a preposition takes.

What case is used in the *dictum*? _____ Why? _____

Here are the forms for *duō*:

	masculine	feminine	neuter
nominative	duo	duae	duo
genitive	duōrum	duārum	duōrum
dative	duōbus	duābus	duōbus
accusative	duōs	duās	duo
ablative	duōbus	duābus	duōbus

1. Why are there no singular forms in this declension?

2. Because numbers express _____, they should *precede* the nouns they modify.

N.B.: Latin sentences usually have this order:

S (and its modifiers) IO (and its modifiers) DO (and its modifiers) ADV and finally V!

V. Historia (*Famous Men of Rome,* Chapter XIX)

In 83 BC, Sulla returns to Rome after defeating Mithridates. He attacks Marius and his followers. He declares himself dictator and kills thousands of real and suspected enemies.

VIII – Octāva   Nōmen: _____

VI. Dēlēgāta

A. *Scrībe* the new Latin *verba* and their meanings.

   Latīnē   *Anglicē*

1. _____   1. _____
2. _____   2. _____
3. _____   3. _____
4. _____   4. _____
5. _____   5. _____
6. _____   6. _____
7. _____   7. _____
8. _____   8. _____
9. _____   9. _____

B. *Variātiōnēs.* *Recitā* these sentence patterns several times.

1. Ad iānuam ambulābit.   (He will walk to the door.)
2. Circum iānuam ambulābit.   (He will walk around the door.)
3. Per iānuam ambulābit.   (He will walk through the door.)
4. Ante iānuam stābit.   (He will stand in front of the door.)
5. Secundum iānuam stābit.   (He will stand beside the door.)
6. Sellae ante mēnsās sunt.   (The chairs are in front of the tables.)
7. Sellae circum mēnsās sunt. (The chairs are around the tables.)
8. Sellae secundum mēnsās sunt. (The chairs are beside the tables.)

C. Translate these sentences.

1. Lampas secundum mēnsam est. _____

2. Duae lampadēs secundum mēnsam sunt. _____

3. Avis per fenestram volat. _____

4. Duae avēs per fenestram volant. _____

5. Ea bene natāre potest. _____

VIII – Octāva					Nōmen: _____

6. Is multum natāre amat.		_____

7. Is trāns flūmen natat.		_____

8. Ea trāns flūmen natābit.		_____

9. Eī trāns flūmen natābunt.		_____

10. Eae trāns flūmen natābunt.		_____

11. Hostēs circum collem movent.	_____

12. Bōs ante puteum cēnat.		_____

13. Duo hominēs ad puteum stant.	_____

14. Mīlitēs super signum pugnant.	_____

D. Fill in the blanks.

1. The objects of Latin prepositions must be written in either the _____ or the _____ case.

2. The prepositions in this *lectiō* all take the _____ case.

3. We must _____ the case(s) each preposition takes.

4. The _____ case is also used for direct objects.

5. Accusative case endings are: 1st: _____(S) _____(P); 2nd M: _____(S) _____(P);

   2nd N: _____(S); _____(P); 3rd M/F: _____(S) _____(P); 3rd N: _____(S) _____(P).

E. *Scrībe* these English sentences *Latīnē*.

1. The king sits above the throne.	_____

2. He moves the stone through two spaces. _____
   _____

3. Legions are standing around two hills. _____

4. The teacher teaches two students.	_____

5. An angel holds two swords.		_____

VIII – Octāva   Nōmen:

6. I see the walls of two towns.   _____

7. I recite words of two languages.   _____

8. The queen will eat two cherries.   _____

9. The boy stands near the church.   _____

10. She will walk through the door.   _____

11. He will walk to the door.   _____

Ex Scriptūrīs:

12. Et septem lampadēs ante thronum sunt septem spīritūs Deī. (Rev. 4:5, alt., spiritūs = nom. pl.)

_____

13. Vidēmus nunc per speculum. (I Cor. 13:12, alt.) _____

14. Deus iūdicābit hominēs secundum evangelium meum per Christum. (Rom. 2:16, alt.)

_____

F. Decline <u>evangelium, -ī, n.</u> (1), and conjugate <u>natō, natāre</u> in future tense (2).

1. _____ _____   2. _____ _____

   _____ _____   _____ _____

   _____ _____   _____ _____

   _____ _____

G. Translate these *verba* and phrases.

1. octāva _____   2. seventh _____

3. ad nauseam _____   4. Vīse medicum. _____

5. The Roman Senate and People. _____

6. Audēmus iūra nostra dēfendere. _____

47

VIII – Octāva   **Nōmen:** _____

7. Quid amās facere? _____

8. Lūdōs facere amō. _____

H. Derivati. Complete each sentence with an English *verbum* chosen from the following *verba*. The italicized *verbum* in the sentence should help you think of the Latin root.

translucent   superb   antebellum   natatorium   evangelist

1. An _____ preaches the *gospel*. Latin root: _____

2. A _____ is an indoor *swimming* pool. Latin root: _____

3. _____ materials permit *light* to pass *across*. Latin root: _____

4. His _____ performance was far *above* our expectations. Latin root: _____

5. _____ homes were built *before* the *war*. Latin root: _____

I. *Verbum* Ladder.
If you write the *octō verba* from this lesson on the right rows, the shaded spaces, read from top to bottom, should show the *quīntum verbum* from this *lectiō*'s list: _____

above

across

around

before

gospel

they will swim

through

toward

J. Historia. Review the history and fill in the blanks.

1. What office does Sulla take when he returns? _____

2. What else does he do after he returns? _____

IX – Nōna   Nōmen:

IX – Nōna lectiō (9 – Ninth lesson)   THE DATIVE

I. Dictum

ante merīdiem / post merīdiem   _____ / _____

II. Colloquium   *Latīnē*   *Anglicē*

Claudia:	Salvē medice.	Hello, doctor.
Medicus:	Salvē. Quid est?	Hello. What's up?
Claudia:	Ego sum aeger!	I am sick!
Medicus:	Manē in lectō trīs diēs.	Stay in bed three days.
	(aeger, aegra, aegrum – sick)	

III. Verba

Latīnē	*Anglicē*	*Scrībe tōtum verbum Latīnum.*	*Dērīvātī*
beātus, -a, -um	happy, blessed		
cāseus, -ī, m.	cheese		
flōs, flōris, m.	flower		
pānis, pānis, m.	bread		
pilleus, -ī, m.	hat		
portō, portāre, portāvī, portātum to carry			
_____	_____	_____	_____
sapientia, -ae, f.	wisdom		
studeō, studēre, studuī to be eager for, to study			
_____	_____	_____	
vērus, -a, -um	true		

1. *Scrībe* N (noun), V (verb), Adj (adjective), or P (preposition) to the left of each *verbum*.

2. Identify the declension of each noun by writing a 1, 2, or 3 next to each.

3. Why do the adjectives have three endings? _____

IX – Nōna	Nōmen: _____

IV. Grammatica

We begin to use the <u>dative case</u> in this *lectiō*. The dative case is usually translated with the words *to* or *for* before the noun and is used to indicate the <u>indirect object</u> of a sentence. An indirect object tells *to whom* or *for whom* an action is done.

Puer <u>puellae</u> flōrēs dat.	The boy is giving flowers to the girl.
Puella <u>puerō</u> flōrēs dat.	The girl is giving flowers to the boy.
Puer <u>sorōribus</u> flōrēs dat.	The boy is giving flowers to (his) sisters.

The indirect object *usually* comes before the direct object in a Latin sentence, but it can appear anywhere in a sentence, because in Latin, the endings indicate the function of the word in the sentence. If something besides the subject comes first in a Latin sentence, or if something besides the verb comes last, that word is emphasized.

Puer flōrēs puellīs dat.	The boy is giving flowers to the girls.
Flōrēs puer puellīs dat.	The boy is giving *flowers* to the girls.
Puellīs puer flōrēs dat.	The boy is giving flowers to the *girls*.

What case is used in the *dictum*? _____ Why? _____

Here's the <u>form for *trēs*</u>.

	masculine	feminine	neuter
nominative	trēs	trēs	tria
genitive	trium	trium	trium
dative	tribus	tribus	tribus
accusative	trīs	trīs	tria
ablative	tribus	tribus	tribus

Why are there no singular forms in this declension? _____

V. Historia (*Famous Men of Rome,* Chapter XX)

In 70 BC, Cneius Pompey is elected consul, and he restores power previously taken from the citizens by Sulla. In 67, he clears the Mediterranean Sea of pirates, and in 66, he goes to Asia to defeat Mithridates and to increase the size of the Empire. After this, he retains the people's favor by funding spectacles with animals and violent fighting.

IX – Nōna   Nōmen: _____

VI. Dēlēgāta

A. *Scrībe* the new Latin *verba* and their meanings.

Latīnē   *Anglicē*

1. _____   1. _____
2. _____   2. _____
3. _____   3. _____
4. _____   4. _____
5. _____   5. _____
6. _____   6. _____
7. _____   7. _____
8. _____   8. _____
9. _____   9. _____

B. *Variātiōnēs.* *Recitā* these sentence patterns several times. Pay attention to the form used for the indirect object of the sentence. Be sure to read the whole Latin line aloud, including the nominative form before the sentence.

1. Puella.   Puer puellae māla dat.   (The boy is giving apples to the girl.)
2. Puellae.   Puer puellīs māla dat.   (The boy is giving apples to the girls.)
3. Magister.   Puer magistrō māla dat.   (The boy is giving apples to the teacher.)
4. Magistrī.   Puer magistrīs māla dat.   (The boy is giving apples to the teachers.)
5. Canis.   Puer canī māla dat.   (The boy is giving apples to the dog.)
6. Canēs.   Puer canibus māla dat.   (The boy is giving apples to the dogs.)

C. Translate these sentences.

1. Servus rēgīnae pānem portat.   _____

2. Servus rēgī pānem portat.   _____

3. Servus dominō pānem portābit.   _____

4. Discipulus magistrō librōs portat. _____

IX – Nōna   Nōmen: _____

5. Iūlia āvibus pānem dat. _____

6. Maria tribus āvibus pānem dabit. _____

7. Anna duābus āvibus pānem dat. _____

8. Pater fīliō pilleum dabit. _____

9. Verbum est vērum. _____

10. Verba Deī semper sunt vēra. _____

11. Rēgīna beāta est. _____

12. Agricola est beātus. _____

13. Amō cāseum et pānem. _____

D. Fill in the blanks.

1. The dative case is used for the _____ of a sentence.

2. The accusative case is most often used for the _____ in a sentence; it can also be used for the object of a _____.

3. The _____ case is used for the subject noun in a sentence.

4. The _____ case shows possession in Latin. It can be translated into English using the preposition _____.

5. Dative case endings: 1st: ____(S) ____(P); 2nd ____(S) ____(P); 3rd: ____(S) ____(P).

E. Translate these sentences (from Latin to English or from English to Latin).

1. Sellam per iānuam portābō. _____

2. Mīlitēs bonī aurum et argentum trāns patriam portābunt.
_____

3. Pānis mihi placet. _____

4. Placentne flōrēs tibi? _____

IX – Nōna   Nōmen:

5. The mother is giving a small book to her pretty daughter.

_____

6. The boy is giving a hat to the girl. _____

7. The boy will give flowers to two girls. _____

Ex Scriptūrīs:

8. Dabō tibi corōnam vītae. (Rev. 2:10) _____

9. Pater meus dat vōbīs pānem vērum. (Jn. 6:32) _____

_____

10. Beātus es Simon. Tū es Petrus et tibi dabō clāvīs regnī caelōrum. (Matt. 16:17-19)

_____

_____

F. Conjugate <u>terreō, terrēre</u> (1) and <u>portō, portāre</u> (2) in future tense.

1._____ _____   2._____ _____

_____ _____   _____ _____

_____ _____   _____ _____

G. Translate these *verba* and phrases.

1. nōna _____   2. eighth _____

3. ante merīdiem _____   4. post merīdiem _____

5. essential ingredient _____   6. ad nauseam _____

7. Velīsne lūdum facere? _____

8. Velīsne pānem? _____

9. Dēlenda est Carthāgo. _____

H. **Dērīvātī.** Complete each sentence with an English *verbum* chosen from the following *verba*. The italicized *verbum* in the sentence should help you think of the Latin root.

IX – Nōna   Nōmen: _____

Beatitudes   veracity   Panera   portable   florist

1. _____ objects can be *carried*. Latin root: _____

2. A _____ sells and arrange *flowers*. Latin root: _____

3. The _____ describe *blessed* people. Latin root: _____

4. _____ *Bread* is a restaurant with sandwiches. Latin root: _____

5. The man's _____ convinced us he spoke *truth*. Latin root: _____

I. **Crossword Puzzle.** Be sure to use the correct form for the grammar indicated. Unscramble the shaded letters to complete the secret message.

RĒCTĒ
1. bean (nom.)
5. you (acc. s.)
6. bread (acc. s.)
7. he
8. I carry
9. end (nom. s.)
11. flowers (acc.)
12. by him (abl. s.)
13. cheese (acc. s.)

DEORSUM
2. happy (m. acc. pl.)
3. coins (acc.)
4. you (s.) give
5. you (acc. s.)
7. of hell
8. hats (acc.)
10. true (n. nom.)
12. she

If Disneyland made a ride based on Pompey's victories in 67 BC, it could be called:

The _ _ _ _ _ _ _ of the _ _ _ _ _ _ _ _ _ _ _ _ _

J. **Historia.** Review the history and fill in the blanks.

1. Whom does Pompey defeat in the Mediterranean Sea? _____

2. Whom does Pompey defeat in Asia? _____

3. What does Pompey start in order to retain popularity? _____

X – Decima   Nōmen: _____

X – Decima lectiō (10 – Tenth lesson)   PREPOSITIONS (+ Ab)

I. Dictum

cum laude
(magnā cum laude; summā cum laude)   (with great praise; with highest praise)

II. Colloquium   *Latīnē*   *Anglicē*

Tiberius:	Quid velīs?	What would you like?
Tullia:	Trāde mihi būtyrum quaesō.	Pass me the butter, please.
Tiberius:	Ecce.	Here it is. (lit., Behold!)

III. Verba

Latīnē	*Anglicē*	*Scrībe tōtum verbum Latīnum.*	*Dērivātī*
ā / ab (+ Abl.)	from, away from		
būtyrum, -ī, n.	butter		
cum (+ Abl.)	with		
dē (+ Abl.)	about, concerning, down from		
ē / ex (+ Abl.)	out of, out from		
laus, laudis, f.	praise		
oleum, -ī, n.	oil		
patientia, -ae, f.	patience		
sine (+ Abl.)	without		

1. *Scrībe* N (noun), V (verb), Adj (adjective), or P (preposition) to the left of each *verbum*.

2. *Scrībe* the declension (1, 2, or 3) of each noun to its right.

3. Objects of prepositions take the _____ or _____ case.

4. What case is used for indirect objects? _____

X – Decima   Nōmen: _____

IV. Grammatica

The new prepositions in this *lectiō* <u>always</u> take nouns in the <u>ablative</u> case as their objects. What case are all the nouns in the dictum? Why?

All languages have funny quirks. One of Latin's oddities is that when *cum* is used with a <u>pronoun</u>, it is attached to the <u>end</u> of the pronoun! So instead of saying *cum mē* or *cum vōbīs*, Latin uses compound words such as *mēcum* (= with me) or *vōbīscum* (= with you all).

In English we use *an* before a vowel and *a* before a consonant: **<u>an</u>** *orange* but **<u>a</u>** *banana*. Similarly, in Latin, use *ab* before a vowel and *ā* before a consonant: **<u>ab</u>** *oppidō* but **<u>ā</u>** *silvā*. Likewise, *ex* is generally used before a vowel, but *ē* before a consonant: **<u>ex</u>** *oppidō* but **<u>ē</u>** *silvā*.

Below are the forms for the very useful Latin pronoun <u>*hic, haec, hoc*</u>, which means *this / these*. Memorize this word horizontally (case by case, left to right). Try not to get the hiccups!

		masculine	feminine	neuter
this (S)	nominative	hic	haec	hoc
	genitive	huius	huius	huius
	dative	huic	huic	huic
	accusative	hunc	hanc	hoc
	ablative	hōc	hāc	hōc
these (P)	nominative	hī	hae	haec
	genitive	hōrum	hārum	hōrum
	dative	hīs	hīs	hīs
	accusative	hōs	hās	haec
	ablative	hīs	hīs	hīs

V. Historia (*Famous Men of Rome*, Chapter XXI, Part I)

Caius Julius Caesar (100 – 44 BC), a patrician, befriends the plebeians and works his way up Rome's political ladder. In 60 BC, he is given an army and proves to be a successful general, invading and conquering Gaul and part of Britain, and growing rapidly in popularity.

X – Decima   Nōmen:

VI. Dēlēgāta

A. *Scrībe* the new Latin *verba* and their meanings.

Latīnē	*Anglicē*
1. _____	1. _____
2. _____	2. _____
3. _____	3. _____
4. _____	4. _____
5. _____	5. _____
6. _____	6. _____
7. _____	7. _____
8. _____	8. _____
9. _____	9. _____

B. *Variātiōnēs.* *Recitā* these sentence patterns several times. Pay attention to the form used for the object of the preposition. Be sure to read the whole Latin line aloud, including the nominative form before the sentence.

1. Pilleus.   Marcus sine pilleō ambulat.   (Mark is walking without a hat.)
2. Oppidum.   Marcus ab oppidō ambulat.   (Mark is walking away from the town.)
3. Amīcus.   Marcus cum amīcō ambulat.   (Mark is walking with a friend.)
4. Collis.   Marcus dē colle ambulat.   (Mark is walking down from the hill.)
5. Culīna.   Marcus ē culīnā ambulat.   (Mark is walking out of the kitchen.)
6. Gladiī.   Mīlitēs sine gladiīs pugnant.   (The soldiers fight without swords.)
7. Montēs.   Mīlitēs dē montibus movent.   (The soldiers move down from the mountains.)

C. Translate these sentences (from Latin to English or from English to Latin).

1. Servus cum patientiā labōrat.   _____

2. Legiō ex Italiā movēbit.   _____

3. Tēla dē vallīs volābunt.   _____

4. Scientia sine cāritate est mala.   _____

X – Decima   Nōmen: _____

5. Nautae ā nāvibus ambulant. _____

6. Mīlitēs sine timōre pugnant. _____

7. We give praise to God. _____

8. Julianna is giving bread to birds. _____

9. The words of the law are holy. _____

10. I like cheese and bread. _____

11. Marcia pānem cum būtyrō amat. _____

12. Titus pānem sine būtyrō cēnāre amat. _____

13. Agricola lampadem cum oleō tenet. _____

14. Many books of the teachers are large. _____

D. Fill in the blanks.

1. *Sine, cum,* and *ex* always take the _____ case.

2. Use *ab* or *ex* before a *verbum* that begins with a _____.

3. List three prepositions that take the accusative case: _____

4. Ablative case endings for each noun declension are:

   1st: _____ (S) _____ (P); 2nd: _____ (S) _____ (P); 3rd: _____ (S) _____ (P).

E. Translate these sentences (from Latin to English or from English to Latin).

1. Canis meus mēcum ambulābit. _____

2. Deus est nōbīscum. _____

3. Hic parvus flōs est bellus. _____

4. Haec clāvis est magna. _____

5. Hoc lātum flūmen tardat. _____

6. Angelī pugnāre sine gladiīs possunt. _____

X – Decima   Nōmen: _____

7. Mary prays with humility. _____

8. I like bread with lots of cheese. _____

9. The legion moves out of Gaul. _____

Ex Scriptūrīs:

10. Nōn timeō malum quoniam tū mēcum es. (Ps. 23:4; *quoniam* = because) _____
_____

11. Pānis Deī est quī descendit dē caelō et dat vītam mundō.

(Jn. 6:33, alt.; *quī* = he who; *descendit* = descends) _____
_____

F. Decline laus, laudis, f. (1) and būtyrum, -ī, n. (2).

1. _____ _____   2. _____ _____

   _____ _____   _____ _____

   _____ _____   _____ _____

   _____ _____   _____ _____

   _____ _____   _____ _____

G. Translate these *verba* and phrases.

1. decima _____   2. ninth _____

3. cum laude _____   4. Quid velis? _____

5. Aperīte librōs. _____ 6. too long _____

7. Trāde mihi pānem quaesō. _____

8. Trāde mihi holera quaesō. _____

9. Trāde mihi cāseum quaesō. _____

10. Hannibal ad portās! _____

X – Decima   Nōmen: _____

H. Dērīvātī. Complete each sentence with an English *verbum* chosen from the following *verba*. The italicized *verbum* in the sentence should help you think of the Latin root.

                    laud   sinecure   impatient

1. "All Glory, _____, and Honor" is a hymn *praising* God. Latin root: _____

2. His *patient* mother was seldom _____. Latin root: _____

3. A _____ gave income *without* the *care* of souls. Latin root: _____

I. Crossword Puzzle. Be sure to use the correct form for the grammar indicated.

RĒCTĒ
  2. away from
  4. with
  5. patience (abl. s.)
  7. oil (abl. s.)
  9. toward
  10. down from
  11. out of
  12. without

DEORSUM
  1. humility (abl. s.)
  3. butter (abl. s.)
  5. snack (nom. s.)
  6. I swim
  8. praise (abl. s.)

J. Historia. Review the history and fill in the blanks.

1. In what year is Julius Caesar born? _____

2. Whose side does he take in the civil unrest? _____

3. What two provinces does he conquer? _____

XI – Ūndecima lectiō   2-CASE PREPOSITIONS
(11 – Eleventh lesson)

I. Dictum

Vēnī, vīdī, vīcī.
   – Julius Caesar

II. Colloquium   *Latīnē*   *Anglicē*

	Latīnē	Anglicē
Magister:	Claudite librōs.	Close your books.
	Hōra est quaestiunculae.	It's time for a quiz.
Discipulus:	Oiei!	Ouch!

III. Verba

Latīnē	*Anglicē*	*Scrībe tōtum verbum Latīnum.*	*Dērīvātī*
ager, agrī, m.	field		
cīvitās, cīvitātis, f.	state		
gemma, -ae, f.	gem, jewel		
in (+ Acc.)	into, onto		
in (+ Abl.)	in, on		
margarīta, -ae, f.	pearl		
porta, -ae, f.	gate		
similis, simile (adj. + Dat.)	similar to, like		
sub (+ Acc. /Abl.)	under, up to, up under		
thēsaurus, -ī, m.	treasure		

1. *Scrībe* N (noun), V (verb), Adj (adjective), or P (preposition) to the left of each *verbum*.

2. *Scrībe* the declension (1, 2, or 3) of each noun to its right.

3. How does one find the stem of a noun? _____

4. How does one find the stem of a verb? _____

XI – Ūndecima   Nōmen: _____

IV. Grammatica

The two new prepositions are tricky because their meaning depends on the case used as object. In general, when they indicate motion *toward* something, they take the accusative; when they indicate motion *within* something or lack of motion, they take the ablative. So, when used with the accusative, *in* means *into* or *onto*, expressing motion toward something. When used with the ablative, it means *in* or *on,* expressing action *within* something or an absence of motion.

Māter in exedrium ambulat.	Mother is walking *into* the living room.
Māter in exedriō ambulat.	Mother is walking *in* the living room.
Māter in exedriō stat.	Mother is standing *in* the living room.

The preposition *sub* operates in the same way, but it's a little harder to see in English, because our language doesn't have two different forms for *under* with which to make the distinction.

Here is the Latin pronoun meaning *that / those*. Memorize it across (like *hic, haec, hoc*).

		masculine	feminine	neuter
that (S)	nominative	ille	illa	illud
	genitive	illīus	illīus	illīus
	dative	illī	illī	illī
	accusative	illum	illam	illud
	ablative	illō	illā	illō
those (P)	nominative	illī	illae	illa
	genitive	illōrum	illārum	illōrum
	dative	illīs	illīs	illīs
	accusative	illōs	illās	illa
	ablative	illīs	illīs	illīs

V. Historia (*Famous Men of Rome,* Chapter XXI, Part IIa)

Caesar, wanting to be master of Rome, gives fortunes to the poor. Pompey, fearing Caesar's popularity, orders Caesar to disband his army. In 49 BC, Caesar crosses the Rubicon River into Italy with his illegal army. He defeats Pompey and the army of the Republic at Pharsalia.

XI – Ūndecima   Nōmen: _____

VI. Dēlēgāta

A. *Scrībe* the new Latin *verba* and their meanings.

Latīnē	*Anglicē*
1. _____	1. _____
2. _____	2. _____
3. _____	3. _____
4. _____	4. _____
5. _____	5. _____
6. _____	6. _____
7. _____	7. _____
8. _____	8. _____
9. _____	9. _____
10. _____	10. _____

B. *Variātiōnēs*. *Recitā* these sentence patterns several times. Be sure to read the whole Latin line aloud, including the nominative form before the sentence. Pay special attention to the form used for *ager, agrī, m* and *porta, portae, f.*

1. Ager.   Ager est magnus.   (The field is large.)
2. Ager.   Flōrēs agrī sunt bellī.   (The flowers of the field are pretty.)
3. Ager.   Rēgnum caelōrum est simile agrō.   (The kingdom of heaven is similar to a field.)
4. Ager.   Agricola agrum arābit.   (The farmer will plow the field.)
5. Ager.   Servus in agrum ambulat.   (The slave is walking into the field.)
6. Ager.   Equus in agrō stat.   (The horse is standing in the field.)
7. Portae.   Portae sunt magnae.   (The gates are large.)
8. Portae.   Dominus portārum nōn est dīves.   (The master of the gates is not a rich man.)
9. Portae.   Portās vidēmus.   (We see the gates.)
10. Portae.   Legiōnēs in portās intrant.   (Legions enter into the gates.)
11. Portae.   Mīlitēs in portīs stant.   (Soldiers stand in the gates.)

C. Translate these sentences (from Latin to English or from English to Latin).

1. Alabāma est cīvitās optima. _____

XI – Ūndecima Nōmen: _____

2. Portae urbis patent. _____

3. Illa margarīta est bella. _____

4. Ille thēsaurus est parvus. _____

5. Lūcius sub aquā natat. _____

6. Augustus sub aquā natāre potest. _____

7. Margarīta rēgīnae est bella. _____

8. Aemīlia is holding a large pearl in [her] right hand.

   _____

9. Many gems are in that treasure. _____

10. Great treasure is under the earth. _____

11. We are watching the city's gates. _____

12. Deus nōbīs lēgem bonam dat. _____

13. Verba eius sunt sancta et vēra. _____

D. Fill in the blanks.

1. When *in* and *sub* indicate motion *toward* something, use the _____ case.

2. When *in* and *sub* indicate motion *within* or lack of motion, use the _____ case.

E. Translate these sentences (from Latin to English or from English to Latin).

1. Urbs duās portās habet. _____

2. Rēx magnum thēsaurum videt. _____

3. Nauta magnās margarītās tenet. _____

4. Hic thēsaurus multum aurum et multōs nummōs habet cum paucīs gemmīs.

   _____

5. Duōs equōs in agrō vidēmus. _____

| XI – Ūndecima | Nōmen: |

6. Duo equī in agrō agricolae stant. _____

7. The keys of the large gates are small.

_____

8. A holy man is entering into the narrow gate.

_____

9. A pretty woman is walking on the narrow road.

_____

10. The queen holds a large gem. _____

11. That pearl is in the treasure. _____

Ex Scriptūrīs:

12. Et urbs sancta Hierusalem habet mūrum magnum et altum et duodecim portās et in portīs

duodecim angelōs. (Rev. 21:12, alt.) _____

_____

13. Simile est rēgnum caelōrum thēsaurō in agrō. (Matt. 13:44) _____

_____

14. Et vōs Dominum habētis in caelō. (Col. 4:1) _____

F. Translate these *verba* and phrases.

1. ūndecima _____   2. tenth _____

3. Oiei! _____   4. cum laude _____

5. Claudite librōs. _____   6. ad nauseam _____

7. Hōra est quaestiunculae. _____

8. Ē plūribus ūnum _____

9. Repetītiō māter memoriae. _____

XI – Ūndecima   Nōmen:

G. Dērīvātī. Complete each sentence with an English *verbum* chosen from the following *verba*. The italicized *verbum* in the sentence should help you think of the Latin root.

gemologist   thesaurus   civilian   agriculture   subterranean

1. __Agriculture__ is the *cultivation* of *fields*. Latin root: __ager__

2. __Subterranean__ mines are *under* the *earth*. Latin root: __terra__

3. A __thesaurus__ is a *treasure* of words. Latin root: __thesaurus__

4. A __civilian__ is a citizen of the *state*. Latin root: __civitas__

5. A __gemologist__ is an authority on *gems*. Latin root: __gemma__

H. Alphabet Code. Unscramble the letters given to form the *verba Latīna* from this *lectiō*. A code letter is under each blank. Use the code to fill in the secret message in the box.

Scrambled	Word	Code
NI	I N	b v
BSU	S U B	h g d
RGAE	A G E R	k n c q
MGAEM	G E M M A	n c a a k
ATOPR	P O R T A	x i q l k
MIILSSI	S I M I L I S	h b a b t b h
VSIITCA	C I V I T A S	j b z b l k h
AARRGITMA	M A R G A R I T A	a k q n k q b l k
RTUEHSASU	T H E S A U R U S	l u c h k g q g h

Secret message:

C A E S A R   C R O S S E S   T H E
j k c h k q   j q i h h c h   l u c

R U B I C O N
q g d b j i v

Doesn't mean "The emperor angers the river!"

I. Historia. Review the history and fill in the blanks.

1. What does Pompey order Caesar to do? _____

2. What illegal act does Caesar commit? _____

XII – Duodecima   Nōmen:

XII – Duodecima lectiō (12 – Twelfth lesson)   QUESTION WORDS

I. Dictum

Et tū, Brūte?
– *Julius Caesar*, Shakespeare

II. Colloquium   *Latīnē*   *Anglicē*

Popilia:	Quota hōra est?	What time is it?
Brūtus:	Octāva hōra est.	It's eight o'clock.

III. Verba

Latīnē	*Anglicē*	*Scrībe tōtum verbum Latīnum.*	*Dērīvātī*
cūr	why		
quandō	when		
quantus, -a, -um	how much		
quid	what		
quis	who		
quōmodō	how		
quot	how many		
quotus, -a, -um	which		
ubi	where		
servō, servāre, servāvī, servātum	to save, to keep, to guard		

Nōtā bene (N.B.):
1. *Quantus* and *quotus* are adjectives that decline. They must agree with nouns they modify.
2. *Quot* is a special adjective that cannot be declined and never changes form.
3. *Quid* can be either the subject or the object of a question. *Quis* must be the subject of the question; it does not mean *whom*. You'll learn more about *quis* and *quid* another year.
4. The rest of the *verba* (except for *servō, servāre*) are adverbs and never change endings.

XII – Duodecima   Nōmen:

IV. Grammatica

You already know how to write a question that can be answered by *yes* or *no*: write the verb first and add the enclitic *–ne* to it. Another way to ask a question in Latin is simply to use the interrogatives, or question words, in this *lectiō*.

Cūr flēs?	Why are you crying?
Quis cantat?	Who is singing?
Quid Marcus habet?	What does Mark have?
Ubi Hanna est?	Where is Hannah?
Quotus pilleus est optimus?	Which hat is best?

The Romans used ordinal numbers (*prīma, secunda, tertia,* etc.) to express time. Now that you know the first twelve ordinal numbers, you can tell time too! Don't forget to specify *ante merīdiem* (before noon) or *post merīdiem* (after noon).

Prīma hōra est.	It's 1 o'clock.	(It's the 1st hour)
Secunda hōra est.	It's 2 o'clock.	(It's the 2nd hour)
Tertia hōra est.	It's 3 o'clock.	(It's the 3rd hour)
Quarta hōra est.	It's 4 o'clock.	(It's the 4th hour)

To be more specific you can add minutes too:

Est prīma hōra et decem minūtae.	It's 1:10	(minūta, -ae, f. = minute)
Est prīma hōra et quadrāns.	It's 1:15	(quadrans, quadrantis, f. = ¼)
Est prīma hōra et dimidia.	It's 1:30	(dimidia, -ae, f. = ½)
Est prīma et dodrāns.	It's 1:45	(dodrāns, dodrantis, f. = ¾)

Some times of day or night have special names:

Est <u>mānē</u>.	It's morning/dawn.	(mānē, adv. = morning)
Est <u>merīdiē</u>.	It's the middle of the day.	(merīdiē, adv. = noon)
Est <u>vesper</u>.	It's evening.	(vesper, vesperī, m. = evening)
Est <u>nox</u>.	It's night.	
Est <u>mediā nocte</u>.	It's the middle of the night.	
Tē <u>mox</u> vidēbō.	I will see you soon.	(mox, adv. = soon)
Tē <u>crās</u> vidēbō.	I will see you tomorrow.	(crās, adv. = tomorrow)
Tē <u>herī</u> vīdī.	I saw you yesterday.	(herī, adv. = yesterday)

V. Historia (*Famous Men of Rome,* Chapter XXI, Part IIb)

After more victories, Julius Caesar is named dictator for life. He improves the city and corrects the calendar. However, some of the nobles fear that he will become a king. He is stabbed to death in Pompey's theatre on March 15, 44 BC (the Ides of March).

XII – Duodecima   Nōmen: _____

VI. Dēlēgāta

A. *Scrībe* the new Latin *verba* and their meanings.

                    Latīnē   *Anglicē*

1. _____   1. _____

2. _____   2. _____

3. _____   3. _____

4. _____   4. _____

5. _____   5. _____

6. _____   6. _____

7. _____   7. _____

8. _____   8. _____

9. _____   9. _____

10. _____   10. _____

B. *Variatiōnēs.* *Recitā* these sentence patterns several times.

1. Quota hōra est?   Quīnta hōra est.   (What time is it? It's 5 o'clock.)
2. Quota hōra est?   Sexta hōra est.   (What time is it? It's 6 o'clock.)
3. Quota hōra est?   Septima hōra est.   (What time is it? It's 7 o'clock.)
4. Quota hōra est?   Octāva hōra est.   (What time is it? It's 8 o'clock.)
5. Quota hōra est?   Ūndecima hōra est.   (What time is it? It's 11 o'clock.)
6. Quota hōra est?   Duodecima hōra est.   (What time is it? It's 12 o'clock.)
7. Quota hōra est?   Prīma hōra post merīdiem.   (What time is it? It's 1:00 pm.)
8. Quota hōra est?   Prīma hōra ante merīdiem.   (What time is it? It's 1:00 am.)
9. Quota hōra est?   Est prīma hōra et dimidia.   (What time is it? It's 1:30.)
10. Quota hōra est? Est prīma hōra et dodrante.   (What time is it? It's 1:45.)

C. Translate these sentences.

1. Cūr festīnās? _____

2. Quis rīdet?   _____

3. Quid dolet?   _____

XII – Duodecima   **Nōmen:** _____

4. Ubi cāseus est? _____

5. Quomodō mīles pugnat? _____

6. Quandō natābis? _____

7. Quot evangelia sunt? _____

8. Quotus liber est optimus? _____

9. Cūr ursa puerōs terret? _____

10. Quis natāre potest? _____

11. Quot spatia habet abacus? _____

12. Quid Gāius in dexterā tenet? _____

13. Quantum aurum in thēsaurō est? _____

D. Translate these sentences. Then find the question in Part C for which each could be an answer. *Scrībe* **the question number in the short blank next to the sentence number.**

_____ 1. Sunt quattuor evangelia. _____

_____ 2. Cāseus est in culīnā. _____

_____ 3. Mīles bene pugnat. _____

_____ 4. Tertius liber est optimus. _____

_____ 5. Multum aurum in thēsaurō est. _____

_____ 6. Ursa terret puerōs quod est magna (*quod* = because).

E. Translate these sentences (from Latin to English of from English to Latin).

1. Sapientia, cāritās, humilitās, et patientia sunt quattuor virtūtēs.

_____

2. Ubi pilleus agricolae est? _____

3. Cūr librōs magistrō portant? _____

XII – Duodecima   Nōmen: _____

4. Quis flōrem puellae bellae dabit? _____

5. Quot gemmās rēx in thēsaurō habet?
_____

6. How many gems are in the king's treasure?
_____

7. Who will walk through fire? _____

8. Quis hunc gladium mīlitī portābit? _____

9. Quis illam mēnsam in culīnam movēre potest?
_____

10. Which man is happy? _____

11. Who has the third jewel? _____

Ex Scriptūrīs:

12. Ubi humilitās, ibi est sapientia. (Prov. 11:2) _____

13. Quis est hic rēx glōriae? (Ps. 23:8 alt.) _____

F. Translate these *verba* and phrases.

1. duodecima _____   2. eleventh _____

3. Et tū, Brūte? _____   4. before noon _____

5. after noon _____   6. Close your books. _____

7. Quota hōra est? _____   8. Quarta hōra est. _____

9. Dēlenda est Carthāgō! _____

10. Vēnī, vīdī, vīcī. _____

G. Dērīvātī. Complete each sentence with an English *verbum* chosen from the following *verba*. The italicized *verbum* in the sentence should help you think of the Latin root.

XII – Duodecima   Nōmen: _____

quantity   quota   ubiquitous

1. Cell phones are _____; they're every*where*. Latin root: _____

2. State troopers may be given a _____ because they are asked *how many* speeding drivers

   they have arrested. Latin root: _____

3. A measure of _____ shows *how much* one has. Latin root: _____

H. *Verbum* Search. Each of the *verba* listed below can be found in this grid, reading forward, backward, up, down, or diagonally. Can you find them all? All the unused letters will spell a crazy message. *Quid est? Scrībe* the crazy message on this line.

_____

```
A  X  S  O  D  N  A  U  Q
T  H  E  S  A  U  R  U  S
I  A  E  A  A  S  O  B  C
R  E  S  G  T  M  I  I  U
A  D  U  M  O  R  M  N  R
G  I  T  D  U  B  O  E  E
R  U  O  M  Q  C  U  P  G
A  Q  U  A  N  T  U  S  A
M  S  Q  U  I  S  U  A  L
```

WORD LIST

AGER	QUID
CUM	QUIS
CUR	QUOMODO
QUANTUS	QUOT
GEMMA	QUOTUS
LAUS	SINE
MARGARITA	SUB
PORTA	UBI
THESAURUS	EX
QUANDO	

I. Historia. Review the history and fill in the blanks.

1. What office do the people give Caesar? _____

2. What does Caesar do with his power? _____

3. What do the patricians fear? _____

4. How does Caesar die? _____

5. On what date does he die? _____

6. What is that date called? _____

XIII – Tertia Decima   Nōmen:

XIII – Tertia decima lectiō   3ᴿᴰ CONJUGATION
(13 – Thirteenth lesson)

I. Dictum

Silent lēgēs inter arma.
– Marcus Tullius Cicero

II. Colloquium   *Latīnē*   *Anglicē*

| Discipulī: | Blā, blā, blā. | Blah, blah, blah. |
| Magistra: | Silēte. Nunc attendite. | Be quiet. Now pay attention. |

III. Verba

Latīnē   *Anglicē*   *Scrībe tōtum verbum Latīnum.*   *Dērīvātī*

ascendō, ascendere, ascendī, ascensum to ascend

crēdō, crēdere, crēdidī, crēditum to believe

dēscendō, dēscendere, dēscendī, dēscensum to descend

dīcō, dīcere, dīxī, dictum to say, to tell, to speak

legō, legere, lēgī, lectum to read

mittō, mittere, mīsī, missum to send

trādō, trādere, trādidī, trāditum to pass, hand over

XIII – Tertia Decima   Nōmen: _____

1. What kind of *verba* are these? _____

2. How can you tell that these *verba* do not belong to 1st or 2nd conjugation?

_____

IV. Grammatica

The new verbs in this *lectiō* belong to 3rd conjugation. In 3rd conjugation, the infinitive ends in –*ere* (*without* a macron), and it is pronounced with a short, rather than a long *e*. You will know to which conjugation a verb belongs by paying close attention to its infinitive and to the stem vowel within the infinitive:

1st conjugation:	**amāre**	(long *ā* stem vowel in the infinitive)
2nd conjugation:	**vidēre**	(long *ē* stem vowel in the infinitive)
3rd conjugation:	**dīcere**	(short *e* stem vowel in the infinitive)

Because the stem vowel of 3rd conjugation is short (not long as in 1st and 2nd conjugations), it changes. The first three forms ought to be *crēdeō, crēdes, crēdet*, but the stem vowel is so short that it gets bullied – and changes to *ō, i,* and *u* just to fit in!

	Singular	Plural	
1st person _____	crēd**ō**	crēd**i**mus	_____
2nd person _____	crēd**i**s	crēd**i**tis	_____
3rd person _____	crēd**i**t	crēd**u**nt	_____

The endings are all familiar, so this conjugation should be easy to learn. Only the stem is odd.

Future tense works differently for 3rd conjugation. You'll learn about it later. For now, you should just know that the future-tense personal endings for 1st and 2nd conjugations don't work for 3rd conjugation.

When used with the verb *dīcō, dīcere*, the preposition *dē* means *about*.

Another way to write *and* in Latin: *-que* is an enclitic that means *and* when added to the second of two words to be joined, e.g., *soror frāterque* = *sister and brother*.

V. Historia (*Famous Men of Rome*, Chapter XXII)

Marcus Tullius Cicero (106-43 BC) lives through the times of Marius, Sulla, Pompey, and Julius Caesar. He is the greatest orator of ancient Roman times. He saves Rome from the conspiracy of Cataline, but also sees the Republic crumble and the beginning of the Empire.

XIII – Tertia Decima   Nōmen:

VI. Dēlēgāta

A. *Scrībe* the new Latin *verba* and their meanings.

Latīnē	*Anglicē*
1. _____	1. _____
2. _____	2. _____
3. _____	3. _____
4. _____	4. _____
5. _____	5. _____
6. _____	6. _____
7. _____	7. _____

B. *Variātiōnēs.* *Recitā* these sentence patterns several times. Pay special attention to the use of the dative case and of ordinal numbers.

1. Aemilia amīcō prīmum librum dat.   (Amelia gives the first book to a friend.)
2. Aemilia amīcae secundum librum legit.   (Amelia reads the second book to a friend.)
3. Aemilia sorōrī tertium librum mittit.   (Amelia sends the third book to her sister.)
4. Aemilia frātrī quartum librum servat.   (Amelia keeps the fourth book for her brother.)
5. Aemilia magistrō quīntum librum portat. (Amelia carries the fifth book to the teacher.)
6. Aemilia mātrī sextum librum tradit.   (Amelia passes the sixth book to her mother.)

C. Translate these sentences (from Latin to English or from English to Latin).

1. Angelus in caelum ascendit.   _____

2. Angelus dē caelō dēscendit.   _____

3. Crēdō amīcum meum.   _____

4. Crēdō in ūnum Deum.   _____

5. A soldier guards the treasure. _____

6. My brother is reading a book.   _____

7. Dīvitēs argentum student.   _____

XIII – Tertia Decima   **Nōmen:** _____

8. The good woman studies wisdom. _____

9. Pastor dē cāritāte dīcit. _____

10. Aemilia amīcae dōnum mittit. _____

11. Rēx fīliō corōnam trādit. _____

12. Cūr Gāius illum librum legit? _____

13. Quotum librum magister legit? _____

14. Quis cīvitātem servābit? _____

15. Servābitne Cicero cīvitātem? _____

D. Fill in the blanks.

1. With what three letters do infinitives of 1st-conjugation verbs end? ____ 2nd? ____ 3rd? ____

2. What is the difference between 2nd- and 3rd-conjugation infinitives? _____
_____

3. Latin prepositions take the _____ or _____ case.

4. The dative case is used for _____.

E. Translate these Latin sentences (from Latin to English or from English to Latin).

1. Soror mea legere amat. _____

2. Servus legere nōn potest. _____

3. Via circum montem dēscendit. _____

4. Mīles glōriam et victōriam studet. _____

5. A new queen ascends to the throne. _____

6. Frāter tuus tibi magna dōna saepe mittit. _____

XIII – Tertia Decima   Nōmen: _____

7. Mīlitēs glōriam victōriamque in bellō semper student. _____

_____

8. Amīcus mihi clāvem parvae iānuae trādit. _____

_____

9. Caesar hostibus gladiōs nōn mittit. _____

_____

10. Mark is reading a good book.   _____

11. Livia believes in God.   _____

12. A slave guards the queen's jewels. _____

Ex Scriptūrīs:

13. Amen dīcō vōbīs, dīves difficile intrābit in rēgnum caelōrum. (Matt. 19:23, alt.; *amen* – truly; *difficile* – with difficulty) _____

_____

F. Conjugate (1) *dīcō, dīcere* and (2) *mittō, mittere* in present tense.

1. _____ _____   2. _____ _____

   _____ _____   _____ _____

   _____ _____   _____ _____

G. Translate these *verba* and phrases.

1. tertia decima _____   2. twelfth _____

3. with praise _____   4. Ouch! _____

5. Silēte. _____   6. Et tū, Brūte? _____

7. Silent lēgēs inter arma. _____

8. What time is it? _____

9. id est _____   10. eleventh _____

XIII – Tertia Decima   Nōmen:

H. Dērīvātī. Complete each sentence with an English *verbum* chosen from the following *verba*. The italicized *verbum* in the sentence should help you think of the Latin root.

predict   missionary   legible   creed   dictates   traditions

1. A _____ is one who is *sent* to share the gospel. Latin root: _____

2. Our forefathers have passed down _____. Latin root: _____

3. The Apostles' _____ states what Christian *believe*. Latin root: _____

4. If a teacher _____ sentences, she *speaks* them aloud. Latin root: _____

5. _____ penmanship is easy to *read*. Latin root: _____

6. To _____ is to *say* or *tell before*. Latin root: _____

I. Crossword Puzzle. Be careful! One answer is very tricky!

RĒCTĒ
2. we are eager for
7. you (s.) believe
8. to read
10. mouths (nom. or acc.)
11. he says
14. you (s.) pass
15. this (m.)

DEORSUM
1. this (n.)
3. it ascends
4. it descends
5. I send
6. they save
9. out of
12. he
13. there
14. you (acc. s.)

J. Historia. Review the history and fill in the blanks.

1. Who is the greatest orator of Roman times? _____

2. What conspiracy does he stop? _____

XIV – Quarta decima lectiō — IMPERFECT TENSE
(14 – Fourteenth lesson)

I. Dictum

Diēs Īrae

II. Colloquium

Latīnē — *Anglicē*

	Latīnē	Anglicē
Magister:	Līvia, converte hanc sententiam ex Anglicā in Latīnam: I prepare.	Livia, translate this sentence from English into Latin: I prepare.
Līvia:	Latīnē dīcimus: Parō.	In Latin we say: I prepare.

III. Verba

Latīnē	Anglicē	Scrībe tōtum verbum Latīnum.	Dērīvātī
albus, -a, -um	white		
avia, -ae, f.	grandmother		
flāvus, -a, -um	yellow		
līberō, līberāre, līberāvī, līberātum to free, to set free			
niger, nigra, nigrum black			
parō, parāre, parāvī, parātum to prepare			
quī	who, he who		
rūfus, -a, -um	red		
salūtō, salūtāre, salūtāvī, salūtātum to greet			

1. To what conjugation do the verbs belong? _____

NB: *niger* has the less common *-er* ending in the masculine singular nominative (like the nouns *magister, puer, culter, ager,* and *liber*). Find its stem in the feminine or neuter form, i.e., *nigr-*.

XIV – Quarta Decima   Nōmen:

IV. Grammatica

You know how to talk about the present and the future in Latin, but in this *lectiō*, you'll learn how to speak about the past. Latin has several past tenses, but the easiest is the imperfect tense.

Here are the personal endings for the imperfect tense. The imperfect tense sign is _____.

	singular	plural
1st person	-bam	-bāmus
2nd person	-bās	-bātis
3rd person	-bat	-bant

And here are the forms for 1st conjugation and 2nd conjugation in imperfect tense. The imperfect is easy! Simply add the imperfect personal endings to the stem.

The *im*perfect tense expresses action that occurred in the past but was *not* completed all at one time. Translate it using the helping verbs *was* or *were* with *–ing* at the end of the verb. It can also be translated using the helping verbs *used to* or *kept*.

	singular	plural
1st person _____	amābam	amābāmus
2nd person _____	amābās	amābātis
3rd person _____	amābat	amābant
1st person _____	manēbam	manēbāmus
2nd person _____	manēbās	manēbātis
3rd person _____	manēbat	manēbant

Ambulābam.	I was walking.	I kept walking.	I used to walk.
Festīnābat.	He was hurrying.	He kept hurrying.	He used to hurry.
Cantābāmus.	We were singing.	We kept singing.	We used to sing.

V. Historia (*Famous Men of Rome,* Chapter XXIII)

Octavian Caesar, grandnephew of Julius Caesar, forms a triumvirate with Mark Antony and Lepidus. Octavian defeats Lepidus in Sicily and defeats Mark Antony at the Battle of Actium in 31 BC. Rejecting the title of king, he is named Emperor and given the title *Augustus* in 27 BC.

XIV – Quarta Decima   Nōmen: _____

VI. Dēlēgāta

A. *Scrībe* the new Latin *verba* and their meanings.

	Latīnē		*Anglicē*
1.	_____	1.	_____
2.	_____	2.	_____
3.	_____	3.	_____
4.	_____	4.	_____
5.	_____	5.	_____
6.	_____	6.	_____
7.	_____	7.	_____
8.	_____	8.	_____
9.	_____	9.	_____

B. *Variātiōnēs.* *Recitā* these sentence patterns several times.

1. Hic equus stābat.   (This horse was standing.)
2. Ille equus cēnābat.   (That horse was eating.)
3. Equus rūfus pugnābat.   (The red horse was fighting.)
4. Equus niger labōrābat.   (The black horse was working.)
5. Equus albus natābat.   (The white horse was swimming.)
6. Equus flāvus ambulābat.   (The yellow horse was walking.)
7. Prīmus equus aquilam spectābat.   (The first horse was looking at an eagle.)
8. Tertius equus mīlitem portābat.   (The third horse was carrying a soldier.)

C. *Converte hās sententiās.*

1. Avia mātrem salūtābat. _____

2. Soror holera parābat. _____

3. Servī fabās rūfās parābant. _____

4. Capillī aviae sunt albī. _____

5. Dominus servōs līberābat. _____

XIV – Quarta Decima Nōmen:

6. Hic flōs est flāvus. _____

7. Illud cerasum est rūfum. _____

8. Quī cāritātem habet pācem habet. _____

9. Ubi in urbe ambulābās? _____

10. Christum laudābāmus. _____

11. Nauta margarītam nigram spectābat. _____

12. Quotus rēx imperābat? _____

13. Quot discipulī rīdēbant? _____

14. Quandō frāter tuus tē terrēbat ? _____

D. *Converte* these imperfect verbs in three different ways.

1. Servābam. _____

2. Dolēbat. _____

3. Stābātis. _____

E. *Converte hās sententiās aut* (or) *scrībe illās Anglicē.*

1. Spectābātisne eōs? _____

2. Cēnābantne canēs? _____

3. Beātus est quī Deum amat. _____

4. Calculum flāvum moveō in hōc lūdō. _____

5. Soror mea calculum rūfum movet. _____

6. Calculum movēbō ē tertiō spatiō ad octāvum spatium. _____

7. Soror mihi āleās trādit. _____

XIV – Quarta Decima   Nōmen:

8. I was giving a red apple to the black horse in the long field. _____

_____

9. *He* was carrying the girls' books. _____

10. This cat is white. _____

11. I have a black dog. _____

12. We were sitting in chairs. _____

Ex Scriptūrīs:

13. Servābant eum. (Matt. 27:36) _____

14. Angelī et serpēns pugnābant. (Rev. 12:7, alt.) _____

15. Beātus est quī legit et quī audit librum sanctum. (*audit* = *hears* Rev. 1:3, alt.)

_____

F. **Conjugate (1)** *parō, parāre* **and (2)** *studeō, studēre* **in imperfect tense.**

1. _____ _____   2. _____ _____

   _____ _____   _____ _____

   _____ _____   _____ _____

G. *Converte* these *verba* and phrases.

1. quarta decima _____   2. thirteenth _____

3. Diēs Īrae _____   4. sine quā nōn _____

5. summā cum laude _____   6. that is _____

7. Converte hanc sententiam ex Anglicā in Latīnam. _____

_____

8. Silent lēgēs inter arma. _____

9. Pay attention now. _____

10. The Roman Senate and People _____

XIV – Quarta Decima **Nōmen:**

H. Dērīvātī. Complete each sentence with an English *verbum* chosen from the following *verba*. The italicized *verbum* in the sentence should help you think of the Latin root.

liberty   salutation   albino

1. An _____ rabbit is all *white*. Latin root: _____

2. _____ is *freedom* we enjoy in America. Latin root: _____

3. "Dear Grandma" is an example of a letter's _____, where the writer *greets* the person to whom he/she is writing. Latin root: _____

I. Anagram. In the spaces provided, *scribe* the *verbum Latinum* corresponding to the clue. Rearrange the shaded letters to spell something Caesar Augustus made and then destroyed.

- he who
- you were greeting
- he was preparing
- I was freeing
- black (f. nom. s.)
- red (m. nom. s.)
- yellow (n. nom. s.)
- white (m. nom. s.)
- grandmother

Caesar Augustus made and then destroyed a:

_ _ _ _ _ _ _ _ _ _ _

J. Historia. Review the history and fill in the blanks.

1. How is Octavian related to Caesar? _____

2. With whom does he form a triumvirate? _____

3. In what battle does he defeat Mark Antony? _____

4. In what year does the Roman Empire officially begin? _____

XV – Quīnta Decima   Nōmen: _____

XV – Quīnta decima lectiō   MORE IMPERFECT
(15 – Fifteenth lesson)

I. Dictum

exemplī grātiā (_____)   _____

II. Colloquium   *Latīnē*   *Anglicē*

| Magister: | Confēcistisne dēlēgātum vestrum? | Did you finish your assignment? |
| Discipulī: | Certē confēcimus! | Of course we finished! |

III. Verba

Latīnē	*Anglicē*	*Scrībe tōtum verbum Latīnum.*	*Dērīvātī*
arcus, -ī, m.	bow, rainbow	_____	_____
aurantius, -a, -um	orange	_____	_____
avus, -ī, m.	grandfather	_____	_____
caeruleus, -a, -um	blue	_____	_____
ecce	behold!	_____	_____
fulvus, -a, -um	brown	_____	_____
mālum aurantium, -ī, n.	(an) orange	_____	_____
purpureus, -a, -um	purple	_____	_____

1. Why do the *verba* for colors have three endings? _____

2. Which *verba* are nouns? _____ What declension? _____

3. The genitive singular case ending for these declensions is:

   a. 1st _____   b. 2nd _____   c. 3rd _____

4. What is the nominative plural for these *verba*?

   a. arcus _____   b. avus _____   c. avia _____   d. ager _____

XV – Quīnta Decima   Nōmen:

IV. Grammatica

Here is the <u>imperfect tense of *sum, esse*</u> and the <u>imperfect tense of *possum, posse*</u>. if you know the imperfect tense of *sum, esse*, the imperfect of *possum, posse* will be easy. Because these are irregular verbs, they must be carefully memorized.

	singular	plural	
1st person _____	eram	erāmus	_____
2nd person _____	erās	erātis	_____
3rd person _____	erat	erant	_____
1st person _____	pot<u>eram</u>	pot<u>erāmus</u>	_____
2nd person _____	pot<u>erās</u>	pot<u>erātis</u>	_____
3rd person _____	pot<u>erat</u>	pot<u>erant</u>	_____

Remember: *esse* is <u>not</u> a helping verb and <u>cannot</u> be used with another verb in a sentence.

Conjugate: (a) *sum, esse*; (b) *habeō, habēre*; (c) *possum, posse*; (d) *amō, amāre* in imperfect.

a. _____ _____   b. _____ _____

   _____ _____   _____ _____

   _____ _____   _____ _____

c. _____ _____   d. _____ _____

   _____ _____   _____ _____

   _____ _____   _____ _____

V. Historia (*Famous Men of Rome,* Chapter XXIV, Parts I and II)

After Augustus dies in 14 A.D., the Empire sees three cruel emperors: Tiberius, Caligula, and Claudius. The fifth emperor, Nero, is even worse. In 54 A.D., Nero's mother, Agrippina, kills emperor Claudius after making him name Nero his successor rather than his own son, Britannicus. Nero becomes emperor, but out of fear, he kills Britannicus and then Agrippina.

XV – Quīnta Decima   Nōmen: _____

VI. Dēlēgāta

A. *Scrībe* the new Latin *verba* and their meanings.

Latīnē   *Anglicē*

1. _____   1. _____

2. _____   2. _____

3. _____   3. _____

4. _____   4. _____

5. _____   5. _____

6. _____   6. _____

7. _____   7. _____

8. _____   8. _____

B. *Variātiōnēs.* *Recitā* these sentence patterns several times.

1. Avus huic puerō dōna dat.   (Grandfather is giving gifts to this boy.)
2. Avus huic puellae dōna dat.   (Grandfather is giving gifts to this girl.)
3. Avus illī puerō dōna dat.   (Grandfather is giving gifts to that boy.)
4. Avus illī puellae dōna dat.   (Grandfather is giving gifts to that girl.)
5. Avus eī dōna dat.   (Grandfather is giving gifts to him / her.)
6. Avus mihi dōna dat.   (Grandfather is giving gifts to me.)
7. Oculī huius puerī fulvī sunt.   (This boy's eyes are brown.)
9. Oculī illīus puellae caeruleī sunt. (That girl's eyes are blue.)
10. Oculī eius caeruleī sunt.   (His / Her eyes are blue.)

C. *Converte hās sententiās.*

1. Hic flōs est aurantius.   _____

2. Illud vīnum est purpureum. _____

3. Caelum est caeruleum.   _____

4. Capillī meī sunt fulvī.   _____

5. Ōs meum est rūfum.   _____

XV – Quīnta Decima   Nōmen:

6. Dentēs meī sunt albī. _____

7. Stellae lūcēbant. _____

8. Ioannes ad mēnsam sedēbat. _____

9. Fēles in bracchiīs meīs erat. _____

10. Pānem in mēnsā habēbāmus. _____

11. Cūr flōrem huic puellae dabās? _____

12. Suntne capillī illīus puellae fulvī? _____

13. Erantne capillī huius puerī flāvī? _____

D. *Converte* **these imperfect verbs in three different ways.**

1. Habēbāmus. _____

2. Vidēbant. _____

3. Movēbās. _____

E. *Converte hās sententiās aut scrībe illās Anglicē.*

1. Avus capillōs fulvōs habēbat. _____

2. Avus capillōs albōs nunc habet. _____

3. Arcum mīlitis tenēre poteram. _____

4. Arcus in caelō est aurantius et purpureus et caeruleus. _____
   _____

5. Tarquinia ūnum canem habēbat. _____

6. Anna duōs canēs habēbat. _____

7. Septimus trīs canēs habēbat. _____

8. That orange was good. _____

9. She was able to carry the gems. _____

XV – Quīnta Decima   Nōmen: _____

10. That flower is purple. _____

11. The sailor used to have a blue jewel. _____

Ex Scriptūrīs:

12. Et tenēbat in dexterā stellās septem et ecce: in ōre eius gladius erat. (Rev. 1:16, alt.)
_____

13. Ecce equus albus et quī sedēbat in illō tenēbat arcum. (Rev. 6:2, alt.) _____
_____

14. Ecce equus rūfus et quī sedēbat in illō tenēbat gladium magnum. (Rev. 6:4, alt.) _____
_____

F. Conjugate (1) *sum, esse* and (2) *possum, posse* in imperfect tense.

1. _____ _____   2. _____ _____

   _____ _____   _____ _____

   _____ _____   _____ _____

G. *Converte* these *verba* and phrases.

   1. quīnta decima _____   2. fourteenth _____

   3. exemplī grātiā _____   4. You, too, Brutus? _____

   5. Claudite librōs. _____   6. Diēs Īrae _____

   7. Confēcistīne dēlēgātum tuum? _____

   8. Quid est tibi? _____

   9. Hōra est quaestiunculae. _____

   10. Translate this sentence. _____

   11. Where do you live? _____

H. **Dērīvātī.** Complete each sentence with an English *verbum* chosen from the following *verba*. The italicized *verbum* in the sentence should help you think of the Latin root.

arch   caerulean

XV – Quīnta Decima   Nōmen: _____

1. _____n_____ is a shade of *blue*. Latin root: _____

2. An _____ is a *bow*-shaped, curved opening. Latin root: _____

I. Crossword Puzzle. When the puzzle is completed, the letters in the shaded squares can be rearranged to show what Roman history taught President James Madison to do with political powers. *Nōtā bene (N.B.)*: All adjectives in this puzzle are masculine singular.

RĒCTĒ:
4. orange (the color)
6. behold
7. grandfather
8. brown
10. purple

DEORSUM
1. secundus imperātor
2. blue
3. prīmus imperātor
5. bow
9. quīntus imperātor

__ __ __ __ __ __ __ __ them!

J. Historia. Review the history and fill in the blanks.

1. Who is the second emperor of Rome? _____

2. Quis tertius imperātor Romae est? _____

3. Quis quartus imperātor Romae est? _____

4. In what year does Nero become emperor? _____

XVI – Sexta Decima   Nōmen: _____

XVI – Sexta decima lectiō   VESTĪMENTA
(16 – Sixteenth lesson)   (Clothes)

I. Dictum

Tē Deum laudāmus.

II. Colloquium   *Latīnē*   *Anglicē*

	Latīnē	*Anglicē*
Semprōnia:	Ubi sunt calceī meī?	Where are my shoes?
Cato:	Hīc sunt!	Here they are!

III. Verba

Latīnē	*Anglicē*	*Scrībe tōtum verbum Latīnum.*	*Dērīvātī*
brācae, brācārum, f.	pants	_____	_____
calceus, -ī, m.	shoe	_____	_____
camisia, -ae, f.	shirt	_____	_____
cingulum, -ī, n.	belt	_____	_____
claudō, claudere, clausī, clausum	to close		_____
_____ _____	_____	_____	
gerō, gerere, gessī, gestum	to wear		_____
_____ _____	_____	_____	
induō, induere, induī, indūtum	to put on		_____
_____ _____	_____	_____	
petō, petere, petīvī, petītum	to seek, to beg, to ask for		_____
_____ _____	_____	_____	
scrībō, scrībere, scrīpsī, scriptum	to write		_____
_____ _____	_____	_____	

Why do you think that *bracae* is plural, when a pair of pants is *one* piece of clothing?

XVI – Sexta Decima   Nōmen:

IV. Grammatica

The imperfect is almost as easy for 3rd conjugation as it is for 1st and 2nd conjugations. In this tense the stem vowel becomes an *ē* (remember that it changes quite a bit in the present tense too), and then add the imperfect personal endings to the stem.

	singular	plural
1st person	crēdē**bam**	crēdē**bāmus**
2nd person	crēdē**bās**	crēdē**bātis**
3rd person	crēdē**bat**	crēdē**bant**

1. How do you find the imperfect stem for 1st- and 2nd-conjugation verbs? _____

2. What does the imperfect tense express? _____

3. The two best helping verbs to use when translating the imperfect tense are _____ and _____.

4. Conjugate (a) *dīcō, dīcere*; (b) *scrībō, scrībere*; (c) *claudō, claudere*; and (d) *mittō, mittere* in imperfect tense.

a. _____   _____   b. _____   _____

c. _____   _____   d. _____   _____

V. Historia (*Famous Men of Rome*, Chapter XXIV, Parts III and IV)

Nero becomes even worse than before. He kills his friends and his wife, and, probably after setting the fire himself, he plays the harp as he watches Rome burn! He then blames Christians for the blaze and has many of them killed. A first plot to kill him fails. Then, in 68 A.D., hiding in fear from a revolt by the army, Emperor Nero dies at the hand of a slave.

XVI – Sexta Decima   Nōmen: _____

VI. Dēlēgāta

A. *Scrībe* the new Latin *verba* and their meanings.

　　　　　　　　　Latīnē　　　　　　　　　　　　　　　　　*Anglicē*

1. _____   1. _____

2. _____   2. _____

3. _____   3. _____

4. _____   4. _____

5. _____   5. _____

6. _____   6. _____

7. _____   7. _____

8. _____   8. _____

9. _____   9. _____

B. *Variātiōnēs.* *Recita* these sentence patterns several times. Be sure to read the whole Latin line aloud, including the nominative at the beginning.

　　1. Brācae.　　　Lūcius brācās induit.　　　　(Pants. Lucius is putting on pants.)
　　2. Calceī.　　　Lūcius calceōs induit.　　　　(Shoes. Lucius is putting on shoes.)
　　3. Camisia.　　 Lūcius camisiam induit.　　　 (Shirt. Lucius is putting on a shirt.)
　　4. Cingulum.　　Lūcius cingulum induit.　　　 (Belt. Lucius is putting on a belt.)
　　5. Pedālia.　　　Lūcius pedālia induit.　　　　(Socks. Lucius is putting on socks.)
　　6. Pilleus.　　　Lūcius pilleum induit.　　　　(Hat. Lucius is putting on a hat.)
　　7. Brācae.　　　Stella brācās gerēbat.　　　　 (Pants. Stella was wearing pants.)
　　8. Calceī.　　　Stella calceōs gerēbat.　　　　(Shoes. Stella was wearing shoes.)
　　9. Camisia.　　 Stella camisiam gerēbat.　　　 (Shirt. Stella was wearing a shirt.)
　10. Cingulum.　　Stella cingulum gerēbat.　　　 (Belt. Stella was wearing a belt.)
　11. Pedālia.　　　Stella pedālia gerēbat.　　　　(Socks. Stella was wearing socks.)
　12. Pilleus.　　　Stella pilleum gerēbat.　　　　(Hat. Stella was wearing a hat.)

C. *Converte hās sententiās.*

1. Antōnius calceōs induēbat.　　_____

2. Vitellius calceōs fulvōs gerit.　_____

XVI – Sexta Decima   Nōmen:

3. Cornēlia brācās fulvās gerēbat. _____

4. Iūlia duo pedālia induit. _____

5. Sextus duōs pilleōs habēbat. _____

6. Lydia used to have two blue hats. _____

7. Marcus trīs camisiās flāvās habēbat. _____

8. Quis camisiam purpuream gerit? _____

9. Cūr Aemilia duās camisiās aurantiās habet?

_____

D. *Converte* **these imperfect verbs in three different ways.**

1. Petēbant. _____

2. Scrībēbās. _____

3. Claudēbātis. _____

E. *Converte hās sententiās aut scrībe illās Latīnē.*

1. Claudēbam fenestram. _____

2. Servī calceōs petunt. _____

3. Ille puer portiōnem petēbat. _____

4. Hic magister librum scrībit. _____

5. The good student was able to write books.

_____

6. Mīlitēs illī rēgī scrībere poterant. _____

7. Avis super nimbōs ascendēbat. _____

8. The king was sending the legion across the country.

_____

XVI – Sexta Decima   Nōmen:

9. Augustus mēcum ambulābat. _____

10. I was wearing a wide hat. _____

11. Titus was writing to Livia. _____

12. We were often happy. _____

Ex Scriptūrīs:

13. Scrībō vōbīs mandātum Dominī. (I Cor. 14:37, alt.; *mandātum, -ī, n.* – commandment)

_____

F. Conjugate (1) *petō, petere* **and (2)** *gerō, gerere* **in imperfect tense.**

1. _____ _____   2. _____ _____

   _____ _____   _____ _____

   _____ _____   _____ _____

G. *Converte* these *verba* and phrases.

1. sexta decima _____   2. fifteenth _____

3. ad nauseam _____   4. ante merīdiem _____

5. Tē Deum laudāmus. _____

6. Laws are silent among arms. _____

7. Quota hōra est? _____

8. Ubi sunt calceī meī? _____

9. Did you finish your assignment? _____

10. I came, I saw, I conquered. _____

H. Dērīvātī. Complete each sentence with an English *verbum* chosen from the following *verba*. The italicized *verbum* in the sentence should help you think of the Latin root.

> camisole   cinch   claustrophobia   petulant   Scripture

XVI – Sexta Decima   Nōmen: _____

1. He liked to _____ up his *belt*. Latin root: _____

2. _____ is God's *written* Word. Latin root: _____

3. A _____ is a woman's sleeveless *shirt*. Latin root: _____

4. The child's _____ *begging* was very annoying. Latin root: _____

5. _____ is the fear of being *closed* in. Latin root: _____

I. *Verbum* **Search.** Each of the *verba* listed below can be found in this grid, reading forward, backward, up, down, or diagonally. The verbs will be in the form given below or in the imperfect tense. All the unused letters, when read row by row from top to bottom, will tell three ways to translate the nonsense word *xēbam*:

Translation: _____

```
B  M  U  L  U  G  N  I  C
C  R  S  M  I  T  T  O  S
A  I  A  I  W  A  H  U  S
M  X  I  C  T  N  M  G  I
I  K  E  P  A  A  A  T  X
S  C  R  I  B  E  B  A  S
I  I  T  E  E  L  E  A  N
A  P  R  O  D  A  U  O  D
G  E  A  G  U  D  D  D  I
G  T  D  E  A  E  N  E  C
I  O  O  L  L  P  I  R  O
U  S  U  E  C  L  A  C  S
E  E  R  A  M  D  T  O  X
```

WORD LIST

BRACAE
CALCEUS
CAMISIA
CINGULUM
CLAUDO
CREDO
DICO
DO (imperf. tense)
GERO
HOC
INDUO
LEGO
MITTO
PEDALE
PETO
SCRIBO
TRADO
SUM

J. Historia. Review the history and fill in the blanks.

1. What does Nero do while Rome burns? _____

2. Whom does he blame for the fire? _____

3. In what year does Nero die? _____

XVII – Septima decima lectiō   **TEMPORA ANNĪ**

(17 – Seventeenth lesson)   (_____ lit.,_____)

I. Dictum

dramatis persōnae _____ (lit., _____)

II. Colloquium   *Latīnē*   *Anglicē*

	Latīnē	*Anglicē*
Flāvius:	Quotum tempus annī tibi maximē placet?	Which season do you like most?
Aurēlia:	Vēr mihi placet. Quotum tempus minimē placet?	I like spring. Which season do you like least?
Flāvius:	Autumnus mihi nōn placet.	I don't like fall.

III. Verba

Latīnē	*Anglicē*	*Scrībe tōtum verbum Latīnum.*	*Dērīvātī*
aestās, aestātis, f.	summer	_____	_____
autumnus, -ī, m.	autumn, fall	_____	_____
hiems, hiemis, f.	winter	_____	_____
vēr, vēris, n.	spring	_____	_____
grātia, -ae, f.	grace	_____	_____
ningit, ningere, ninxit	to snow		_____
_____ _____ _____			
nix, nivis, f.	snow	_____	_____
pluit, pluere, pluit	to rain		_____
_____ _____ _____			
pluvia, -ae, f.	rain	_____	_____

1. From which conjugation are the verbs above? ___ How can you tell? _____

2. Which nouns are from 1st declension? From 2nd? From 3rd?

N.B.: *Pluit* and *ningit* are <u>only</u> used in the 3rd-person singular and the infinitive forms.

XVII – Septima Decima   Nōmen:

IV. Grammatica

Here is the future tense of *3rd conjugation*. It does not use the ordinary future tense endings. Instead, we change the stem vowel to an *a* (for 1st person singular) or to a long *ē* (for all others). When you learn 4th conjugation you will see that it works the same way. Memorize this silly rhyme about future tense: *"Bo, bi, bu for one and two; a and e for four and three!"*

This means that in the future tense of conjugations one and two, we see the endings *bō, bi* and *bu* (e.g.: *amābō, anābis, amābunt*). In conjugations four and three, however, we simply change the stem vowel to *a* and *ē* (e.g.: *crēdam, crēdēs*) and leave the usual personal endings in place.

	singular	plural
1st person	crēdam	crēdēmus
2nd person	crēdēs	crēdētis
3rd person	crēdet	crēdent

The ablative case has many uses besides being used for objects of prepositions. It is used with *dīgnus, -a, -um* to express the idea of being worthy *of* (something).

Deus est laude dīgnus.	God is worthy of praise.

And in expressions of time, the ablative case is used without any preposition: *in* is not needed.

Hieme ningit.	It snows in winter.

Conjugate (a) *dīcō, dīcere* and (b) *scrībō, scrībere* in future tense.

a. _____ _____   b. _____ _____

_____ _____   _____ _____

_____ _____   _____ _____

V. Historia (*Famous Men of Rome,* Chapter XXV)

After Nero dies, three generals—Galba, Otho, and Vitellius—become emperor, each for just a few months. Then in 69 A.D., General Titus Flavius Vespasian, known as Vespasian, takes advantage of the turmoil and becomes emperor. In 70 A.D., his son Titus destroys Jerusalem, and in 79 A.D., he becomes emperor. Titus builds the Colosseum and the Baths of Titus. During his reign, Pompeii and Herculaneum are destroyed by the eruption of Mt. Vesuvius.

XVII – Septima Decima   Nōmen: _____

VI. Dēlēgāta

A. *Scrībe* the new Latin *verba* and their meanings.

          Latīnē   *Anglicē*

1. _____ 1. _____

2. _____ 2. _____

3. _____ 3. _____

4. _____ 4. _____

5. _____ 5. _____

6. _____ 6. _____

7. _____ 7. _____

8. _____ 8. _____

9. _____ 9. _____

B. *Variātiōnēs.* *Recitā* these sentence patterns several times. (N.B. Sentences 1-8 are idiomatic Latin, i.e., they are written as the Romans expressed these ideas, but they are not translated literally.)

1. Aestās mihi placet.   (I like summer. Lit., Summer is pleasing to me.)
2. Autumnus mihi placet.   (I like autumn.)
3. Hiems mihi placet.   (I like winter.)
4. Vēr mihi placet.   (I like spring.)
5. Placetne tibi aestās?   (Do you like summer?)
6. Placetne tibi autumnus?   (Do you like autumn?)
7. Placetne tibi hiems?   (Do you like winter?)
8. Placetne tibi vēr?   (Do you like spring?)
9. Hieme ningit.   (It snows in winter.)
10. Aestāte numquam ningit.   (It never snows in summer.)
11. Vēre saepe pluit.   (It often rains in spring.)
12. Autumnō non saepe pluit. (It does not often rain in autumn.)

C. *Converte hās sententiās.*

1. Ningit super montēs. _____

2. Ningēbat ad flūmen. _____

XVII – Septima Decima   Nōmen: _____

3. Vēre multum pluit. _____

4. Autumnō parum pluēbat. _____

5. Hiems erat bona. _____

6. Autumnus erat bonus. _____

7. Vēr est bonum. _____

8. Lūcius brācās in cubiculō induēbat. _____

9. Cūr rēx hostibus nūntium mittit? _____

10. Amāsne natāre aestāte? _____

11. Ille rēx erat laude dīgnus. _____

D. *Converte hās sententiās aut scrībe illās Latīne.*

1. Hiems est tempus annī optimum. _____

2. Nix dē caelō dēscendēbat. _____

3. Nix et pluvia dē caelō dēscendent. _____

4. Haec nix est bella. _____

5. Illa nix erat bella. _____

6. Arcus illīus mīlitis valēbat. _____

7. Mendācia huius rēgis erant magna. _____

8. Deus meus est glōriā dīgnus. _____

9. Brācae huius puellae flāvae erant. _____

10. The flowers were blue. _____

11. The snow was white. _____

XVII – Septima Decima   Nōmen: _____

12. It was raining in the winter! _____

Ex Scriptūrīs:

13. Grātia vōbīs et pax ab eō quī est, et quī erat, et quī ventūrus est. (Rev. 1:4; *ventūrus* – coming)

_____

_____

14. In principiō erat Verbum, et Verbum erat apud Deum, et Deus erat Verbum. (John 1:1; *apud [+ Ac]* – with, in the presence of)

_____

_____

15. Hoc erat in principiō apud Deum. (John 1:2) _____

16. In eō vīta erat, et vīta erat lūx hominum. (John 1:4, alt.)

_____

E. *Converte* these *verba* and phrases.

1. septima decima _____   2. sixteenth _____

3. dramatis persōnae _____   4. post merīdiem _____

5. Diēs Īrae _____   6. tempora annī _____

7. Quotum tempus annī tibi maximē placet? _____

F. Conjugate (1) *placeō, -ēre*; and (2) *dīcō, dīcere* in future tense.

1. _____ _____   2. _____ _____

   _____ _____   _____ _____

   _____ _____   _____ _____

XVII – Septima Decima   Nōmen:

G. Conjugate (1) *mittō, mittere;* and (2) *sum, esse* in the present tense.

1. _____ _____ 2. _____ _____

   _____ _____   _____ _____

   _____ _____   _____ _____

H. Anagrams. Unscramble each *verbum*, and *scribe* it in the squares. When you finish, unscramble the letters in the shaded squares to finish *hanc sententiam Latīnam*:

Vēr est __ __ __ __ __ __ __ __ __ __ .

- XNI
- EVR
- MHESI
- TULIP
- TGAARI
- TSAASE
- GTIINN
- UAVLIP
- USUTNUAM

I. Historia. Review the history and fill in the blanks.

1. What three emperors have short reigns (68-69 AD)? _____

2. Who becomes emperor after them? _____

3. Although the ninth and tenth emperors have the same name, the son is known in history as

   _____

4. What does Titus do in 70 A.D.? _____

5. What disaster happens during Titus's reign? _____

XVIII – Duodēvīcēsima   Nōmen: _____

XVIII – Duodēvīcēsima lectiō   MENSĒS
(18 – Eighteenth lesson)   (Months)

I. Dictum

nōtā bene (_____)   _____

II. Colloquium   *Latīnē*   *Anglicē*

	Latīnē	*Anglicē*
Valeria:	Quō mēnse nātus es?	In what month were you born?
Quīntus:	Mēnse Augustō nātus sum.	I was born in the month of August.
	Quō mēnse nāta es tū?	In what month were you born?
Valeria:	Mēnse Februāriō nāta sum.	I was born in the month of February.

III. Verba

Latīnē	*Anglicē*	*Scrībe tōtum verbum Latīnum.*	*Dērīvātī*
mēnsis, mēnsis, m.	month		
Iānuārius, -ī, m.	January		
Februārius, -ī, m.	February		
Martius, -ī, m.	March		
Aprīlis, Aprīlis, m.	April		
Māius, -ī, m.	May		
Iūnius, -ī, m.	June		
Iūlius, -ī, m.	July		
Augustus, -ī, m.	August		
September, -bris, m.	September		
Octōber, -bris, m.	October		
November, -bris, m.	November		
December, -bris, m.	December		

XVIII – Duodēvīcēsima   Nōmen:

IV. Grammatica

You have probably noticed that the last four months are named after numbers: *septem, octō, novem,* and *decem*. But they aren't the seventh, eighth, ninth, and tenth months! The Roman calendar originally began in *Martius*. Thus, September *was* the seventh month, and the leap day (which is now in February every fourth year) was added at the end of the year. At some point, the Romans decided to start the year in *Iānuārius*. Plutarch, a first-century Greek writer, tells us that King Numa Pompilius made the decision because he thought it was more appropriate to begin the year honoring Janus, the god who looks backward and forward, than Mars, the god of war. We still use the new year as a time to think back on what has happened and to plan ahead and make resolutions for the coming year.

Plutarch also tells us about other months. *Māius* and *Iūnius*, he says, were either named for the goddesses Maia and Juno *or* to honor older people, *māiōrēs*, and younger people, *iūniōrēs*. According to the calendar, who do you think is greater: older people or younger people?

Julius Caesar named the seventh month after himself. Caesar Augustus followed suit and took the eighth month for himself. They each wanted a long month to reflect their greatness!

The seasons and the months can both be expressions of time, so, as with the seasons, the ablative case is used when one means *in___*, e.g., *Februāriō nāvigābit = He will sail in February*.

Conjugate (a) *possum, posse* and (b) *legō, legere* in imperfect tense.

a. _____ _____   b. _____ _____

_____ _____   _____ _____

_____ _____   _____ _____

Conjugate (a) *lūceō, lūcēre* and (b) *dīcō, dīcere* in future tense.

a. _____ _____   b. _____ _____

_____ _____   _____ _____

_____ _____   _____ _____

V. Historia (*Famous Men of Rome,* Chapter XXVI)

Titus is followed by his brother Domitian, who amuses himself by killing flies, and Nerva. In 98 A.D. Nerva's adopted son, Trajan, becomes the thirteenth emperor of Rome. Trajan achieves great military victories in Dacia, Armenia, and Mesopotamia. He also promotes public works and literature. Plutarch and Tacitus live during his time.

XVIII – Duodēvīcēsima   Nōmen: _____

VI. Dēlēgāta

A. *Scrībe* the new Latin *verba* and their meanings.

Latīnē	*Anglicē*
1. _____	1. _____
2. _____	2. _____
3. _____	3. _____
4. _____	4. _____
5. _____	5. _____
6. _____	6. _____
7. _____	7. _____
8. _____	8. _____
9. _____	9. _____
10. _____	10. _____
11. _____	11. _____
12. _____	12. _____
13. _____	13. _____

B. *Variātiōnēs.* *Recitā* these sentence patterns several times. (N.B.: *nātus* vs. *nāta*)

1. Mēnse Iānuāriō nātus / nāta sum.   (I was born in the month of January.)
2. Mēnse Februāriō nātus / nāta sum.   (I was born in the month of February.)
3. Mēnse Martiō nātus / nāta sum.   (I was born in the month of March.)
4. Mēnse Aprīle nātus / nāta sum.   (I was born in the month of April.)
5. Mēnse Māiō nātus / nāta sum.   (I was born in the month of May.)
6. Mēnse Iūniō nātus / nāta sum.   (I was born in the month of June.)
7. Mēnse Iūliō nātus / nāta sum.   (I was born in the month of July.)
8. Mēnse Augustō nātus / nāta sum.   (I was born in the month of August.)
9. Mēnse Septembre nātus / nāta sum.   (I was born in the month of September.)
10. Mēnse Octōbre nātus / nāta sum.   (I was born in the month of October.)
11. Mēnse Novembre nātus / nāta sum.   (I was born in the month of November.)
12. Mēnse Decembre nātus / nāta sum.   (I was born in the month of December.)

XVIII – Duodēvīcēsima Nōmen:

C. *Converte hās sententiās.*

1. Iānuārius est prīmus mensis. _____

2. September est nōnus mensis. _____

3. Iūniō multum natābimus. _____

4. Decembre multum cantābāmus. _____

5. Iūliō natāre saepe poterāmus. _____

6. Aprīle natāre nōn poterāmus. _____

7. Augustō sine calceīs ambulāre poterās.

_____

8. Līvia semper pilleum Martiō gerit. _____

9. Quotus mensis tibi maximē placet? _____

10. Quis natāre Februāriō amat? _____

D. *Converte hās sententiās aut scrībe illās Latīne.*

1. Annus duodecim mensēs habet. _____

2. Māius est mensis vēris. _____

3. November est mensis autumnī. _____

4. Nivēs Decembris semper bellae sunt.

_____

5. Aprīle multum pluit. _____

6. Augustō parum pluet. _____

7. Four gospels tell about the life of Christ.

_____

8. Rhea was born in April. _____

XVIII – Duodēvīcēsima Nōmen: _____

9. We were able to swim in September. _____

10. May is the fifth month. _____

11. The farmers were not able to plow in March.

_____

Ex Scrīptūrīs:

12. "Ego sum Alpha et Omega, principium et fīnis," dīcit Dominus Deus quī est, et quī erat, et quī ventūrus est. (*ventūrus est – who is coming* Rev. 1:8)

_____

_____

E. *Converte* **these** *verba* **and phrases.**

1. duodēvīcēsima _____ 2. seventeenth _____

3. nōtā bene _____ 4. for example _____

5. Quō mense nātus / nāta es? _____

F. Conjugate (1) *dō, dare* **and (2)** *dīcō, dīcere* **in imperfect tense.**

1. _____ _____   2. _____ _____

   _____ _____   _____ _____

   _____ _____   _____ _____

G. Conjugate (1) *possum, posse* **in the present and (2) imperfect tenses.**

1. _____ _____   2. _____ _____

   _____ _____   _____ _____

   _____ _____   _____ _____

H. Mixed-Up Calendar. The printer forgot to put the names of the months on this calendar and then got them all out of order. Can you figure out which month is which? (N.B. Two months in every year look exactly the same.)

XVIII – Duodēvīcēsima   Nōmen: _____

			1	2	3
4	5	6	7	8	9	10
11	12	13	14	15	16	17
18	19	20	21	22	23	24
25	26	27	28	29	30	31

				1	2	3	4
5	6	7	8	9	10	11
12	13	14	15	16	17	18
19	20	21	22	23	24	25
26	27	28	29	30	31	

1	2	3	4	5	6	7
8	9	10	11	12	13	14
15	16	17	18	19	20	21
22	23	24	25	26	27	28
29	30	31				

			1	2	3
4	5	6	7	8	9	10
11	12	13	14	15	16	17
18	19	20	21	22	23	24
25	26	27	28	29	30	

1	2	3	4	5	6
7	8	9	10	11	12	13
14	15	16	17	18	19	20
21	22	23	24	25	26	27
28	29	30	31			

1	2	3	4	5	6
7	8	9	10	11	12	13
14	15	16	17	18	19	20
21	22	23	24	25	26	27
28	29	30	31			

1	2	3	4	5	6	7
8	9	10	11	12	13	14
15	16	17	18	19	20	21
22	23	24	25	26	27	28
29	30					

						1
2	3	4	5	6	7	8
9	10	11	12	13	14	15
16	17	18	19	20	21	22
23	24	25	26	27	28	29
30						

						1
2	3	4	5	6	7	8
9	10	11	12	13	14	15
16	17	18	19	20	21	22
23	24	25	26	27	28	29
30	31					

					1	2
3	4	5	6	7	8	9
10	11	12	13	14	15	16
17	18	19	20	21	22	23
24	25	26	27	28	29	30

				1	2	3
4	5	6	7	8	9	10
11	12	13	14	15	16	17
18	19	20	21	22	23	24
25	26	27	28			

		1	2	3	4	5
6	7	8	9	10	11	12
13	14	15	16	17	18	19
20	21	22	23	24	25	26
27	28	29	30	31		

I. Historia. Review the history and fill in the blanks.

1. What does Domitian do for fun? _____

2. Who is the twelfth emperor of Rome? _____

3. In what year does Trajan's reign begin? _____

4. What two historians live during Trajan's reign? _____

XIX – Ūndēvīcēsima   Nōmen:

XIX – Ūndēvīcēsima lectiō   QUID ERIT ERIT.
(19 – Nineteenth lesson)   (What will be will be.)

I. Dictum

　　　　　Ecce homō!
　　　　　　– Pilate

II. Colloquium　　　*Latīnē*　　　　　*Anglicē*

| **Publius:** | Manē dum, quaesō! | Wait a minute, please! |
| **Līvia:** | Minimē! Festīnā! | No! Hurry! |

III. Verba

Latīnē	*Anglicē*	*Scrībe tōtum verbum Latīnum.*	*Dērīvātī*
fatuus, -a, -um	foolish, silly		
labor, labōris, m.	work, labor, effort		
nēmo, nēminis, m./f.	no one		
opus, operis, n.	(a) work		
pauper, pauperis, m.	poor man		
piscātor, piscātōris, m.	fisherman		
piscis, piscis, m.	fish		
prophetia, -ae, f.	prophecy		
virgō, virginis, f.	young woman, maiden, virgin		

1. How many *verba* are nouns? Adjectives? Verbs?

2. How many *verba* are 1st-declension nouns? 2nd? 3rd?

3. How many nouns name people? Places? Things? Ideas?

4. What important detail distinguishes one declension from another? _____

XIX – Ūndēvīcēsima   Nōmen:

IV. Grammatica

The future tense of *sum, esse* is easy, but because it is an irregular verb you must memorize it.

Sum, esse also a _____ verb, and it means _____.

	singular	plural	
1st person _____	erō	erimus	_____
2nd person _____	eris	eritis	_____
3rd person _____	erit	erunt	_____

The future tense of *possum, posse* is also easy once you know the future tense of *sum, esse*.

	singular	plural	
1st person _____	poterō	poterimus	_____
2nd person _____	poteris	poteritis	_____
3rd person _____	poterit	poterunt	_____

A. *Scrībe* the future tense conjugation of *sum, esse* two times.

1. _____ _____   2. _____ _____

B. *Scrībe* the future tense conjugation of *possum, posse* two times.

1. _____ _____   2. _____ _____

V. Historia (*Famous Men of Rome*, Chapter XXVII, Part I)

Beginning in 117, Trajan's cousin Hadrian governs well and builds a wall in Britain. He is followed by Antoninus Pius, who allows Christian worship. In 161, Marcus Aurelius, a Stoic philosopher, becomes emperor.

XIX – Ūndēvīcēsima

VI. Dēlēgāta

A. *Scrībe* the new Latin *verba* and their meanings.

Latīnē	*Anglicē*
1. _____	1. _____
2. _____	2. _____
3. _____	3. _____
4. _____	4. _____
5. _____	5. _____
6. _____	6. _____
7. _____	7. _____
8. _____	8. _____
9. _____	9. _____

B. *Variātiōnēs.* *Recitā* these sentence patterns several times.

1. Pauper erat fatuus. (The poor man was foolish.)
2. Pauper est fatuus. (The poor man is foolish.)
3. Pauper erit fatuus. (The poor man will be foolish.)
4. Virgō erat fatua. (The young woman was foolish.)
5. Virgō est fatua. (The young woman is foolish.)
6. Virgō erit fatua. (The young woman will be foolish.)
7. Piscātōrēs erant fatuī. (The fishermen were foolish.)
8. Piscātōrēs sunt fatuī. (The fishermen are foolish.)
9. Piscātōrēs erunt fatuī. (The fishermen will be foolish.)
10. Fatuae erāmus. (We were foolish.)
11. Fatuae sumus. (We are foolish.)
12. Fatuae erimus. (We shall be foolish.)

C. *Converte has sententiās.*

1. Virgō erit rēgīna. _____

2. Labōrēs meī erunt magnī. _____

3. Hoc erit meum magnum opus. _____

XIX – Ūndēvīcēsima   Nōmen:

4. Prophetia dē Christō dīcit. _____
5. Nēmo portās claudēbat. _____
6. Nēmo portās claudere poterit. _____
7. Ursa piscem cēnābat. _____
8. Piscātor numquam labōrat. _____
9. Ille piscātor fatuus est. _____
10. Is erit pauper. _____
11. Hominēs beātī in caelō erunt. _____
12. Cum Christō ascendēmus. _____

D. *Converte hās sententiās aut scrībe illās Latīnē.*

1. Christus erit rēx mundī huius. _____
2. Piscātor aestāte erit dīves. _____
3. It will rain a lot in March. _____
4. Virgō argentum nōn habet. _____
5. Quandō rēx erit beātus? _____
6. Cūr aleās tenēbās? _____
7. The fishermen are eager for work. _____
8. No one will be happy in January. _____
9. The fisherman used to have many fish. _____
10. The young women will be rich. _____

Ex Scriptūrīs:

11. Simile erit rēgnum caelōrum decem virginibus. (Matt. 25:1) _____

XIX – Ūndēvīcēsima   Nōmen: _____

12. Quīnque ex eīs erant fatuae. (Matt. 25:2, alt.) _____
13. Eritis piscātōrēs hominum. (Matt. 4:19, alt.) _____

E. Decline dīves fatuus. N.B.: These words are from different declensions!

_____   _____
_____   _____
_____   _____
_____   _____
_____   _____

F. Conjugate (1) *sum, esse* **and (2)** *possum, posse* **in future tense.**

1. _____ _____   2. _____ _____
   _____ _____   _____ _____
   _____ _____   _____ _____

G. *Converte* **these** *verba* **and phrases.**

1. ūndēvīcēsima _____   2. eighteenth _____
3. Ecce homō! _____   4. Festīnā! _____
5. We praise You, O God. _____
6. Manē dum quaesō. _____
7. Confēcistīne dēlēgātum tuum? _____
8. Vēnī, vīdī, vīcī. _____
9. In which month were you born? _____

H. Dērīvātī. Complete each sentence with an English *verbum* chosen from the following *verba*. The italicized *verbum* in the sentence should help you think of the Latin root.

pauper   virgin   fatuous   laboratory   magnum opus

1. A _____ is a place where *work* is done. Latin root: _____

XIX – Ūndēvīcēsima   Nōmen: _____

2. The _____ of the spider Charlotte, in *Charlotte's Web* was a *great work*.

   Latin roots: _____ and _____

3. A _____ is a poor man. Latin root: _____

4. The _____ Mary was a *young woman* when she became Jesus' mother.

   Latin root: _____

5. The _____ child was so *foolish* and *silly*. Latin root: _____

I. **Crossword Puzzle.** Be sure to use the endings for the grammar indicated. Unscramble the letters in the shaded squares to find out *when* what will be will be.

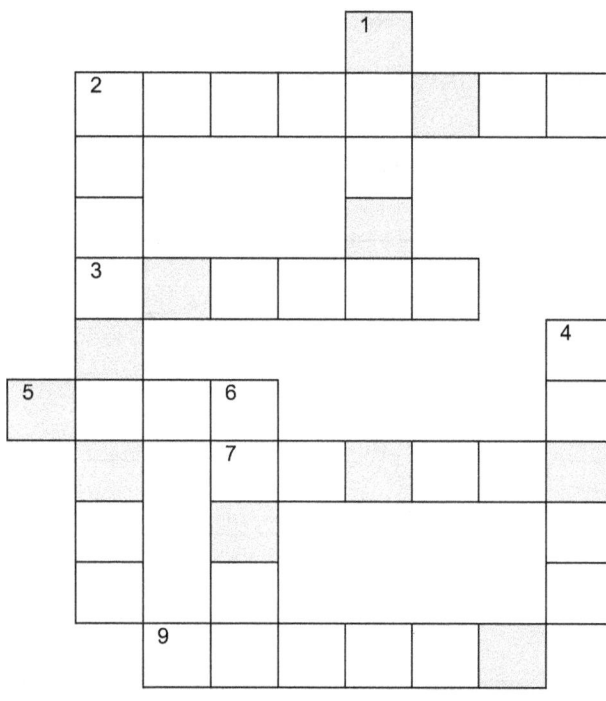

RĒCTĒ
2. fisherman (nom.)
3. of the fish (s.)
5. no one (s.)
7. poor man
9. effort (abl. s.)

DEORSUM
1. of a foolish man
2. prophecy
4. young woman (nom.)
6. works (nom. or acc.)

What will be, will be   __ __   __ __ __   __ __ __ __ __ .

J. **Historia.** Review the history and fill in the blanks.

1. Who builds a defensive wall in Britain? _____

2. Who first allows Christian worship? _____

3. In what year does Marcus Aurelius become emperor? _____

4. What kind of philosopher is Marcus? _____

XX – Vīcēsima   Nōmen:

XX – Vīcēsima lectiō   **PERFECT TENSE**
(20 – Twentieth lesson)

I. Dictum

        terra fīrma   _____(lit.)_____

II. Colloquium   *Latīnē*   *Anglicē*

Iūlia:	Potesne venīre domum meam?	Can you come to my house?
Tiberius:	Certē! Quid possumus facere?	Sure! What can we do?

III. Verba

Latīnē	*Anglicēe*	*Scrībe tōtum verbum Latīnum.*	*Dērīvātī*
diēs, diēī, m. (Ab – diē)	day		
diēs Sōlis	Sunday		
Dominica, -ae, f.	Lord's Day		
diēs Lūnae	Monday		
diēs Martis	Tuesday		
diēs Mercuriī	Wednesday		
diēs Iovis	Thursday		
diēs Veneris	Friday		
diēs Sāturnī	Saturday		
epistula, -ae, f.	letter		
septimāna, -ae, f.	a week		

<u>N.B.</u>: *Diēs* is from 5th declension. For now, just learn the nominative, genitive, and ablative.

1. There are no *verba Latīna* for _____ and _____.

2. *sum, esse* is a _____ and a _____ verb.

3. Adverbs cannot be _____ or _____.

XX – Vīcēsima   Nōmen: _____

IV. Grammatica

In this *lectiō*, we begin the <u>perfect tense</u>. The word *perfect* is used in the sense of *complete*. An action (or state of being) described in the perfect tense happened in the past and is now completed. The perfect tense expresses action that happened in the past but was completed quickly or in a short period of time. Consider the different sense of *walk* in these two sentences:

1. When we lived at the other house, *I used to walk* to school.
2. On Tuesday, *I walked* to school.

The first sentence tells about a repeated action, one that wasn't completed all at one time. It would be written using the *imperfect* tense: *ambulābam*. The second sentence tells about a single, completed action. It would be written using the *perfect* tense: *ambulāvī*.

The perfect tense is most often translated using the *–ed* form of the English verb, e.g., *ambulāvī* = I walk*ed*. It can also be translated using the helping verb *did*, e.g., *I did walk*. <u>N.B.</u>: Many English verbs have irregular perfect-tense forms. Compare *I think* vs. *I thought*; *I sing* vs. *I sang*; *I write* vs. *I wrote*; *I lead* vs. *I led*. Latin, however, has <u>no</u> irregular perfect tense forms!

The perfect tense uses a new set of personal endings *and* a different stem. The stem for the perfect tense is the third principal part of the verb, minus the *–ī* ending. E.g., the third principal part of *ambulō, ambulāre, ambulāvī, ambulātum* is *ambulāvī*, so the perfect stem is *ambulāv-*. Here are the personal endings and a model verb.

	singular	plural
1st person	-ī	-imus
2nd person	-istī	-istis
3rd person	-it	-ērunt

	singular	plural
1st person	ambulāv<u>ī</u>	ambulāv<u>imus</u>
2nd person	ambulāv<u>istī</u>	ambulāv<u>istis</u>
3rd person	ambulāv<u>it</u>	ambulāv<u>ērunt</u>

V. Historia (*Famous Men of Rome,* Chapter XXVII, Parts II and III)

The reign of Marcus Aurelius is full of troubles, but he writes that God makes everything happen for the good of all existence and that we must keep sober by remembering that we are only a small part of everything. Marcus is very impressed with the Thundering Legion, some Christian soldiers whose prayer is apparently answered, but he remains a pagan.

XX – Vīcēsima   Nōmen: _____

VI. Dēlēgāta

A. *Scrībe* the new Latin *verba* and their meanings.

Latīnē   *Anglicē*

1. _____   1. _____

2. _____   2. _____

3. _____   3. _____

4. _____   4. _____

5. _____   5. _____

6. _____   6. _____

7. _____   7. _____

8. _____   8. _____

9. _____   9. _____

10. _____   10. _____

11. _____   11. _____

B. *Variātiōnēs.* *Recitā* these sentence patterns several times. (Note the ablative of time.)

1. Diē Sōlis ad ecclēsiam ambulāvī.   (On Sunday I walked to church.)
2. Diē Lūnae in cubiculō meō labōrāvī.   (On Monday I worked in my bedroom.)
3. Diē Martis spectaculum spectāvī.   (On Tuesday I watched a show.)
4. Diē Mercuriī serpentem vīdī.   (On Wednesday I saw a snake.)
5. Diē Iovis gallīnam cēnāvī.   (On Thursday I ate chicken.)
6. Diē Veneris librum lēgī.   (On Friday I read a book.)
7. Diē Sāturnī epistulam scrīpsī.   (On Saturday I wrote a letter.)
8. Diē Sāturnī epistulam scrīpsistī.   (On Saturday you wrote a letter.)
9. Diē Sāturnī epistulam scrīpsit.   (On Saturday he wrote a letter.)

C. *Converte hās sententiās.*

1. Duo puerī pugnāvērunt.   _____

2. Duae legiōnēs pugnāvērunt.   _____

XX – Vīcēsima Nōmen: _____

3. Mīlitēs lēgem novam lēgērunt. _____
4. Soror et frāter ambulāvērunt. _____
5. Diē Lūnae nāvigāvimus. _____
6. Diē Iovis dē grātiā dīximus. _____
7. Dominicā ad ecclēsiam ambulāvimus. _____
8. Fīlia huic puerō epistulam mīsit. _____
9. Diē Mercuriī librōs bonōs lēgistis. _____
10. Diē Sāturnī natāvimus. _____

D. *Converte hās sententiās aut scrībe illās Latīnē.*

1. Māter mihi būtyrum trādidit. _____
2. Lydia tibi āleās trādidit. _____
3. Prophetiae dē Christō dīxērunt. _____
4. Quandō natāre poteris? _____
5. Quandō trāns flūmen natāvistī? _____
6. Diē Veneris trāns flūmen natāvī. _____
7. Why did you swim across the river? _____
8. On the Lord's Day we will write. _____
9. On Tuesday we worked in the kitchen. _____
10. On Friday my brothers wrote a letter. _____
11. On Saturday Tullia read my letter. _____

Ex Scriptūrīs:

12. Deus nōs amāvit et Fīlium mīsit. (I Jn. 4:10) _____

XX – Vīcēsima   Nōmen:

E. Conjugate *natō, natāre, natāvī, natātum* **and** *dīcō, dīcere, dīxī, dictum* **in perfect tense.**

1. _____ _____   2. _____ _____

   _____ _____   _____ _____

   _____ _____   _____ _____

F. Conjugate (1) *sum, esse, fuī, futūrum* **and (2)** *possum, posse, potuī* **in perfect tense.**

1. _____ _____   2. _____ _____

   _____ _____   _____ _____

   _____ _____   _____ _____

G. Conjugate *doceō, docēre, docuī, doctum* **and** *legō, legere, lēgī, lectum* **in perfect tense.**

1. _____ _____   2. _____ _____

   _____ _____   _____ _____

   _____ _____   _____ _____

H. *Converte* **these** *verba* **and phrases.**

1. vīcēsima _____   2. nineteenth _____

3. terra fīrma _____   4. cast of characters _____

5. Et tū, Brūte? _____   6. Wait a minute! _____

7. Potesne venīre domum meam diē Martis? _____

8. Potesne venīre domum meam diē Sōlis? _____

9. with great praise _____

10. ē plūribus ūnum _____   14. sine quā nōn _____

11. after noon _____   15. with praise _____

12. too long _____   16. Behold the Man! _____

13. Pray and work. _____   17. Lamb of God _____

XX – Vīcēsima   Nōmen: _____

I. Crossword Puzzle. Use the grammar indicated. Letters in the shaded squares, when read from top to bottom and left to right, will make seven days: _____

RĒCTĒ
1. day (nom.)
6. away from
7. me (acc.)
8. in front of
11. *Dies* ___ (Wed.)
12. You (pl.) walked
14. in, into
15. you (acc.)
16. *Dies* ___ (Sun.)
19. She passed
20. this (f.)
21. He wrote
22. my (f. sing.)
23. They said
24. where?

DEORSUM
2. *Dies* ___ (Sat.)
3. *Dies* ___ (Fri.)
4. You (pl.) worked
5. They read (perf.)
9. this (n.)
10. letter
13. toward, near
17. I watched
18. We saw
23. You give

J. Historia. Review the history and fill in the blanks.

1. Marcus Aurelius believed everything happened for the good of _____

2. What was the name of Marcus's Christian legion? _____

XXI – Vīcēsima Prīma   Nōmen: _____

XXI – Vīcēsima prīma lectiō　　　　　　　　　　*-iō* VERBS
(21 – Twenty-first lesson)

I. Dictum

Dominus vōbīscum.　　　　　　　_____

Et tēcum.　　　　　　　　　　　_____

II. Colloquium　　　　*Latīnē*　　　　　　*Anglicē*

Magister:	Quis rēsponsum scit?	Who knows the answer?
Discipulī:	Ō! Ego! Sciō! Ego!	Oh! Me! I know! Me!
Magister:	Attollite manūs.	Raise your hands.

III. Verba

Latīnē　　　　*Anglicē*　　　*Scrībe tōtum verbum Latīnum.*　　　*Dērīvātī*

accipiō, accipere, accēpī, acceptum to receive　　　_____

_____ _____ _____ _____

capiō, capere, cēpī, captum to seize, to take　　　_____

_____ _____ _____ _____

dēficiō, dēficere, dēfēcī, dēfectum to fail　　　_____

_____ _____ _____ _____

ēripiō, ēripere, ēripuī, ēreptum to rescue　　　_____

_____ _____ _____ _____

faciō, facere, fēcī, factum to make, to do　　　_____

_____ _____ _____ _____

iaciō, iacere, iēcī, iactum to throw, to cast　　　_____

_____ _____ _____ _____

1. Most verbs have _____ principal parts. Be sure to _____ them!

N.B.: *faciō, facere, fēcī, factum* can mean *to play* when used with *lūdus, -ī, m.*

XXI – Vīcēsima Prīma   Nōmen:

IV. Grammatica

The –iō verbs of 3rd conjugation end in –iō in the 1st-person singular present-tense form. Notice that present tense keeps the *i* in the 3rd-person plural.

	singular	plural	
1st person _____	**capiō**	**capimus**	_____
2nd person _____	**capis**	**capitis**	_____
3rd person _____	**capit**	**capi̱unt**	_____

The imperfect tense of –iō verbs of 3rd conjugation keeps the *i* in the stem in all forms, and like all 3rd conjugation verbs also has the usual long *ē* stem vowel. Pronounce *iē* like this: "Yay!"

1st person _____	**capiēbam**	**capiēbāmus**	_____
2nd person _____	**capiēbās**	**capiēbātis**	_____
3rd person _____	**capiēbat**	**capiēbant**	_____

In future tense of –iō verbs of 3rd conjugation keep the *i* in the stem in all forms. Even though it looks funny, it still follows the rhyme: "*Bō, bi, bu* for one and two; *a* and *e* for four and three!"

1st person _____	**capiam**	**capiēmus**	_____
2nd person _____	**capiēs**	**capiētis**	_____
3rd person _____	**capiet**	**capient**	_____

3rd conjugation -iō verbs are so much fun! The perfect tense is the same as for other verbs.

Conjugate *capiō, capere* in (a) present tense and (b) future tense.

a. _____ _____   b. _____ _____

   _____ _____   _____ _____

   _____ _____   _____ _____

V. Historia (*Famous Men of Rome*, Chapter XXVIII)

A period of many bad emperors is known as the Military Anarchy (180-285). The next emperor, Diocletian, decides the Empire is too large, and he divides it into the Eastern Roman Empire, ruled by himself at Nicomedia, and the Western Roman Empire, ruled by Maximian at Milan. Diocletian's attempts to reform the corrupt government fail, and within five years of his resignation, five men fight a civil war for the prize of the title of Emperor.

XXI – Vīcēsima Prīma   Nōmen: _____

VI. Dēlēgāta

A. *Scrībe* the new Latin *verba* and their meanings.

        Latīnē   *Anglicē*

1. _____   1. _____

2. _____   2. _____

3. _____   3. _____

4. _____   4. _____

5. _____   5. _____

6. _____   6. _____

B. *Variātiōnēs.* *Recitā* these sentence patterns several times.

1. Āleās iaciō.   (I'm throwing the dice.)   7. Āleās iēcī.   (I threw the dice.)
2. Āleās iacis.   (You're throwing the dice.)   8. Āleās iēcistī.   (You threw the dice.)
3. Āleās iacit.   (She's throwing the dice.)   9. Āleās iēcit.   (He threw the dice.)
4. Āleās iacimus.   (We're throwing the dice.)   10. Āleās iēcimus.   (We threw the dice.)
5. Āleās iacitis.   (Y'all are throwing the dice.) 11. Āleās iēcistis.   (Y'all threw the dice.)
6. Āleās iaciunt.   (They're throwing the dice.)   12. Āleās iēcērunt.   (They threw the dice.)

C. *Converte hās sententiās.*

1. Soror mea epistulam accēpit.   _____

2. Epistulās accipere amō.   _____

3. Legiōnēs oppidum capiunt.   _____

4. Diē Lūnae, legiōnēs signum hostium cēpērunt.

   _____

5. Diē Veneris, legiōnēs oppidum capere dēfēcērunt.

   _____

6. Portam facimus.   _____

7. Quotum lūdum faciēbant?   _____

XXI – Vīcēsima Prīma   Nōmen: _____

8. Diē Martis lūdum fēcimus. _____

9. Mīlitēs tēla iēcērunt. _____

10. Mīlitēs tēla iaciēbant. _____

11. Mīlitēs tēla iacient. _____

D. *Converte hās sententiās aut scrībe illās Latīnē.*

1. Rēx multās epistulās accipit. _____

2. Agricola duās epistulās accēpit. _____

3. Mīlitēs tēla dē vallō iaciēbant. _____

4. Claudius āleās cēpit et eās iacit. _____

5. My brothers are playing that game. _____

6. Christus nōs ē peccātō ēripuit. _____

7. Servī portam facere nōn poterant. _____

8. The slaves were able to close the windows. _____

9. Cato is throwing the dice. _____

10. I received two letters on Thursday. _____

11. The farmer was making a bow. _____

Ex Scriptūrīs:

12. Petitis et nōn accipitis. (James 4:3) _____

13. Dīgnus es, Domine, accipere glōriam. (Rev. 4:11)

_____

E. Conjugate *accipiō, accipere, accēpī, acceptum* **in present (1) and imperfect (2) tenses.**

1. _____ _____   2. _____ _____

   _____ _____   _____ _____

   _____ _____   _____ _____

XXI – Vīcēsima Prīma   Nōmen:

F. Conjugate *dēficiō, dēficere, dēfēcī, dēfectum* **in imperfect (1) and perfect (2) tenses.**

1. _____ _____   2. _____ _____

   _____ _____   _____ _____

   _____ _____   _____ _____

G. Conjugate *ēripiō, ēripere, ēripuī, ēreptum* **in present (1) and perfect (2) tenses.**

1. _____ _____   2. _____ _____

   _____ _____   _____ _____

   _____ _____   _____ _____

H. *Converte hās sententiās aut scrībe illās Latīnē.*

1. Your friends are preparing bread. _____

2. Vallum urbis quattuor portās habet. _____

3. Trēs portae nigrae sunt. _____

4. The fourth gate is red. _____

5. Fenestrae trium portārum nigrārum sunt parvae.

   _____

6. The window of the fourth gate is large.

   _____

7. Geram ūnum pedāle album et ūnum pedāle flāvum.

   _____

I. Translate these words and phrases.

1. vīcēsima prīma _____   2. twentieth _____

3. Note well. _____   4. Dominus vōbīscum. _____

5. Attollite manūs. _____

XXI – Vīcēsima Prīma   Nōmen: _____

6. Quotum tempus annī tibi maximē placet? _____

7. Can you come to my house? _____

J. Dērīvātī. Complete each sentence with an English *verbum* chosen from the following *verba*. The italicized *verbum* in the sentence should help you think of the Latin root.

   trajectory   deficient   accept   manufactured   captured

1. In earlier times, _____ products were *made* by *hand*.

   Latin roots: _____ and _____

2. Wild animals are sometimes _____ by scientists so that they can study

   them more closely. Latin root: _____

3. A _____ effort is in some way a *failure*. Latin root: _____

4. A _____ is the path of an object that is *thrown*. Latin root: _____

5. To _____ a gift is to *receive* it. Latin root: _____

K. *Verbum* Ladder. If you fill in five of this *lectiō*'s *verba* correctly in the horizontal spaces, the shaded spaces running vertically will spell the remaining *sextum verbum*: _____

L. Historia. Review the history and fill in the blanks.

1. What are the dates of the Military Anarchy? _____

2. Who divides the Empire into two parts? _____

3. What are the two capital cities of the divided Empire? _____

XXII – Vīcēsima Secunda   Nōmen: _____

XXII – Vīcēsima secunda lectiō   4th CONJUGATION
(22 – Twenty-second lesson)

I. Dictum

In hōc signō vincēs. _____

II. Colloquium   *Latīnē*   *Anglicē*

| **Iūlius:** | Scīsne natāre? | Do you know how to swim? |
| **Calpurnia:** | Ita, sciō natāre. | Yes, I know how to swim. |

III. Verba

Latīnē   *Anglicē*   *Scrībe tōtum verbum Latīnum.*   *Dērīvātī*

aperiō, aperīre, aperuī, apertum to open   _____

_____ _____ _____ _____

audiō, audīre, audīvī, audītum to hear, to listen   _____

_____ _____ _____ _____

dormiō, dormīre, dormīvī, dormītum to sleep   _____

_____ _____ _____ _____

veniō, venīre, vēnī, ventum to come   _____

_____ _____ _____ _____

sciō, scīre, scīvī, scītum to know   _____

_____ _____ _____ _____

inveniō, invenīre, invēnī, inventum to find by accident   _____

_____ _____ _____ _____

1. How are these verbs different from verbs in other conjugations?
2. How do we know from what conjugation a verb comes?
3. The present, imperfect, and future tenses find their stem in the _____.
4. The 3rd principal part provides the stem for the _____ tense.

XXII – Vīcēsima Secunda   Nōmen: _____

IV. Grammatica

The new verbs are all from 4th conjugation. They are like -iō verbs of 3rd conjugation, except that in present tense, the *i* will be long when possible. 4th conjugation verbs are known by the infinitive ending *-īre* and the long stem vowel *ī*. Here's the form for the present tense of 4th conjugation.

	singular	plural
1st person	audiō	audīmus
2nd person	audīs	audītis
3rd person	audit	audiunt

Here's the form for the imperfect tense of 4th conjugation. It's just like 3rd *-iō*!

1st person	audiēbam	audiēbāmus
2nd person	audiēbās	audiēbātis
3rd person	audiēbat	audiēbant

Just like *-io* verbs of 3rd conjugation, the Future tense of 4th conjugation keeps an *i* in the stem. Remember: "bō, bi, bu for one and two; a and ē for four and three."

1st person	audiam	audiēmus
2nd person	audiēs	audiētis
3rd person	audiet	audient

The perfect tense is the same as for other verbs.

N.B. *Sciō* with an infinitive can mean *I know how*. E.g., *Sciō natāre* = *I know how to swim*.

V. Historia (*Famous Men of Rome,* Chapter XXIX, Part I)

Although five men claim the title of Roman Emperor, Maxentius rules in Rome. Constantine decides to do battle with him. In 312, he sees a vision of a cross and hears a voice saying, "In this sign you will conquer." He has crosses painted on his soldiers' shields and banners, and he wins the Battle of Milvian Bridge. Constantine then becomes the first Christian emperor.

XXII – Vīcēsima Secunda   Nōmen: _____

VI. Dēlēgāta

A. *Scrībe* **the new Latin** *verba* **and their meanings.**

Latīnē	*Anglicē*
1. _____	1. _____
2. _____	2. _____
3. _____	3. _____
4. _____	4. _____
5. _____	5. _____
6. _____	6. _____

B. *Variātiōnēs*. *Recitā* these sentence patterns several times.

1. Rēgīna legere scit.   (Regina knows how to read.)
2. Rēgīna scrībere scit.   (Regina knows how to write.)
3. Rēgīna lūdōs facere scit. (Regina knows how to play games.)
4. Rēgīna holera parāre scit. (Regina knows how to prepare vegetables.)

C. *Converte hās sententiās.*

1. Magistrum audīmus. _____

2. Quis avem audit? _____

3. Pastōrēs angelōs audīvērunt. _____

4. Sextus iānuam claudit. _____

5. Iūlia iānuam aperiet. _____

6. Discipula fenestram aperiēbat. _____

7. Titus amīcum meum scit. _____

8. Sorōrēs meae amīcam meam sciunt. _____

9. Marcus natāre nōn scit. _____

10. Marcus natāre nōn potest. _____

XXII – Vīcēsima Secunda   Nōmen:

11. Puerī thēsaurum invēnērunt. _____

12. Sanctus Nicolaus ad oppidum venit. _____

13. Grātia Dominī est magna. _____

14. Dormīvistisne bene? _____

D. *Converte hās sententiās aut scrībe illās Latīnē.*

1. Tulia in cubiculō dormit. _____

2. Eā diē Veneris in exedriō dormīvit. _____

3. Servus in focō dormiēbat. _____

4. A soldier sent a letter to the king. _____

5. Nummōs antīquōs in agrō invēnī. _____

6. The shepherd stood in front of the church. _____

7. Christus caelum nōbīs aperuit. _____

8. Lydia is opening the door. _____

9. My friends came on Wednesday. _____

10. Titus does not know how to sing. _____

11. Iēsus nōs ēripiet ex infernō. _____

12. The keys of the gates are large. _____

13. The farmer will plow the field. _____

14. Gaius is a poor man; Publius is a rich man. _____

15. Lampās agricolae oleum nōn habet. _____

16. Aurum in montibus vīdimus. _____

17. The girls were not sleeping well. _____

18. Imperātor et mīlitēs hostīs vincent. _____

XXII – Vīcēsima Secunda   Nōmen: _____

Ex Scriptūrīs:

19. Veniet Fīlius hominis. (Matt. 25:31, alt.) _____

20. Beātus homō quī invenit sapientiam. (Prov. 3:13)

_____

21. Sciō opera tua et labōrem et patientiam tuam. (Rev. 2:2)

_____

22. Et nēmo poterat in caelō neque in terrā neque sub terrā aperīre librum. (Rev. 5:3 *neque* = nor)

_____

_____

E. Conjugate *audiō, audīre, audīvī, audītum* in present (1) and future (2) tenses.

1. _____ _____   2. _____ _____

   _____ _____   _____ _____

   _____ _____   _____ _____

F. Conjugate *sciō, scīre, scīvī, scītum* in imperfect (1) and perfect (2) tenses.

1. _____ _____   2. _____ _____

   _____ _____   _____ _____

   _____ _____   _____ _____

G. *Converte* these *verba* and phrases.

1. vīcēsima secunda _____   2. twenty-first _____

3. Behold the Man! _____   4. Diēs Īrae _____

5. In hōc signō vincēs. _____

6. Scīsne natāre? _____

7. Raise your hands. _____

8. Silent lēgēs inter arma. _____

XXII – Vīcēsima Secunda   Nōmen: _____

H. Dērīvātī. Complete each sentence with an English *verbum* chosen from the following *verba*. The italicized *verbum* in the sentence should help you think of the Latin root.

aperture   dormitories   dormant   invent   auditory

1. Creative people *find* new gadgets when they _____ them.

   Latin root: _____

2. _____ learners learn best by *hearing*. Latin root: _____

3. A camera's _____ is a small *opening*. Latin root: _____

4. _____ plants *sleep* during the winter. Latin root: _____

5. College students *sleep* in _____. Latin root: _____

I. *Verbum* Search. Each of the *verba* listed below can be found in this grid, reading forward, backward, up, down, or diagonally. All the unused letters, when read row by row from top to bottom, will tell you the best way to remember a verb's conjugation.

Secret message: _____

A	U	D	I	O	Y	O	O	O
U	C	M	I	U	S	I	I	T
D	M	C	E	M	P	R	O	I
E	A	O	I	A	E	R	I	A
F	D	I	C	P	Z	E	P	C
I	S	O	A	O	I	T	I	I
C	H	C	R	E	I	O	R	O
I	I	N	I	M	F	N	E	I
O	N	I	T	O	I	I	E	V
I	N	V	E	N	I	O	E	V

WORD LIST

ACCIPIO
APERIO
AUDIO
CAPIO
DEFICIO
DORMIO
ERIPIO
FACIO
INVENIO
IACIO
SCIO
VENIO

J. Historia. Review the history and fill in the blanks.

1. Who is the first Christian emperor of Rome? _____

2. What words does he hear in a vision? _____

3. What is the year of the battle of Milvian Bridge? _____

XXIII – Vīcēsima tertia lectiō   NEW ADJECTIVES
(23 – Twenty-third lesson)

I. Dictum

Fortīs fortūna adiuvat.
— Terence

II. Colloquium

Latīnē   *Anglicē*

Catherīna:	Est frīgidum! (Decembre)	It's cold!
Lūcius:	Est calidum! (Augustō)	It's hot!

III. Verba

Latīnē	*Anglicē*	*Scrībe tōtum verbum Latīnum.*	*Dērīvātī*
brevis, breve (brevis, -e)	short		
fortis, forte (fortis, -e)	strong, brave		
longus, -a, -um	long		
omnis, omne (omnis, -e)	all, every		
prūdēns, prūdentis	wise		
tristis, triste (tristis, -e)	sad		
viridis, viride (viridis, -e)	green		

1. What kind of *verba* are these? _____

2. How are most of these *verba* different from other *verba* of this kind we have learned?

3. Adjectives must agree with the nouns they modify in _____

4. Therefore, unlike adverbs, adjectives must be _____.

XXIII – Vīcēsima Tertia Nōmen:

IV. Grammatica

Most of the adjectives in this *lectiō* are from 3rd declension. Before now, we used only 1st and 2nd declension adjectives, so called because all their endings fit into those declensions. You can tell a 1st and 2nd declension adjective by its nominative endings: *-us, -a, -um*.

The endings for 3rd declension adjectives are similar to those for 3rd declension i-stem nouns. Most show two endings in the dictionary entry: *-is* for masculine and feminine nominative singular, and *-e* for neuter nominative singular. Adjectives of any declension may be used with any noun of any declension. Their endings do not need to *look* the same, but they *must* agree with the nouns they modify in gender, number, and case.

Here are the forms for the 3rd-declension adjectives:

		masculine	feminine	neuter
Singular	nominative	omnis	omnis	omne
	genitive	omnis	omnis	omnis
	dative	omnī	omnī	omnī
	accusative	omnem	omnem	omne
	ablative	omnī	omnī	omnī
Plural	nominative	omnēs	omnēs	omnia
	genitive	omnium	omnium	omnium
	dative	omnibus	omnibus	omnibus
	accusative	omnīs	omnīs	omnia
	ablative	omnibus	omnibus	omnibus

Which case endings are different from those for 3rd-declension nouns? _____

V. Historia (*Famous Men of Rome*, Chapter XXIX, Part II)

Constantine improves Roman laws and government. In 324, the last remaining claimant to the title, Licinius, dies, leaving Constantine sole ruler and the first Christian emperor of the whole Roman Empire. Constantine then moves the capital to Byzantium and renames it Constantinople.

XXIII – Vīcēsima Tertia			Nōmen:

VI. Dēlēgāta

A. *Scrībe* **the new Latin** *verba* **and their meanings.**

      Latīnē   *Anglicē*

1. _____ 1. _____

2. _____ 2. _____

3. _____ 3. _____

4. _____ 4. _____

5. _____ 5. _____

6. _____ 6. _____

7. _____ 7. _____

B. *Variātiōnēs.* *Recitā* these sentence patterns several times.

1. Via est longa. (The road is long.) 6. Vallum est breve. (The wall is short.)
2. Arcus est longus. (The bow is long.) 7. Lectus est viridis. (The couch is green.)
3. Vallum est longum. (The wall is long.) 8. Herba est viridis. (The plant is green.)
4. Via est brevis. (The way is short.) 9. Pōculum est viride. (The cup is green.)
5. Arcus est brevis. (The bow is short.) 10. Iānua est viridis. (The door is green.)

C. *Converte hās sententiās.*

1. Cāritās Deī est longa. _____

2. Cāritās Deī est alta. _____

3. Cāritās Deī est fortis. _____

4. Pauper erat beātus. _____

5. Dīves erit tristis. _____

6. Omnia māla nōn sunt rūfa. _____

7. Hoc mālum viride est. _____

8. Illud mālum est flāvum. _____

XXIII – Vīcēsima Tertia   Nōmen:

9. Hic nauta est fatuus. _____

10. Ille nauta est prūdēns. _____

11. Fēmina prūdēns Deum laudat. _____

12. Homō prūdēns sapientiam studet. _____

13. Omnis flōs est bellus. _____

14. Hic liber brevis est. _____

D. *Converte hās sententiās aut scrībe illās Latīnē.*

1. Fēles sub sellā dormiēbat. _____

2. Canis sub sellam ambulāvit. _____

3. Fēles nunc nōn dormit. _____

4. Spectāculum triste spectāvimus. _____

5. Vīdistisne gemmam viridem? _____

6. Quomodō gemmam viridem invēnistis? _____

7. Homō fortis mē ex igne ēripuit. _____

8. Avus omnibus puellīs dōna dābat. _____

9. Puerī Iūniō in flūmine natāvērunt. _____

10. The sailors will see land on Sunday. _____

11. The strong farmer is carrying a table. _____

12. The sad man works without patience. _____

13. Every lamp has oil. _____

14. The green apple is large. _____

Ex Scriptūrīs:

15. Omnēs scientiam habēmus. (I Cor. 8:1). _____

XXIII – Vīcēsima Tertia   Nōmen:

16. Deus dedit illī nōmen super omne nōmen. (Phil. 2:9, alt.; *illī* – to that one – to Him)

_____

17. Deus, quī fēcit mundum et omnia in eō, caelī et terrae Dominus est. (Ac. 17:24 alt.;)

_____

_____

E. Decline *fortis, -e* **in masculine (1), feminine (2), and neuter (3), singular (S) and plural (P).**

(S) 1._____ 2._____ 3._____

_____ _____ _____

_____ _____ _____

_____ _____ _____

_____ _____ _____

(P) 1._____ 2._____ 3._____

_____ _____ _____

_____ _____ _____

_____ _____ _____

_____ _____ _____

F. *Converte* **these** *verba* **and phrases.**

1. vīcēsima tertia _____ 2. twenty-second _____

3. dry land _____ 4. exemplī grātiā _____

5. Est frīgidum. _____ 6. Manē dum! _____

G. Derivati. Complete each sentence with an English *verbum* chosen from the following *verba*. The italicized *verbum* in the sentence should help you think of the Latin root.

        verdant   fortitude   prudent   omnipotent   brief

1. God is _____; i.e., He is *all-powerful*. Latin root: _____

XXIII – Vīcēsima Tertia   Nōmen:

2. _____ students *wisely* take responsibility for their homework.

   Latin root: _____

3. The *green* of spring provides beautiful _____ scenery.

   Latin root: _____

4. _____ reports are *short*. Latin root: _____

5. The _____ of *brave* soldiers is admirable. Latin root: _____

H. Alphabet Code. Unscramble the letters given to write the *feminine singular* form of the *verba* in this *lectiō*. Use the code letters under each blank to find the secret message.

AOLNG L O N G A
       q k p o v

MSOIN O M N I S
       k d p b c

ITFSRO F O R T I S
       u k g h b c

VESBRI B R E V I S
       x g w r b c

IVRSDII V I R I D I S
        r b g b a b c

TTISRSI T R I S T I S
        h g b c h b c

PSNRUED P R U D E N S
        t g n a w p c

The difference between the 3rd declension adjective forms
and the 3rd declension noun forms is mostly in the…

A B L A T I V E   S I N G U L A R
v x q v h b r w   c b p o n q v g

I. Historia. Review the history and fill in the blanks.

1. When does Constantine become sole ruler of Rome? _____

2. To where does he move the capital? _____

3. What does he rename the capital? _____

XXIV – Vīcēsima Quarta   Nōmen: _____

XXIV – Vīcēsima quarta lectiō   COMMANDS
(24 – Twenty-fourth lesson)

I. Dictum

Tempus fugit.   _____

II. Colloquium   *Latīnē*   *Anglicē*

Aemilia:	Quotus diēs mēnsis est?	What's the date?
Lūcius:	Vīcēsimus quartus diēs Iānuāriī est.	It's the 24th of January.

III. Verba

Latīnē	*Anglicē*	*Scrībe tōtum verbum Latīnum.*	*Dērīvātī*
canticum, -ī, n.	song	_____	_____
cārissimus, -a, -um	beloved	_____	_____
honor, honōris, m.	honor	_____	_____

1. Which *verba* are nouns? _____

2. *Scrībe* the declension of each noun to its left.

3. What kind of *verbum* is *cārissimus, -a, -um*? _____

4. How does one find the stem of a Latin noun? _____

5. What is the genitive singular case ending for 1st declension? __ 2nd? __ 3rd? __

6. Which declension has no neuter nouns? _____

7. What are two ways to ask a question *Latīnē*? a. _____

   b. _____

8. What detail differentiates one conjugation from another? _____

9. There are _____ conjugations of Latin verbs.

10. What vowel identifies 1st conjugation? _____ 2nd? _____ 3rd? _____ 4th? _____

XXIV – Vīcēsima Quarta   Nōmen: _____

IV. Grammatica

Commands are very easy in Latin. In general, to use a verb in the *imperative mood* (command form) when commanding *one* person, just use the stem. To make a negative command, use the irregular verb *nōlō* (which looks like it belongs in the 4th conjugation) with an infinitive. Here are some examples:

Labōrā!	**Work!**
Manē!	**Stay!**
Sedē!	**Sit!**
Lege!	**Read!**
Venī!	**Come!**
Nōlī cantāre	**Don't sing!**

To command more than one person, add *–te* to the stem. In 3rd conjugation, the stem vowel changes to an *–i* in the plural. Here are some examples of plural imperatives:

Labōrāte!	**Work!**
Manēte!	**Stay!**
Sedēte!	**Sit!**
Legite!	**Read!**
Venīte!	**Come!**
Nōlīte cantāre	**Don't sing!**

Now you can train your dog in a foreign language!

A. *Scrībe* these commands to one person *Latīnē*.

1. Write! _____

2. Sing! _____

3. Rejoice! _____

4. Don't talk! _____

B. *Scrībe* these commands to more than one person *Latīnē*.

1. Believe! _____

2. Hurry! _____

3. Be silent! _____

4. Don't fight! _____

V. Historia (*Famous Men of Rome,* Chapter XXX)

In 364, Emperor Valentinian again divides the Empire into eastern and western sections. Then Bishop Ambrose of Milan makes Emperor Theodosius do penance. Barbarian tribes pour into western Europe, and in 476, the last Emperor, Romulus Augustus, is taken prisoner, and the Roman Empire in the west falls. The Byzantine Empire survives until 1453.

XXIV – Vīcēsima Quarta   Nōmen:

VI. Dēlēgāta

A. *Scrībe* the new Latin *verba* and their meanings.

Latīnē   *Anglicē*

1. _____   1. _____

2. _____   2. _____

3. _____   3. _____

B. *Variātiōnēs.* *Recitā* these sentence patterns several times.

1. Tertius diēs Iānuāriī est.   (It's the 3rd of January.)
2. Quartus diēs Februāriī est.   (It's the 4th of February.)
3. Octāvus diēs Martiī est.   (It's the 8th of March.)
4. Nōnus diēs Aprīlis est.   (It's the 9th of April.)
5. Duodecimus diēs Maiī est.   (It's the 12th of May.)
6. Quīntus decimus diēs Iuniī est.   (It's the 15th of June.)
7. Ūndēvīcēsimus diēs Iuliī est.   (It's the 19th of July.)
8. Vīcēsimus prīmus diēs Augustī est.   (It's the 21st of August.)
9. Duodētrīcēsimus diēs Septembris est. (It's the 28th of September.)
10. Ūndetrīcēsimus diēs Octōbris est.   (It's the 29th of October.)
11. Trīcēsimus diēs Novembris est.   (It's the 30th of November.)
12. Trīcēsimus prīmus diēs Decembris est. (It's the 31st of December.)

C. *Converte hās sententiās.*

1. Cantāte canticum bellum. _____

2. Cārissimō meō canticum cantābō. _____

3. Cārissimae meae canticum cantābō. _____

4. Laudā Deum! _____

5. Laudāte Dominum! _____

6. Dīves sine honōre est pauper. _____

7. Dā mihi pānem quaesō. _____

8. Trāde mihi mālum quaesō. _____

9. Tenē equōs tuōs! _____

XXIV – Vīcēsima Quarta   Nōmen: _____

10. Salūtā aviam tuam, Maria. _____

11. Salūtā avum, Secunde. _____

12. Parāte viam Dominī. (Matt. 3:3) _____

13. Patellās in culīnam portā, quaesō. _____

D. *Converte hās sententiās aut scrībe illās Latīnē.*

1. Dominus super omnem terram regnat. _____

2. Spectāte porcum meum. _____

3. Cēnāte omnia holera vestra. _____

4. Cēnā omnīs fābās tuās. _____

5. Epistulam mihi mitte. _____

6. Claudite ōra et aperīte librōs. _____

7. Marcus calculum sub lectō invēnit. _____

8. Tarquinia librum bonum leget. _____

9. Rēx et rēgīna ad oppidum meum vēnient.

_____

10. Mīles cum duōbus arcīs est fortis. _____

11. We were listening to a song. _____

12. Now I hear a sad song. _____

13. My beloved is happy. _____

14. The good soldier fights with honor. _____

15. I know how to sing a song. _____

16. Rejoice (P) in the Lord! _____

17. Carry (S) the books to the table, please. _____

XXIV – Vīcēsima Quarta   Nōmen:

Ex Scriptūrīs:

18. Hic est Fīlius meus cārissiumus; audīte illum. (Mark 9:7; *illum* – to him).

19. Quod vidēs, scrībe in librō et mitte septem ecclesiīs. (Rev. 1:11; *quod* – *that which*)

20. Timēte Deum et dāte illī honōrem. (Rev. 14:7; *illī* – to him)

21. Iēsus dīxit, "Dāte quae sunt Caesāris Caesārī, et quae sunt Deī Deō." (Mark 12:17, alt.; *quae* – the things which)

E. Decline **canticum triste**. Be careful!

F. *Converte* these *verba* and phrases.

1. vīcēsima quarta _____ 2. twenty-third _____

3. Tempus fugit. _____ 4. too long _____

5. dramatis persōnae _____ 6. It's cold. _____

7. Fortune favors the bold. _____

8. Quotus diēs mensis est? _____

9. Manē dum quaesō! _____

XXIV – Vīcēsima Quarta   Nōmen: _____

10. Vēnī, vīdī, vīcī. _____

11. Tē Deum laudāmus. _____

G. **Dērīvātī.** Complete each sentence with an English *verbum* chosen from the following *verba*. The italicized *verba* in the sentence should help you think of the Latin root.

cantor   canticle

1. A _____ is a *song*. Latin root: _____

2. A _____ *sings* during a Jewish worship service. Latin root: _____

H. **Crossword Puzzle.** All nouns and adjectives are in the nominative case.

RĒCTĒ
1. beloved (f.)
4. honor
5. red cherry
6. of the snow
7. across
9. brown fish (sing.)
10. every (f. sing.)
11. brave (m. sing.)

DEORSUM
1. with
2. green chair
3. yellow flower
5. song
8. I hear

I. **Historia.** Review the history and fill in the blanks.

1. Who divides the Empire in 364? _____

2. Who is the last western emperor? _____

3. In what year does the Roman Empire end? _____

Glossary – Latin to English

Roman numeral indicates lesson number.
Vocabulary from *Schola Latina Book I* are marked (BI)

Nōtā bene: Noun dictionary entries are often shortened by listing only the genitive singular *ending* rather than the full genitive singular *form*. So **lectus, lectī, m.** would become **lectus, -ī, m.** and **vallum, vallī, n.** would become **vallum, -ī, n.** This seems confusing at first, but you can still see the stem of these nouns in the nominative singular forms <u>lectus</u> and <u>vallum</u>. However, nouns like **culter, cultrī, m.** and **māter, mātris, f.** will *not* be abbreviated, because their stems are not visible in the nominative singular form.

A

ā / ab (+Abl)	from, away from (X)
abacus, -ī, m.	gameboard (IV)
accipiō, accipere, accēpī, acceptum	to receive (XXI)
ad (+Acc)	to, toward, at (VIII)
aestās, aestātis, f.	summer (XVII)
aeternus, -a, -um	eternal (BI)
ager, agrī, m.	farm field (XI)
agnus, -ī, m.	lamb (BI)
agricola, -ae, m.	farmer (BI)
albus, -a, -um	white (XIV)
ālea, -ae, f.	(game) die (IV)
altus, -a, -um	high, deep (BI)
ambulō, ambulāre, ambulāvī, ambulātum	to walk (BI)
amīcus, -ī, m.	friend (BI)
amō, amāre, amāvī, amātum	to love, to like (BI)
angelus, -ī, m.	angel (II)
angustus, -a, -um	narrow (BI)
annus, -ī, m.	year (BI)
ante (+Acc)	before, in front of (VIII)
antīquus, -a, -um	old, ancient (BI)
aperiō, aperīre, aperuī, apertum	to open (XXII)
Aprīlis, -is, m.	April (XVIII)
aqua, -ae, f.	water (BI)
aquila, -ae, f.	eagle (BI)
arcus, -ī, m.	bow, rainbow (XV)
argentum, -ī, n.	silver (III)
arō, arāre, arāvī, arātum	to plow (BI)
ascendō, ascendere, ascendī, ascensum	to ascend (XIII)
audiō, audīre, audīvī, audītum	to hear (XXII)
Augustus, -ī, m.	August (XVIII)
aurantius, -a, -um	orange (XV)
auris, auris, f.	ear (BI)
aurum, -ī, n.	gold (III)
autumnus, -ī, m.	autumn (XVII)
avia, -ae, f.	grandmother (XIV)
avis, avis, f.	bird (BI)
avus, -ī, m.	grandfather (XV)

B

beātus, -a, -um	happy, blessed (IX)
bellus, -a, -um	pretty (BI)
bellum, -ī, n.	war (BI)
bene	well (BI)
bonus, -a, -um	good (BI)
bōs, bovis, m./f.	ox, cow (BI)
brācae, -ārum, f.	pants (XVI)
bracchium, -ī, n.	arm (BI)
brevis, -e	short (XXIII)
būtyrum, -ī, n.	butter (X)

C

caelum, ī, n.	sky, heaven (BI)
Caesar, Caesaris, m.	Caesar (BI)
caeruleus, -a, -um	blue (BI)
calamus, -ī, m.	pen (BI)
calceus, -ī, m.	shoe (XVI)
calculus, -ī, m.	stone, gamepiece (IV)

Latin	English
camisia, -ae, f.	shirt (XVI)
canis, canis, m./f.	dog (BI)
canticum, -ī, n.	song (XXIV)
cantō, cantāre, cantāvī, cantātum	to sing (BI)
capillus, -ī, m.	(a) hair (BI)
capiō, capere, cēpī, captum	to seize (XXI)
caput, capitis, n.	head (BI)
cārissimus, -a, -um	beloved (XXIV)
cāritās, cāritātis, f.	love (V)
cāseus, -ī, m.	cheese (IX)
cēnō, cēnare, cēnāvī, cēnātum	to dine, to eat (BI)
cerasum, -ī, n.	cherry (VII)
charta, -ae, f.	paper (BI)
Christus, -ī, m.	Christ (BI)
cingulum, -ī, n.	belt (XVI)
circum (+ Acc)	around, about (VIII)
cīvitās, cīvitātis, f.	state (XI)
claudō, claudere, clausī, clausum	to close (XVI)
clāvis, clāvis, f.	key (VII)
cochleāre, cochleāris, n.	spoon (BI)
cōgitō, cōgitāre, cōgitāvī, cōgitātum	to think (BI)
collis, collis, m.	hill (BI)
corōna, -ae, f.	crown (BI)
corpus, corporis, n.	body (BI)
crēdō, crēdere, crēdidī, crēditum	to believe (XIII)
crūs, crūris, n.	leg (BI)
crux, crucis, f.	cross (BI)
cubiculum, -ī, n.	bedroom (BI)
cubīle, cubīlis, n.	bed (BI)
culīna, -ae, f.	kitchen (BI)
culpa, -ae, f.	fault (BI)
culter, cultrī, m.	knife (BI)
cum (+ Ab)	with (X)
cūr	why (XII)

D

dē (+Abl)	about, concerning down from (X)
December, Decembris, m.	December (XVIII)
dēficiō, dēficere, dēfecī, dēfectum	to fail (XXI)
dēns, dentis, m.	tooth (BI)
dēscendō, -ere, dēscendī, dēscensum	to descend (XIII)
Deus, -ī, m.	God (BI)
dextera, -ae, f.	right hand (IV)
dīcō, dīcere, dīxī, dictum	to say, to tell (XIII)
diēs, diēī, m.	day (XX)
diēs Iovis	Thursday (XX)
diēs Lūnae	Monday (XX)
diēs Martis	Tuesday (XX)
diēs Mercuriī	Wednesday (XX)
diēs Sāturnī	Saturday (XX)
diēs Sōlis	Sunday (XX)
diēs Veneris	Friday (XX)
dīgnus, -a, -um	worthy (VI)
digitus, -ī, m.	finger, toe (BI)
discipula, -ae, f.	student (BI)
discipulus, -ī, m.	student (BI)
dīves, dīvitis, m./f.	rich person (V)
dō, dare, dedī, datum	to give (III)
doceō, docēre, docuī, doctum	to teach (BI)
doleō, dolēre, doluī, dolitūrum	to ache (BI)
Dominica, -ae, f.	Lord's Day (XX)
dominus, -ī, m.	lord, master (BI)
domus, domūs, f.	house (BI)
dōnum, -ī, n.	gift (BI)
dormiō, dormīre, dormīvī, dormītum	to sleep (XXII)
dubitō, dubitāre, dubitāvī, dubitātum	to doubt (BI)
dūrō, dūrāre, dūrāvī, dūrātum	to endure (BI)

E

ē / ex (+Abl)	out of, out from, from (X)
ecce	behold! (XV)
ecclēsia, -ae, f.	church (BI)
ego	I, me (II)
epistula, -ae, f.	letter (XX)
equus, -ī, m.	horse (BI)
ēripiō, ēripere,	to rescue (XXI)

ēripuī, ēreptum		**H**	
errō, errāre, errāvī, errātum	to err, to wander, be mistaken (BI)	habeō, habēre, habuī, habitum	to have, to possess (III)
et	and (BI)	septimāna, septimānae, f.	a week
evangelium, -ī, n.	gospel (VII)	herba, -ae, f.	plant, herb (BI)
exedrium, -ī, n.	living room (BI)	hīc	here (BI)
		hic, haec, hoc	this (X)
F		hiems, hiemis, f.	winter (XVII)
fāba, -ae, f.	bean (VI)	Hispania, -ae, f.	Spain (BI)
faciō, facere, fēcī, factum	to make, to do (XXI)	holus, holeris, n.	vegetable (VI)
fatuus, -a, -um	foolish (XIX)	homō, hominis, m.	person, man, human (BI)
Februārius, -ī, m.	February (XVIII)	honor, honōris, m.	honor (XXIV)
fēles, fēlis, f.	cat (BI)	hōra, -ae, f.	hour (BI)
fēmina, -ae, f.	woman (BI)	hostis, hostis, m./f.	enemy (BI)
fenestra, -ae, f.	window (BI)	humilitās, humilitātis, f.	humility (V)
festīnō, festīnāre, festīnāvī, festīnātum	to hurry (BI)		
fīlia, -ae, f.	daughter (BI)	**I**	
fīlius, -ī, m.	son (BI)	iaciō, iacere, iēcī, iactum	to throw, to cast (XXI)
fīnis, fīnis, m.	end, border (VII)	iānua, -ae, f.	door (BI)
flāvus, -a, -um	yellow (XIV)	Iānuārius, -ī, m.	January (XVIII)
fleō, flēre, flēvī, flētum	to weep, to cry (BI)	ibi	there (BI)
flōs, flōris, m.	flower (IX)	ignis, ignis, m.	fire (BI)
flūmen, flūminis, n.	river (BI)	ille, illa, illud	that (XI)
focus, -ī, m.	fireplace (BI)	imperātor, imperātōris, m.	commander (BI)
fortis, -e	strong, brave (XXIII)		
frāter, frātris, m.	brother (BI)	imperō, imperāre, imperāvī, imperātum	to rule, to order (BI)
fulvus, -a, -um	brown (XV)		
furca, -ae, f.	fork (BI)	in (+Abl)	in, on (XI)
		in (+Acc)	into, onto (XI)
G		indō, induere, induī, indūtum	to put on (XVI)
Gallia, -ae, f.	Gaul (France) (BI)		
gallīna, -ae, f.	chicken (BI)	infernus, -ī, m.	underworld, hell (VII)
gaudeō, gaudēre, gāvīsus sum	to rejoice (BI)	īnsula, -ae, f.	island (BI)
gaudium, -ī, n.	joy (BI)	intrō, intrāre, intrāvī, intrātum	to enter (III)
gemma, -ae, f.	gem, jewel (XI)		
gerō, gerere, gessī, gestum	to wear, to manage (XVI)	inveniō, invenīre, invēnī, inventum	to find (XXII)
gladius, -ī, m.	sword (BI)	is, ea, id	he, she, it; they
glōria, -ae, f.	glory (BI)	Ītalia, -ae, f.	Italy (IV)
grātia, -ae, f.	grace (XVII)	iūdicō, iūdicāre, iūdicāvī, iūdicātum	to judge (II)

L

labor, labōris, m.	labor, effort (XIX)
labōrō, labōrāre, labōrāvī, labōrātum	to work (BI)
lacūnar, lacūnāris, n.	ceiling (BI)
lampas, lampadis, f.	lamp, torch (VII)
lātus, -a, -um	wide (BI)
laudō, laudāre, laudāvī, laudātum	to praise (III)
laus, laudis, f.	praise (X)
lectus, -ī, m.	couch, bed (BI)
legiō, legiōnis, f.	legion (BI)
legō, legere, lēgī, lectum	to read (XIII)
lēx, lēgis, f.	law (BI)
liber, librī, m.	book (BI)
līberō, līberāre, līberāvī, līberātum	to free (XIV)
lingua, -ae, f.	language, tongue (BI)
longus, -a, -um	long (XXIII)
lūceō, lucēre, lūxī	to shine (BI)
lūdus, -ī, m.	game, school (IV)
lūna, -ae, f.	moon (BI)
lūx, lūcis, f.	light (BI)

M

magister, magistrī, m.	teacher (BI)
magistra, -ae, f.	teacher (BI)
magnus, -a, -um	large, great (BI)
Māius, -ī, m.	May (XVIII)
male	badly (BI)
mālum, -ī, n.	apple (III)
mālum aurantium	orange (XV)
malus, -a, -um	bad, evil (BI)
maneō, manēre, mānsī, mānsum	to stay, to remain (BI)
manus, manūs, f.	hand (BI)
margarīta, -ae, f.	pearl (XI)
Maria, -ae, f.	Mary (BI)
Martius, -ī, m.	March (XVIII)
māter, mātris, f.	mother (BI)
mendācium, -ī, n.	lie, falsehood (BI)
mēnsa, -ae, f.	table (BI)
mensis, mensis, m.	month (XVIII)
meus, -a, -um	my (BI)
mīles, mīlitis, m.	soldier (BI)
misereō, miserēre,	to be sorry (BI)
mittō, mittere, mīsī, missum	to send (XIII)
mōns, montis, m.	mountain (BI)
mors, mortis, f.	death (BI)
moveō, movēre, mōvī, mōtum	to move (BI)
multum	a lot (BI)
multus, -a, -um	much, many (BI)
mundus, -ī, m.	world (BI)
mūrus, -ī, m.	wall (BI)

N

nāsus, -ī, m.	nose (BI)
natō, natāre, natāvī, natātum	to swim (VIII)
nauta, -ae, m.	sailor (BI)
nāvigō, nāvigāre, nāvigāvī, nāvigātum	to sail (BI)
nāvis, nāvis, f.	ship (BI)
nēmo, nēminis, m./f.	no one, nobody (XIX)
niger, nigra, nigrum	black (XIV)
nimbus, -ī, m.	cloud (BI)
ningit, ningere	to snow (XVII)
nix, nivis, f.	snow (XVII)
nōmen, nōminis, n.	name (BI)
nōn	not (BI)
nōs	us (II)
November, Novembris, m.	November (XVIII)
novus, -a, -um	new (BI)
nox, noctis, f.	night (BI)
nummus, -ī, m.	coin (VI)
numquam	never (BI)
nunc	now (BI)
nūntius, -ī, m.	messenger, message (BI)

O

Octōber, Octōbris, m.	October (XVIII)
oculus, -ī, m.	eye (BI)
oleum, -ī, n.	oil (X)

Latin	English
omnis, -e	all, every (XXIII)
oppidum, -ī, n.	town (BI)
optimus, -a, -um	best (BI)
opus, operis, n.	work (XIX)
ōrō, ōrāre, ōrāvī, ōrātum	to pray, to speak (BI)
ōs, ōris, n.	mouth (BI)

P

pānis, pānis, m.	bread (IX)
parō, parāre, parāvī, parātum	to prepare (XIV)
pars, partis, f.	part (BI)
parum	a little (BI)
parvus, -a, -um	small (BI)
pastor, pastōris, m.	shepherd (BI)
patella, -ae, f.	plate (BI)
pateō, patēre, patuī	to be open (BI)
pater, patris, m.	father (BI)
patientia, -ae, f.	patience (X)
patria, -ae, f.	fatherland country (BI)
pauper, pauperis, m.	poor man (XIX)
pax, pācis, f.	peace (BI)
peccātum, -ī, n.	sin (BI)
peccō, peccāre, peccāvī, peccātum	to sin (BI)
pecūnia, -ae, f.	money (BI)
pedāle, pedālis, n.	sock (V)
per (+ Acc)	through (VII)
pēs, pedis, m.	foot (BI)
petō, petere, petīvī, petītum	to seek, to beg, to ask for (XVI)
pilleus, -ī, m.	hat (IX)
piscātor, piscātōris, m.	fisherman (XIX)
piscis, piscis, m.	fish (XIX)
placeō, placēre, placuī, placitum	to please (BI)
pluit, pluere	to rain (XVII)
pluvia, -ae, f.	rain (XVII)
pōculum, -ī, n.	cup (BI)
pōmum, -ī, n.	fruit (VI)
porcus, -ī, m.	pig (BI)
porta, -ae, f.	gate (XI)
portiō, portiōnis, f.	portion, snack (V)
portō, portāre, portāvī, portātum	to carry (IX)
possum, posse, potuī	to be able, can (BI)
praemium, -ī, n.	reward (BI)
prīmus, -a, -um	first (BI)
principium, -ī, n.	beginning (VII)
prophetia, -ae, f.	prophecy (XIX)
prūdēns, prūdentis	wise (XXIII)
puella, -ae, f.	girl (BI)
puer, puerī, m.	boy (BI)
pugnō, pugnāre, pugnāvī, pugnātum	to fight (BI)
purpureus, -a, -um	purple (XV)
puteus, -ī, m.	a well (BI)

Q

quandō	when (XII)
quantus, -a, um	how much (XII)
quī	who; (he) who (XIV)
quid	what? (XII)
quis	who? (XII)
quōmodo	how? (XII)
quot	how many? (XII)
quotus, -a, -um	which? (XII)

R

recitō, recitāre, recitāvī, recitātum	to recite, to read aloud (BI)
rēgīna, -ae, f.	queen (BI)
rēgnō, rēgnāre, rēgnāvī, rēgnātum	to reign (BI)
rēgnum, -ī, n.	kingdom (BI)
resurrectiō, resurrectiōnis, f.	resurrection (V)
rēx, rēgis, m.	king (BI)
rīdeō, rīdēre, rīsī, rīsum	to laugh (VII)
Rōma, -ae, f.	Rome (BI)
rūfus, -a, -um	red (XIV)

S

saepe	often (XV)
salūtō, salūtāre, salūtāvī, salūtātum	to greet (XIV)
salveō, salvēre	to be well (BI)
sanctus, -a, -um	holy (BI)

sapientia, -ae, f.	wisdom (III)
scientia, -ae, f.	knowledge (VII)
sciō, scīre, scīvī, scītum	to know (XXII)
scrībō, scrībere, scrīpsī, scrīptum	to write (XVI)
secundum (+ Acc)	beside, according to (VIII)
secundus, -a, -um	second (BI)
sedeō, sedēre, sēdī, sessum	to sit (BI)
sella, -ae, f.	chair (BI)
semper	always (BI)
September, Septembris, m.	September (XVIII)
serpens, serpentis, m./f.	snake (BI)
servō, servāre, servāvī, servātum	to save, to keep, to guard (XIII)
servus, -ī, m.	slave, servant (BI)
signum, -ī, n.	sign (BI)
sileō, silēre, siluī	to be silent (BI)
silva, -ae, f.	forest (BI)
similis, -e (+ Dat)	similar to (XI)
sine (+ Abl)	without (X)
solum, -ī, n.	floor (BI)
soror, sorōris, f.	sister (BI)
spatium, -ī, n.	space (IV)
spectāculum, -ī, n.	sight, show (VI)
spectō, spectāre, spectāvī, spectātum	to look at, to observe (VI)
speculum, -ī, n.	mirror (BI)
spīritus, spīritūs, m.	spirit (BI)
stella, -ae, f.	star (BI)
stīlus, -ī, m.	pencil (BI)
stō, stāre, stetī, statum	to stand (BI)
stomachus, -ī, m.	stomach (BI)
studeō, -ēre, studuī	to be eager for, to study (XIII)
sub (+ Acc/Abl)	under, up to, up under (XI)
sum, esse, fuī, futūrum	to be (BI)
super (+ Acc)	above, over (VII)
superō, superāre, superāvī, superātum	to overcome, to conquer (III)

T

tardō, tardāre, tardāvī, tardātum	to be slow (BI)
taurus, -ī, m.	bull (BI)
tēlum, -ī, n.	weapon (BI)
tempus, tempōris, n.	time (BI)
teneō, tenēre, tenuī, tentum	to hold (IV)
terra, -ae, f.	land, earth (BI)
terreō, terrēre, terruī, territum	to frighten (VI)
thēsaurus, -ī, m.	treasure (XI)
thronus, -ī, m.	throne (II)
timeō, timēre, timuī	to fear, to be afraid (BI)
timor, timōris, m.	fear (VII)
tōtus, -a, -um	whole (BI)
trādō, trādere, trādidī, trāditum	to pass, to hand over (XIII)
trāns (+Acc)	across (VII)
tristis, -e	sad (XXIII)
tū	you (sing.) (III)
tūtus, -a, -um	safe (BI)
tuus, -a, -um	your (sing.) (BI)

U

ubi	where? (XII)
urbs, urbis, f.	city (BI)
ursa, -ae, f.	bear (BI)

V

valeō, valēre, valuī, valitūrum	to be strong, to have power (BI)
vallum, -ī, n.	wall, rampart (BI)
velim	I would like (III)
velīsne	Would you like? (IV)
veniō, venīre, vēnī, ventum	to come (XXII)
vēr, vēris, n.	spring (XVII)
verbum, -ī, n.	word (BI)
vēritās, vēritātis, f.	truth (BI)
vērus, -a, -um	true (IX)

via, -ae, f.	road, way (BI)
victōria, -ae, f.	victory (BI)
videō, vidēre, vīdī, vīsum	to see (III)
vīnum, -ī, n.	wine (BI)
virgō, virginis, f.	young woman, maiden (XIX)
viridis, -e	green (XXIII)
virtūs, virtūtis, f.	courage, virtue, manliness (BI)
vīta, -ae, f.	life (BI)
volō, volāre, volāvī, volātum	to fly (BI)
vōs	you (pl.) (III)
vōx, vōcis, f.	voice (BI)

Glossary – English to Latin
Roman numeral indicates lesson number.
Vocabulary from *Schola Latina Book I* are marked (BI)

<u>Nōtā bene</u>: Noun dictionary entries are often shortened by listing only the genitive singular *ending* rather than the full genitive singular *form*. So **lectus, lectī, m.** would become **lectus, -ī, m.** and **vallum, vallī, n.** would become **vallum, -ī, n.** This seems confusing at first, but you can still see the stem of these nouns in the nominative singular forms **lectus** and **vallum**. However, nouns like **culter, cultrī, m.** and **māter, mātris, f.** will *not* be abbreviated, because their stems are not visible in the nominative singular form.

A
able, to be	possum, posse, potuī (XVII)
about	circum (+ Acc) (VII)
	dē (+ Abl) (X)
above	super (+ Acc) (VIII)
according to	secundum (+ Acc) (VIII)
ache, to	doleō, dolēre, doluī, olitūrum (BI)
across	trāns (+ Acc) (VIII)
all	omnis, -e (XXIII)
a lot	multum (BI)
always	semper (BI)
ancient	antīquus, -a, -um (BI)
and	et (BI)
angel	angelus, -ī, m. (II)
apple	mālum, -ī, n. (III)
April	Aprīlis, -is, m. (XVIII)
arm	bracchium, -ī, n. (BI)
around	circum (+ Acc) (VII)
ascend, to	ascendō, ascendere, ascendī, ascensum (XIII)
ask for, to	petō, petere, petīvī, petītum (XVI)
at	ad (+ Acc) (VIII)
August	Augustus, -ī, m. (XVIII)
autumn	autumnus, -ī, m. (XVII)

B
bad	malus, -a, -um (BI)
be, to	sum, esse, fuī, futūrum (BI)
bean	fāba, -ae, f. (VI)
badly	male (BI)
bear	ursa, -ae, f. (BI)
bed	cubīle, cubīlis, n. (BI)
	lectus, -ī, m. (BI)
bedroom	cubiculum, -ī, n. (BI)
before	ante (+ Ac) (VIII)
beg for, to	petō, petere, petīvī, petītum (XVI)
beginning	principium, -ī, n. (VII)
behold!	ecce (XV)
believe, to	crēdō, crēdere, crēdidī, crēditum (XIII)
beloved	cārissimus, -a, -um (XXIV)
belt	cingulum, -ī, n. (XVI)
beside	secundum (+ Acc) (VIII)
best	optimus, -a, -um (BI)
bird	avis, avis, f. (BI)
black	niger, nigra, nigrum (XIV)
blessed	beātus, -a, -um (IX)
blue	caeruleus, -a, -um (XV)
body	corpus, corporis, n. (BI)
book	liber, librī, m. (BI)
border	fīnis, fīnis, m. (VII)
bow	arcus, -ī, m. (XV)
boy	puer, puerī, m. (BI)
brave	fortis, -e (XXIII)
bread	pānis, pānis, m. (IX)
breath	spīritus, spīritūs, m. (BI)
brother	frāter, frātris, m. (BI)
brown	fulvus, -a, -um (XV)
bull	taurus, -ī, m. (BI)
butter	būtyrum, -ī, n. (X)

Glossary			**English to Latin**
C			(BI)
Caesar	Caesar, Caesaris, m. (BI)	dog	canis, canis, m./f. (BI)
carry, to	portō, portāre, portāvī, portātum (IX)	door	iānua, -ae, f. (BI)
cat	fēles, fēlis, f. (BI)	doubt, to	dubitō, dubitāre, dubitāvī, dubitātum (BI)
ceiling	lacūnar, lacūnāris, n. (BI)	down from	dē (+ Abl) (X)
chair	sella, -ae, f. (BI)		
cheese	cāseus, -ī, m. (IX)		
cherry	cerasum, -ī, n. (VII)	**E**	
chicken	gallīna, -ae, f. (BI)	eager, to be	studeō, studēre, studuī (XIII)
Christ	Christus, -ī, m. (BI)	eagle	aquila, -ae, f. (BI)
church	ecclesia, -ae, f. (BI)	ear	auris, auris, f. (BI)
city	urbs, urbis, f. (BI)	earth	terra, -ae, f. (BI)
close, to	claudō, claudere, clausī, clausum (XVI)	eat, to	cēnō, cēnāre, -āvī, -ātum (BI)
		effort	labor, labōris, m. (XIX)
cloud	nimbus, -ī, m.(BI)	end	fīnis, fīnis, m. (VII)
coin	nummus, -ī, m. (VI)	endure, to	dūrō, durāre, -āvī, -ātum (BI)
come, to	veniō, venīre, vēnī, ventūrum (XXII)	enemy	hostis, hostis, m./f. (BI)
		enter, to	intrō, intrāre, -āvī, -ātum (BI)
commander	imperātor, imperātōris, m. (BI)	eternal	aeternus, -a, -um (BI)
		every	omnis, -e (XXIII)
concerning	dē (+ Abl) (X)	evil	malus, -a, -um (XIII)
conquer, to	superō, superāre, superāvī, superātum (BI)	eye	oculus, -ī, m. (BI)
		F	
couch	lectus, -ī, m. (BI)	fail, to	dēficiō, dēficere, dēfēcī, dēfectum (XXI)
country	patria, -ae, f. (BI)		
courage	virtūs, virtūtis, f. (BI)	farmer	agricola, -ae, m. (BI)
cow	bōs, bovis, m./f. (BI)	father	pater, patris, m. (BI)
cross	crux, crucis, f. (BI)	fatherland	patria, -ae, f. (BI)
crown	corōna, -ae, f. (BI)	fault	culpa, -ae, f. (BI)
cup	pōculum, -ī, n. (BI)	fear	timor, timōris, m. (VII)
cry, to	fleō, flēre, flēvī, flētum (BI)	fear, to	timeō, timēre, timuī (BI)
		February	Februārius, -ī, m. (XVIII)
		field	ager, agrī, m. (XI)
D		fight, to	pugnō, pugnāre, pugnāvī, pugnātum (BI)
daughter	fīlia, -ae, f. (BI)		
day	diēs, diēī, m. (XX)	find, to	inveniō, invenīre, invēnī, inventum (XXII)
death	mors, mortis, f. (BI)		
December	December, Decembris (XVIII)	finger	digitus, -ī, m. (BI)
		fire	ignis, ignis, m. (BI)
deep	altus, -a, -um (BI)	fireplace	focus, -ī, m. (BI)
descend, to	dēscendō, dēscendere, dēscendī, dēscensum (XIII)	first	prīmus, -a, -um (BI)
		fish	piscis, piscis, m. (XIX)
		fisherman	piscātor, piscātōris, m. (XIX)
die (game)	ālea, -ae, f. (IV)	floor	solum, -ī, n. (BI)
dine, to	cēnō, cēnāre, -āvī, -ātum	flower	flōs, flōris, m. (IX)

fly, to	volō, volāre, -āvī, -ātum (BI)	**hand over, to**	tradō, trādere, trādidī, trāditum (XIII)
foolish	fatuus, -a, -um (XIX)	**happy**	beātus, -a, -um (IX)
foot	pēs, pedis, m. (BI)	**hat**	pilleus, -ī, m. (IX)
forest	silva, -ae, f. (BI)	**have, to**	habeō, habēre, habuī, habitum (III)
fork	furca, -ae, f. (BI)		
free, to	līberō, līberāre, līberāvī, līberātum (XIV)	**he**	is (see is, ea, id)
		he who	quī (XIV)
		head	caput, capitis, n. (BI)
friend	amīcus, -ī, m. (BI) amīca, -ae, f.	**hear, to**	audiō, audīre, audīvī, audītum (XXII)
frighten, to	terreō, terrēre, terruī, territum (VI)	**heaven**	caelum, -ī, n. (BI)
		hell	infernus, -ī, m. (VII)
from	ā / ab (+ Abl) (X)	**here**	hīc (BI)
in front of	ante (+ Acc) (VIII)	**high**	altus, -a, -um (BI)
fruit	pōmum, -ī, n. (VI)	**hill**	collis, collis, m. (BI)
		hold, to	teneō, tenēre, tenuī, tentum (IV)

G

game	lūdus, -ī, m. (IV)	**holy**	sanctus, -a, -um (BI)
gameboard	abacus, -ī, m. (IV)	**honor**	honor, honōris, m. (XXIV)
game piece	calculus, -ī, m. (IV)	**horse**	equus, -ī, m. (BI)
gate	porta, -ae, f. (XI)	**hour**	hōra, -ae, f. (BI)
Gaul	Gallia, -ae, f. (BI)	**house**	domus, domūs, f. (BI)
gift	dōnum, -ī, n. (BI)	**how**	quōmodo (XII)
girl	puella, -ae, f. (BI)	**how many**	quot (XII)
give, to	dō, dare, dedī, datum (III)	**how much**	quantus, -a, -um (XII)
glory	glōria, -ae, f. (BI)	**humility**	humilitās, humilitātis, f. (V)
God	Deus, -ī, m. (BI)	**hurry, to**	festīnō, festināre, festīnāvī, festīnātum (BI)
gold	aurum, -ī, n. (III)		
good	bonus, -a, -um (BI)		
gospel	evangelium, -ī, n. (VIII)		
grace	grātia, -ae, f. (XVII)		I
grandfather	avus, -ī, m. (XV)	**I**	ego
grandmother	avia, -ae, f. (XIV)	**in**	in (+ Abl) (XI)
great	magnus, -a, -um (BI)	**into**	in (+ Acc) (XI)
green	viridis, -e (XXIII)	**island**	īnsula, -ae, f. (BI)
greet, to	salūtō, salūtāre, salūtāvī, salūtātum (XIV)	**it**	id (see is, ea, id)
		Italy	Ītalia, -ae, f. (BI)

J

guard, to	servō, servāre, servāvī, servātum (XIII)

		January	Iānuārius, -ī, m. (XVIII)
		jewel	gemma, -ae, f. (XI)
		joy	gaudium, -ī, n. (BI)

H

hair (a)	capillus, -ī, m. (BI)	**judge, to**	iūdicō, iūdicāre, iūdicāvī, iūdicātum (BI)
hand	manus, manus, f. (4th d., BI)	**July**	Iūlius, -ī, m. (XVIII)
		June	Iūnius, -ī, m. (XVIII)

Glossary — English to Latin

K

keep, to	servō, servāre, servāvī, servātum (XIII)
key	clāvis, clāvis f. (VII)
king	rēx, rēgis, m. (BI)
kingdom	rēgnum, -ī, n. (BI)
kitchen	culīna, -ae, f. (BI)
knife	culter, cultrī, m. (BI)
know, to	sciō, scīre, scīvī, scītum (XXII)
knowledge	scientia, -ae, f. (VII)

L

labor	labor, labōris, m. (XIX)
lamb	agnus, -ī, m. (BI)
lamp	lampas, lampadis, f. (VII)
land	terra, -ae, f. (BI)
language	lingua, -ae, f. (BI)
large	magnus, -a, -um (BI)
laugh, to	rideō, ridēre, rīsī, rīsum (BI)
law	lēx, lēgis, f. (BI)
leg	crūs, crūris, n. (BI)
legion	legiō, legiōnis, f. (BI)
letter	epistula, -ae, f. (XX)
lie	mendācium, -ī, n. (BI)
life	vīta, -ae, f. (BI)
light	lūx, lūcis, f. (BI)
like	similis, -e (XI)
like, to	amō, amāre, -āvī, -ātum (BI)
little, a	parum (BI)
living room	exedrium, -ī, n. (BI)
long	longus, -a, -um (BI)
look at, to	spectō, spectāre, spectāvī, specātum (VI)
lord	dominus, -ī, m. (BI)
Lord's Day	Dominica, -ae, f. (XX)
lot, a	multum (BI)
love, to	amō, amāre, -āvī, -ātum (BI)
love	cāritās, cāritātis, f. (V)

M

maiden	virgō, virginis, f. (XIX)
make, to	faciō, facere, fēcī, factum (XXI)
man	homō, hominis, m. (BI)
manage, to	gerō, gerere, gessī, gestum (XVI)
March	Martius, -ī, m. (XVIII)
manliness	virtūs, virtūtis, f. (BI)
many	multus, -a, -um (BI)
Mary	Maria, -ae, f. (BI)
master	dominus, -ī, m. (BI)
me	ego (II)
message	nūntius, -ī, m. (BI)
messenger	nūntius, -ī, m. (BI)
mirror	speculum, -ī, n. (BI)
Monday	diēs Lūnae (XX)
money	pecūnia, -ae, f. (BI)
month	mensis, mensis, m. (XVIII)
moon	lūna, -ae, f. (BI)
mother	māter, mātris, f. (BI)
mountain	mōns, montis, m. (BI)
mouth	ōs, ōris, n. (BI)
move, to	moveō, movēre, mōvī, mōtum (BI)
much	multus, -a, -um (BI)
my	meus, -a, -um (BI)

N

name	nōmen, nōminis, n. (BI)
narrow	angustus, -a, -um (BI)
never	numquam (BI)
new	novus, -a, -um (BI)
night	nox, noctis, f. (BI)
nobody	nēmo, nēminis, m./f. (XIX)
no one	nēmō, nēminis, m./f. (XIX)
nose	nāsus, -ī, m. (BI)
not	nōn (BI)
November	November, Novembris, m. (XVIII)
now	nunc (BI)

O

October	Octōber, Octōbris, m. (XVIII)
often	saepe (BI)
oil	oleum, -ī, n. (X)
old	antīquus, -a, -um (BI)
on	in (+ Abl) (XI)

open, to	aperiō, aperīre, aperuī, apertum (XXII)	**purple**	purpureus, -a, -um (XV)
open, to be	pateō, patēre, patuī (BI)	**put on, to**	induō, induere, induī, indūtum (XVI)
orange	aurantius, -a, -um (XV)		
orange	mālum aurantium, -ī, n. (XV)	**Q**	
		queen	rēgīna, -ae, f. (BI)
order, to	imperō, imperāre, imperāvī, imperātum (BI)	**R**	
		rain	pluvia, -ae, f. (XVII)
out from	ē / ex (+ Abl) (X)	**rainbow**	arcus, -ī, m. (XV)
out of	ē / ex (+ Abl) (X)	**rain, to**	pluit, pluere (XVII)
over	super (+ Ac) (VIII)	**rampart**	vallum, -ī, n. (BI)
overcome, to	superō, superāre, -āvī, superātum (BI)	**read, to**	legō, legere, lēgī, lectum (XIII)
ox	bōs, bovis, m./f. (BI)	**read aloud, to**	recitō, recitāre, -āvī, -ātum (BI)
P		**receive, to**	accipiō, accipere, accēpī, acceptum (XXI)
pants	brācae, -ārum, f. (XVI)		
paper	charta, -ae, f. (BI)	**recite, to**	recitō, recitāre, recitāvī, recitātum (BI)
part	pars, partis, f. (BI)		
pass, to	trādō, trādere, trādidī, trāditum (XIII)	**red**	rūfus, -a, -um (XIV)
		reign, to	rēgnō, rēgnāre, rēgnāvī, rēgnātum (BI)
patience	patientia, -ae, f. (X)		
peace	pax, pācis, f. (BI)	**rejoice, to**	gaudeō, gaudēre, gāvīsus sum (BI)
pearl	margarīta, -ae, f. (XI)		
pen	calamus, -ī, m. (BI)	**remain, to**	maneō, manēre, mansī, mansum (BI)
pencil	stīlus, -ī, m. (BI)		
pig	porcus, -ī, m. (BI)	**rescue, to**	ēripiō, ēripere, ēripuī, ēreptum (XXI)
plant	herba, -ae, f. (BI)		
plate	patella, -ae, f. (BI)	**resurrection**	resurrectiō, resurrectiōnis, f. (V)
please, to	placeō, placēre, placuī (BI)		
		reward	praemium, -ī, n. (BI)
plow, to	arō, arāre, arāvī, arātum (BI)	**rich person**	dīves, dīvitis, m./f. (V)
		right hand	dextera, -ae, f. (IV)
poor man	pauper, pauperis, m. (XIX)	**river**	flūmen, flūminis, n. (BI)
		road	via, -ae, f. (BI)
portion	portiō, portiōnis, f. (V)	**Rome**	Rōma, -ae, f. (BI)
praise, to	laudō, laudāre, -āvī, laudātum (X)	**rule, to**	imperō, imperāre, imperāvī, imperātum (BI)
praise	laus, laudis, f. (X)		
pray, to	ōrō, ōrāre, -āvī, -ātum (BI)	**S**	
		sad	tristis, -e (XXIII)
prepare, to	parō, parāre, -āvī, -ātum (XIV)	**safe**	tūtus, -a, -um (BI)
		sail, to	nāvigō, nāvigāre, nāvigāvī, nāvigātum (BI)
pretty	bellus, -a, -um (BI)		
prophecy	prophetia, -ae, f. (XIX)	**sailor**	nauta, -ae, m. (BI)

Saturday	diēs Sāturnī (XX)	snack	portiō, portiōnis, f. (V)
save, to	servō, servāre, servāvī, servātum (XIII)	snake	serpens, serpentis, m./f. (BI)
		snow	nix, nivis, f. (XVII)
say, to	dīcō, dīcere, dīxī, dictum (XIII)	snow, to	ningit, ningere (XVII)
		sock	pedāle, pedālis, n. (V)
school	lūdus, -ī, m. (IV)	soldier	mīles, mīlitis, m. (BI)
second	secundus, -a, -um (BI)	son	fīlius, -ī, m. (BI)
see, to	videō, vidēre, vīdī, vīsum (III)	song	canticum, -ī, n. (XXIV)
		sorry, to be	misereō, miserēre (BI)
seize, to	capiō, capere, cēpī, ceptum (XXI)	space	spatium, -ī, n. (IV)
		Spain	Hispania, -ae, f. (BI)
send, to	mittō, mittere, mīsī, missum (XIII)	speak, to	ōrō, ōrāre, -āvī, -ātum (BI) dīcō, dīcere, dīxī, dictum (XIII)
September	September, Septembris, m. (XVIII)	spirit	spīritus, spīritūs, m. (XXIV)
		spoon	cochleāre, cochleāris, n. (BI)
servant	servus, -ī, m. (BI)	spring	vēr, vēris, n. (XVII)
she	ea (see is, ea, id)	stand, to	stō, stāre, stetī, statum (BI)
shepherd	pastor, pastōris, m. (BI)	star	stella, -ae, f. (BI)
shine, to	luceō, lucēre, lūxī (BI)	state	cīvitās, cīvitātis, f. (XI)
ship	nāvis, nāvis, f. (BI)	stay, to	maneō, manēre, mansī, mansum (BI)
shirt	camisia, -ae, f. (XVI)		
shoe	calceus, -ī, m. (XVI)	stomach	stomachus, -ī, m. (BI)
short	brevis, -e (XXIII)	stone	calculus, -ī, m. (IV)
show	spectāculum, -ī, n. (VI)	strong	fortis, -e (XXIII)
sight	spectāculum, -ī, n. (VI)	strong, to be	valēre, valuī, valitūrum (BI)
sign	signum, -ī, n. (BI)	student	discipulus, -ī, m. discipula, -ae, f. (BI)
silent, to be	sileō, silēre, siluī (BI)		
silver	argentum, -ī, n. (III)	study, to	studeō, studēre, studuī (XIII)
similar	similis, -e (+ Dat) (XI)	summer	aestās, aestātis, f. (XVII)
sin	peccātum, -ī, n. (BI)	Sunday	diēs Sōlis (XX)
sin, to	peccō, peccāre, peccāvī, peccātum (BI)	swim, to	natō, natāre, natāvī, natātum (VIII)
sing, to	cantō, cantāre, cantāvī, cantātum (BI)	sword	gladius, -ī, m. (BI)
sister	soror, sorōris, f. (BI)		**T**
sit, to	sedeō, sedēre, sēdī, sessum (BI)	table	mēnsa, -ae, f. (BI)
		teach, to	doceō, docēre, docuī, doctum (BI)
sky	caelum, -ī, n. (BI)		
slave	servus, -ī, m. (BI)	teacher	magister, magistrī, m. magistra, -ae, f. (BI)
sleep, to	dormiō, dormīre, dormīvī, dormītum (XXII)		
		tell, to	dīcere, dīxī, dictum (XIII)
		that	ille, illa, illlud (XI)
slow, to be	tardō, tardāre, tardāvī, tardātum (BI)	there	ibi (BI)
		they	(see: is, ea, id)
small	parvus, -a, -um (BI)	think, to	cogitō, cogitāre, cōgitāvī, cōgitātum (BI)

English	Latin
this	hic, haec, hoc (X)
throne	thronus, -ī, m. (II)
through	per (+ Acc) (VII)
throw, to	iaciō, iacere, iēcī, iactum (XXI)
Thursday	diēs Iovis (XX)
time	tempus, temporis, n. (BI)
to	ad (+ Acc) (VIII)
toe	digitus, -ī, m. (BI)
tongue	lingua, -ae, f. (BI)
tooth	dēns, dentis, m. (BI)
torch	lampas, lampadis, f. (VII)
toward	ad (+ Ac) (VIII)
town	oppidum, -ī, n. (BI)
treasure	thēsaurus, -ī, m. (XI)
true	vērus, -a, -um (IX)
truth	vēritās, vēritātis, f. (BI)
Tuesday	diēs Martis (XX)

U

uncertain, to be	dubitō, dubitāre, dubitāvī, dubitātum (BI)
under	sub (+ Acc / Abl) (XI)
underworld	infernus, -ī, m. (VII)
us	nōs (II)

V

vegetable	holus, holeris, n. (VI)
victory	victōria, -ae, f. (BI)
virgin	virgō, virginis, f. (XIX)
virtue	virtūs, virtūtis, f. (BI)
voice	vōx, vōcis, f. (BI)

W

walk, to	ambulō, ambulāre, ambulāvī, ambulātum (BI)
wall	vallum, -ī, n. (BI) (of a fortress)
wall	mūrus, -ī, m. (BI) (of a building or room)
wander, to	errō, errāre, -āvī, -ātum (BI)
war	bellum, -ī, n. (BI)
watch, to	spectō, spectāre, spectāvī, spectātum (VI)
water	aqua, -ae, f. (BI)
way	via, -ae, f. (BI)
we	nōs (II)
weapon	tēlum, -ī, n. (BI)
wear, to	gerō, gerere, gessī, gestum (XVI)
Wednesday	diēs Mercuriī (XX)
week	septimāna, septimānae, f. (XX)
weep, to	fleō, flēre, flēvī, flētum (BI)
well, to be	salveō, salvēre (BI)
well	puteus, -ī, m. (BI)
well	bene (BI)
what	quid (XII)
when	quandō (XII)
where	ubi (XII)
which	quotus, -a, -um (XII)
white	albus, -a, -um (XIV)
who	quis (XII)
whole	tōtus, -a, -um (BI)
why	cūr (XII)
wide	lātus, -a, -um (BI)
window	fenestra, -ae, f. (BI)
wine	vīnum, -ī, n. (BI)
winter	hiems, hiemis, f. (XVII)
wisdom	sapientia, -ae, f. (III)
wise	prūdens, prūdentis (XXIII)
with	cum (+ Abl) (X)
without	sine (+ Abl) (X)
woman	fēmina, -ae, f. (BI)
word	verbum, -ī, n. (BI)
work	labor, labōris, m. (XIX)
work, to	labōrō, labōrāre, labōrāvī, labōrātum (BI)
world	mundus, -ī, m. (BI)
worthy	dīgnus, -a, -um (VI)
write, to	scrībō, scrībere, scrīpsī, scriptum (XVI)

Y

year	annus, -ī, m. (BI)
yellow	flāvus, -a, -um (XIV)
you	tū (sing.), vōs (pl.) (III)
young woman	virgō, virginis, f. (XIX)
your (sing.)	tuus, -a, -um (BI)

Numbers

	Cardinals	Ordinals	Roman Numerals
1	ūnus, -a, -um	prīmus, -a, -um	I
2	duo, duae, duo	secundus, -a, -um	II
3	trēs, trēs, tria	tertius, -a, -um	III
4	quattuor	quartus, -a, -um	IV
5	quīnque	quīntus, -a, -um	V
6	sex	sextus, -a, -um	VI
7	septem	septimus, -a, -um	VII
8	octō	octāvus, -a, -um	VIII
9	novem	nōnus, -a, -um	IX
10	decem	decimus, -a, -um	X
11	ūndecim	ūndecimus, -a, -um	XI
12	duodecim	duodecimus, -a, -um	XII
13	tredecim	tertius decimus, -a, -um	XIII
14	quattuordecim	quartus decimus, -a, -um	XIV
15	quīndecim	quīntus decimus, -a, -um	XV
16	sēdecim	sextus decimus, -a, -um	XVI
17	septendecim	septimus decimus, -a, -um	XVII
18	duodēvīgintī	duodēvīcēsimus, -a, -um	XVIII
19	ūndēvīgintī	ūndēvīcēsimus, -a, -um	XIX
20	vīgintī	vīcēsimus, -a, -um	XX
21	vīgintī ūnus, -a, -um	vīcēsimus prīmus, -a, -um	XXI
22	vīgintī duo, duae, duo	vīcēsimus secundus, -a, -um	XXII
23	vīgintī trēs, trēs, tria	vīcēsimus tertius, -a, -um	XXIII
24	vīgintī quattuor	vīcēsimus quartus, -a, -um	XXIV
25	vīgintī quīnque	vīcēsimus quīntus, -a, -um	XXV
26	vīgintī sex	vīcēsimus sextus, -a, -um	XXVI
27	vīgintī septem	vīcēsimus septimus, -um	XXVII
28	duodētrīginta	duodētrīcēsimus, -a, -um	XXVIII
29	undētrīginta	undētrīcēsimus, -a, -um	XXIX
30	trīginta	trīcēsimus, -a, -um	XXX
40	quadrāgintā	quadrāgēsimus, -a, -um	XL
50	quīnquāgintā	quīnquāgēsimus, -a, -um	L
60	sexāgintā	sexāgēsimus, -a, -um	LX
70	septuāgintā	septuāgēsimus, -a, -um	LXX
80	octōgintā	octōgēsimus, -a, -um	LXXX
90	nōnāgintā	nōnāgēsimus, -a, -um	XC
100	centum	centēsimus, -a, -um	C
1000	mīlle	mīlēsimus, -a, -um	M

Vocabulary by Lectio

<u>Nōtā bene</u>: Noun dictionary entries are often shortened by listing only the genitive singular *ending* rather than the full genitive singular *form*. So **lectus, lectī, m.** would become **lectus, -ī, m.** and **vallum, vallī, n.** would become **vallum, -ī, n.** This seems confusing at first, but you can still see the stem of these nouns in the nominative singular forms <u>lectus</u> and <u>vallum</u>.

However, nouns like **culter, cultrī, m.** and **māter, mātris, f.** will *not* be abbreviated, because their stems are not visible in the nominative singular form.

II – Secunda lectiō

angelus, -ī, m.	angel
thronus, -ī, m.	throne
ego	I, me; us, we

III – Tertia lectiō

argentum, -ī, n.	silver
aurum, -ī, n.	gold
mālum, -ī, n.	apple
dō, dare, dedī, datum	to give
laudō, laudāre, laudāvī, laudātum	to praise
habeō, habēre, habuī, habitum	to have, to possess
videō, vidēre, vīdī, vīsum	to see
tū	you

IV – Quarta lectiō

abacus, -ī, m.	gameboard
ālea, -ae, f.	(game) die
calculus, -ī, m.	stone, game piece
dextera, -ae, f.	right hand
lūdus, -ī, m.	game, school
spatium, -ī, n.	space
teneō, tenēre, tenuī, tentum	to hold

V – Quīnta lectiō

cāritās, cāritātis, f.	(Christian) love
dīves, dīvitis, m./f.	rich person
humilitās, humilitātis, f.	humility
pedāle, pedālis, n.	sock (pl. – pedālia)
portiō, portiōnis, f.	portion, snack
resurrectiō, resurrectiōnis, f.	resurrection

VI – Sexta lectiō

dignus, -a, um	worthy
faba, -ae, f.	bean
holus, holeris, n.	vegetable
nummus, -ī, m.	coin
pōmum, -ī, n.	fruit
spectaculum, -ī, n.	sight, show
spectō, spectāre, spectāvī, spectātum	to look at, to watch
terreō, terrēre, terruī, territum	to frighten

VII – Septima lectiō

cerasum, -ī, n.	cherry
clāvis, clāvis, f.	key
fīnis, fīnis, m.	end, border
infernus, -ī, m.	hell, underworld
lampās, lampadis, f.	lamp, torch
principium, -ī, n.	beginning
scientia, -ae, f.	knowledge
timor, timōris, m.	fear

VIII – Octava lectiō

ad (+ Acc)	to, toward, near, at
ante (+ Acc)	before, in front of
circum (+ Acc)	around, about

Vocabulary by Lectio

per (+ Acc)	through	sub (+ Acc /Abl)	under
secundum (+ Acc)	beside, according to	thēsaurus, -ī, m.	treasure

XII – Duodecima lectiō

super (+ Acc)	above, over
trāns (+ Acc)	across
evangelium, -ī, n.	gospel
natō, natāre, natāvī, natātum	to swim

cūr	why
quandō	when
quantus, -a, -um	how much
quid	what
quis	who
quōmodō	how
quot	how many
quotus, -a, -um	which
ubi	where, when
servō, servāre, servāvī, servātum	to save, keep, guard

IX – Nōna lectiō

beātus, -a, -um	happy, blessed
cāseus, -ī, m.	cheese
flōs, flōris, m.	flower
pānis, pānis, m.	bread
pilleus, -ī, m.	hat
portō, portāre, portāvī, portātum	to carry
sapientia, -ae, f.	wisdom
studeō, studēre, studuī	to be eager for, to study
vērus, -a, -um	true

XIII – Tertia decima lectiō

ascendō, ascendere, ascendī, ascensum	to ascend
crēdō, crēdere, crēdidī, crēditum	to believe
dēscendō, dēscendere, dēscendī, dēscensum	to descend
dīcō, dīcere, dīxī, dictum	to say, to tell, to speak
legō, legere, lēgī, lectum	to read
mittō, mittere, mīsī, mīssum	to send
servō, servāre, servāvī, servātum	to save, to keep, to guard
studeō, studēre, studuī, ---	to be eager for, to study
trādō, trādere, trādidī, trāditum	to pass, to hand over

X – Decima lectiō

ā / ab (+ Abl)	from, away from
būtyrum, -ī, n.	butter
cum (+ Abl)	with
dē (+ Abl)	about, concerning, down from
ē / ex (+ Abl)	out of, out from
laus, laudis, f.	praise
oleum, -ī, n.	oil
patientia, -ae, f.	patience
sine (+ Abl)	without

XI – Ūndecima lectiō

XIV – Quarta decima lectiō

ager, agrī, m.	field (on farm)
cīvitās, cīvitātis, f.	state
gemma, -ae, f.	gem, jewel
in (+ Acc)	into, onto
in (+ Abl)	in, on
margarīta, -ae, f.	pearl
porta, -ae, f.	gate
similis, simile (+Dat)	similar to, like

albus, -a, -um	white
avia, -ae, f.	grandmother
flāvus, -a, -um	yellow
līberō, līberāre, līberāvī, līberātum	to free
niger, nigra, nigrum	black

Vocabulary by Lectio

parō, parāre, parāvī, parātum	to prepare		pluvia, -ae, f.	rain

XVIII – Duodēvīcēsima lectiō

quī	who; (he) who
rūfus, -a, -um	red
salūtō, salūtāre, salūtāvī, salūtātum	to greet

XV – Quīnta decima lectiō

arcus, -ī, m.	bow, rainbow
aurantius, -a, -um	orange
avus, -ī, m.	grandfather
caeruleus, -a, -um	blue
ecce	behold! (a command)
fulvus, -a, -um	brown
mālum aurantium, -ī, n.	(an) orange
purpureus, -a, -um	purple

XVIII – Duodēvīcēsima lectiō

mensis, mensis, m.	month
Iānuārius, -ī, m.	January
Februārius, -ī, m.	February
Martius, -ī, m.	March
Aprīlis, Aprīlis, m.	April
Māius, -ī, m.	May
Iūnius, -ī, m.	June
Iūlius, -ī, m.	July
Augustus, -ī, m.	August
September, -bris, m.	September
Octōber, -bris, m.	October
November, -bris, m.	November
December, -bris, m.	December

XVI – Sexta decima lectiō

brācae, brācārum, f.	pants
calceus, -ī, m.	shoe
camisia, -ae, f.	shirt
cingulum, -ī, n.	belt
claudō, claudere, clausī, clausum	to close
gerō, gerere, gessī, gestum	to wear, to manage
induō, induere, induī, indūtum	to put on
petō, petere, petīvī, petitum	to seek, to beg to ask for
scrībō, scrībere, scrīpsī, scrīptum	to write

XIX – Ūndēvīcēsima lectiō

fatuus, -a, -um	foolish, silly
labor, labōris, m.	work, labor, effort
nēmō, nēminis, m./f.	no one, nobody
opus, operis, n.	(a) work
pauper, pauperis, m.	poor man
piscātor, -is, m.	fisherman
piscis, piscis, m./f.	fish
prophetia, -ae, f.	prophecy
virgō, virginis, f.	young woman, maiden, virgin

XVII – Septima decima lectiō

aestās, aestātis, f.	summer
autumnus, -ī, m.	autumn, fall
hiems, hiemis, f.	winter
vēr, vēris, n.	spring
grātia, -ae, f.	grace
ningit, ningere	to snow
nix, nivis, f.	snow
pluit, pluere, pluit	to rain

XX – Vīcēsima lectiō

diēs, diēī, m.	day (Abl – diē)
diēs Sōlis	Sunday
Dominica, -ae, f.	Lord's Day
diēs Lūnae	Monday
diēs Martis	Tuesday
diēs Mercuriī	Wednesday
diēs Iovis	Thursday
diēs Veneris	Friday
diēs Sāturnī	Saturday
epistula, -ae, f.	letter
septimāna, septimānae, f.	week

Vocabulary by Lectio

XXI – Vīcēsima prīma lectiō

accipiō, accipere, accēpī, acceptum	to receive
capiō, capere, cēpī, captum	to seize
dēficiō, dēficere, dēfēcī, dēfectum	to fail
ēripiō, ēripere, ēripuī, ēreptum	to rescue
faciō, facere, fēcī, factum	to make, to do
iaciō, iacere, iēcī, iactum	to throw, to cast

XXII – Vīcēsima secunda lectiō

aperiō, aperīre, aperuī, apertum	to open
audiō, audīre, audīvī, audītum	to hear, to listen
dormiō, dormīre, dormīvī, dormītum	to sleep
veniō, venīre, vēnī, ventum	to come
sciō, scīre, scīvī, scītum	to know
inveniō, invenīre, invēnī, inventum	to find

XXIII – Vīcēsima tertia lectiō

brevis, breve (brevis, -e)	short
fortis, forte (fortis, -e)	strong, brave
longus, -a, -um	long
omnis, omne (omnis, -e)	all, every
prūdēns, prūdentis	wise
tristis, triste (tristis, -e)	sad
viridis, viride (viridis, -e)	green

XXIV – Vīcēsima quarta lectiō

canticum, -ī, n.	song
cārissimus, -a, um	beloved
honor, honōris, m.	honor

Paradigms

I: amō, amāre – 1ˢᵗ conjugation
present tense

	SINGULAR	PLURAL
1ˢᵗ PERSON	amō	amāmus
2ⁿᵈ PERSON	amās	amātis
3ʳᵈ PERSON	amat	amant

present tense personal endings

1ˢᵗ PERSON	-ō	-mus
2ⁿᵈ PERSON	-s	-tis
3ʳᵈ PERSON	-t	-nt

ursa, -ae, f. – 1ˢᵗ declension m./f.

NOM.	ursa	ursae
GEN.	ursae	ursārum
DAT.	ursae	ursīs
ACC.	ursam	ursās
ABL.	ursā	ursīs

1ˢᵗ-declension m./f. case endings

NOM.	-a	-ae
GEN.	-ae	-ārum
DAT.	-ae	-īs
ACC.	-am	-ās
ABL.	-ā	-īs

II: sum, esse
present tense

	SINGULAR	PLURAL
1ˢᵗ PERSON	sum	sumus
2ⁿᵈ PERSON	es	estis
3ʳᵈ PERSON	est	sunt

nimbus, -ī, m. – 2ⁿᵈ declension m./f.

NOM.	nimbus	nimbī
GEN.	nimbī	nimbōrum
DAT.	nimbō	nimbīs
ACC.	nimbus	nimbōs
ABL.	nimbō	nimbīs

2ⁿᵈ-declension m./f. case endings

NOM.	-us	-ī
GEN.	-ī	-ōrum
DAT.	-ō	-īs
ACC.	-um	-ōs
ABL.	-ō	-īs

dōnum, -ī, n. – 2ⁿᵈ declension N

NOM.	dōnum	dōna
GEN.	dōnī	dōnōrum
DAT.	dōnō	dōnīs
ACC.	dōnum	dōna
ABL.	dōnō	dōnīs

2ⁿᵈ declension n. case endings

NOM.	-um	-a
GEN.	-ī	-ōrum
DAT.	-ō	-īs
ACC.	-um	-a
ABL.	-ō	-īs

ego

NOM.	ego	nōs
GEN.	meī	nostrī
DAT.	mihi	nōbīs
ACC.	mē	nōs
ABL.	mē	nōbīs

Paradigms

III: maneō, manēre – 2nd conjugation
present tense

	SINGULAR	PLURAL
1st PERSON	maneō	manēmus
2nd PERSON	manēs	manētis
3rd PERSON	manet	manent

tū

NOM.	tū	vōs
GEN.	tuī	vestrī
DAT.	tibi	vōbīs
ACC.	tē	vōs
ABL.	tē	vōbīs

IV: amō, amāre – 1st conjugation
future tense

1st PERSON	amābō	amābimus
2nd PERSON	amābis	amābitis
3rd PERSON	amābit	amābunt

maneō, manēre – 2nd conjugation
future tense

1st PERSON	manēbō	manēbimus
2nd PERSON	manēbis	manēbitis
3rd PERSON	manēbit	manēbunt

future tense personal endings

1st PERSON	-bō	-bimus
2nd PERSON	-bis	-bitis
3rd PERSON	-bit	-bunt

possum, posse
present tense

1st PERSON	possum	possumus
2nd PERSON	potes	potestis
3rd PERSON	potest	possunt

V: pater, patris, m. – 3rd decl. M/F

	SINGULAR	PLURAL
NOM.	pater	patrēs
GEN.	patris	patrum
DAT.	patrī	patribus
ACC.	patrem	patrēs
ABL.	patre	patribus

3rd declension m./f. case endings

NOM.	(varies)	-ēs
GEN.	-is	-um
DAT.	-ī	-ibus
ACC.	-em	-ēs
ABL.	-e	-ibus

flūmen, flūminis, n. – 3rd decl. N

NOM.	flūmen	flūmina
GEN.	flūminis	flūminum
DAT.	flūminī	flūminibus
ACC.	flūmen	flūmina
ABL.	flūmine	flūminibus

3rd-declension n. case endings

NOM.	(varies)	-a
GEN.	-is	-um
DAT.	-ī	-ibus
ACC.	(varies)	-a
ABL.	-e	-ibus

feles, felis, f. 3rd decl. M/F i-stem

NOM.	fēles	fēlēs
GEN.	fēlis	fēlium
DAT.	fēlī	fēlibus
ACC.	fēlem	fēlīs
ABL.	fēle	fēlibus

3rd decl. m./f. i-stem case endings

NOM.	(varies)	-ēs
GEN.	-is	-ium
DAT.	-ī	-ibus
ACC.	-em	-īs
ABL.	-e	-ibus

Paradigms

VI: is, ea, id

SINGULAR

	M.	F.	N.
NOM.	is	ea	id
GEN.	eius	eius	eius
DAT.	eī	eī	eī
ACC.	eum	eam	id
ABL.	eō	eā	eō

PLURAL

	M.	F.	N.
NOM.	eī	eae	ea
GEN.	eōrum	eārum	eōrum
DAT.	eīs	eīs	eīs
ACC.	eōs	eās	ea
ABL.	eīs	eīs	eīs

VII: ūnus, -a, -um (singular only)

	M.	F.	N.
NOM.	ūnus	ūna	ūnum
GEN.	ūnīus	ūnīus	ūnīus
DAT.	ūnī	ūnī	ūnī
ACC.	ūnum	ūnam	ūnum
ABL.	ūnō	ūnā	ūnō

VIII: duo, duae, duo (plural only)

	M.	F.	N.
NOM.	duo	duae	duo
GEN.	dōrum	duārum	duōrum
DAT.	duōbus	duābus	duōbus
ACC.	duōs	duās	duo
ABL.	duōbus	duābus	duōbus

IX: trēs, trēs, tria (plural only)

	M.	F.	N.
NOM.	trēs	trēs	tria
GEN.	trium	trium	trium
DAT.	tribus	tribus	tribus
ACC.	trīs	trīs	tria
ABL.	tribus	tribus	tribus

X: hic, haec, hoc

SINGULAR

	M.	F.	N.
NOM.	hic	haec	hoc
GEN.	huius	huius	huius
DAT.	huic	huic	huic
ACC.	hunc	hanc	hoc
ABL.	hōc	hāc	hōc

PLURAL

	M.	F.	N.
NOM.	hī	hae	haec
GEN.	hōrum	hārum	hōrum
DAT.	hīs	hīs	hīs
ACC.	hōs	hās	haec
ABL.	hīs	hīs	hīs

XI: ille, illa, illud

SINGULAR

	M.	F.	N.
NOM.	ille	illa	illud
GEN.	illīus	illīus	illīus
DAT.	illī	illī	illī
ACC.	illum	illam	illud
ABL.	illō	illā	illō

PLURAL

	M.	F.	N.
NOM.	illī	illae	illa
GEN.	illōrum	illārum	illōrum
DAT.	illīs	illīs	illīs
ACC.	illōs	illās	illa
ABL.	illīs	illīs	illīs

XIII: crēdō, crēdere – 3rd conjugation present tense

1ST PERSON	crēdō	crēdimus
2ND PERSON	crēdis	crēditis
3RD PERSON	crēdit	crēdunt

Paradigms

XIV: amō, amāre – 1st conjugation
imperfect tense

	SINGULAR	PLURAL
1ST PERSON	amābam	amābāmus
2ND PERSON	amābās	amābātis
3RD PERSON	amābat	amābant

maneō, manēre – 2nd conjugation
imperfect tense

1ST PERSON	monēbam	monēbāmus
2ND PERSON	monēbās	monēbātis
3RD PERSON	monēbat	monēbant

imperfect tense personal endings

1st PERSON	-bam	-bāmus
2nd PERSON	-bās	-bātis
3rd PERSON	-bat	-bant

XV: sum esse
imperfect tense

1ST PERSON	eram	erāmus
2ND PERSON	erās	erātis
3RD PERSON	erat	errant

possum, posse
imperfect tense

1ST PERSON	poteram	poterāmus
2ND PERSON	poterās	poterātis
3RD PERSON	poterat	poterant

XVI: crēdō credere – 3rd conjugation
imperfect tense

1ST PERSON	crēdēbam	crēdēbāmus
2ND PERSON	crēdēbās	crēdēbātis
3RD PERSON	crēdēbat	crēdēbant

XVII: crēdō credere – 3rd conjugation
future tense

1ST PERSON	crēdam	crēdēmus
2ND PERSON	crēdēs	crēdētis
3RD PERSON	crēdet	crēdent

XIX: sum, esse
future tense

	SINGULAR	PLURAL
1ST PERSON	erō	erimus
2ND PERSON	eris	eritis
3RD PERSON	erit	erunt

possum, posse
future tense

1st PERSON	poterō	poterimus
2ND PERSON	poteris	poteritis
3RD PERSON	poterit	poterunt

XX: amō, amāre, amāvī, amātum –
1st conjugation, perfect tense

1ST PERSON	amāvī	amāvimus
2ND PERSON	amāvistī	amāvistis
3RD PERSON	amāvit	amāvērunt

perfect tense personal endings

1ST PERSON	-ī	-imus
2ND PERSON	-istī	-istis
3RD PERSON	-it	-ērunt

XXI: capiō, capere – 3rd conj.- iō verbs
present tense

1ST PERSON	capiō	capimus
2ND PERSON	capis	capitis
3RD PERSON	capit	capiunt

capiō, capere
imperfect tense

1ST PERSON	capiēbam	capiēbāmus
2ND PERSON	capiēbās	capiēbātis
3RD PERSON	capiēbat	capiēbant

capiō, capere
imperfect tense

1ST PERSON	capiam	capiēmus
2ND PERSON	capiēs	capiētis
3RD PERSON	capiet	capient

Paradigms

XXII: audiō, audīre – 4th conjugation
present tense

	SINGULAR	PLURAL
1ST PERSON	audiō	audīmus
2ND PERSON	audīs	audītis
3RD PERSON	audit	audiunt

audiō, audīre
imperfect tense

1ST PERSON	audiēbam	audiēbāmus
2ND PERSON	audiēbās	audiēbātis
3RD PERSON	audiēbat	audiēbant

audio, audīre
future tense

1ST PERSON	audiam	audiēmus
2ND PERSON	audiēs	audiētis
3RD PERSON	audiēt	audient

XXIII: omnis, omne (3rd-decl. adjectives)

	SINGULAR	
	M./F.	N.
NOM.	omnis	omne
GEN.	omnis	omnis
DAT.	omnī	omnī
ACC.	omnem	omne
ABL.	omnī	omnī

	PLURAL	
NOM.	omnēs	omnia
GEN.	omnium	omnium
DAT.	omnibus	omnibus
ACC.	omnīs	omnia
ABL.	omnibus	omnibus

Dicta

Roman numeral indicates lesson number.

I	Audēmus iūra nostra dēfendere.	We dare to defend our rights.
II	Hannibal ad portās!	Hannibal [is] at the gates!
III	Ē plūribus ūnum.	Out of many, one.
IV	Carthāgō dēlenda est! - Cato the Censor	Carthage must be destroyed!
V	Senātus Populusque Rōmānus (SPQR)	The Roman Senate and People
VI	sine quā nōn	essential ingredient (lit., "without which not)
VII	id est (i.e.)	that is
VIII	ad nauseam	too long (lit., to the point of seasickness)
IX	ante merīdiem (a.m.) post merīdiem (p.m.)	before noon after noon
X	cum laude magnā cum laude summā cum laude	with praise with great praise with the highest praise
XI	Vēnī, vīdī, vīcī - Julius Caesar	I came, I saw, I conquered.
XII	Et tū, Brūte? -*Julius Caesar*, Shakespeare	You too, Brutus? (lit., and you, Brutus?)
XIII	Silent lēgēs inter arma. -Marcus Tullius Cicero	Laws are silent among arms.
XIV	Diēs Īrae	Day of Wrath
XV	exemplī grātiā	for the sake of example
XVI	Tē Deum laudāmus.	We praise you, O God.
XVII	dramatis persōnae	cast of characters (lit., masks of the drama)
XVIII	nōtā bene (N.B.)	note well (*or* pay attention!)

Dicta

XIX	Ecce Homō! 　　　-Pontius Pilate	Behold the Man!
XX	terra firma	dry land (lit., stable/firm land)
XXI	Dominus vōbīscum. Et tēcum.	The Lord be with you. And with you.
XXII	In hōc signō vincēs.	In this sign you will conquer.
XXIII	Fortēs Fortūna adiuvat.	Fortune favors the bold.
XXIV	Tempus fugit.	Time flies.

Colloquia
Roman numeral indicates lesson number.

I	Salvē! Quōmodō aestās erat?	Hi! How was the summer?
	Optimē! Et quōmodō tē habēs?	Great! And how are you?
	Bene mē habeō.	I'm well.
	Optimē mē habeō.	I'm great.
	Pessimē mē habeō.	I'm feeling terrible.
	Male mē habeō.	I'm not well.
	Satis bene mē habeō.	I'm well enough.
II	Ubi habitās?	Where do you live?
	In Alabāmā.	In Alabama.

N.B.: the preposition *in* takes the Ablative case. Here are the names of all the states:

Alabāma, -ae, f.	AL	Illinoesia, -ae, f.	IL	Novum Eborācum, -ī, n.	NY
Alaska, -ae, f.	AK	Indiāna, -ae, f.	IN	Ohiōa, -ae, f.	OH
Arizōna, -ae, f.	AZ	Īnsula Rhodēnsia, -ae, f.	RI	Ōklahōma, -ae, f.	OK
Arkānsia, -ae, f.	AR	Īova, -ae, f.	IA	Oregōnia, -ae, f.	OR
California, -ae, f.	CA	Kānsia, -ae, f.	KS	Pennsilvānia, -ae, f.	PA
Carolīna, -ae Merīdiōnālis, -is, f	SC	Kentukia, -ae, f.	KY	Tennessia, -ae, f.	TN
Carolīna, -ae Septentriōnālis, -is, f.	NC	Ludovīciāna, -ae, f.	LA	Terra, -ae, f. Mariae	MD
Cenomannica, -ae, f.	ME	Massachuseta, -ae, f.	MA	Texia, -ae, f.	TX
Nivāta, -ae, f.	NV	Michigānia, -ae, f.	MI	Ūta, -ae, f.	UT
Colorāta, -ae, f.	CO	Minnesōta, -ae, f.	MN	Vasingtōnia, -ae, f.	WA
Connecticūta, -ae, f.	CT	Mississippia, -ae, f.	MS	Viominga, -ae, f.	WY
Dakōta, -ae Merīdiōnālis, -is, f.	SD	Missūria, -ae, f.	MO	Virginia Occidentālis f.	WV
Dakōta, -ae Septentriōnālis, -is, f.	ND	Mons Viridis, -is, m.	VT	Virginia, -ae, f.	VA
Delevāria, -ae, f.	DE	Montāna, -ae, f.	MT	Viscōnsinia, -ae, f.	WI
Flōrida, -ae, f.	FL	Nebraska, -ae, f.	NE		
Georgia, -ae, f.	GA	Nova Caesarēa, -ae, f.	NJ		
Havaiī, -ōrum, m.	HI	Nova Hantōnia, -ae, f.	NH		
Idahōa, -ae, f.	ID	Nova Mexica, -ae, f.	NM		

III	Salvē, bone vir. Possumne tibi ministrāre?	Hello, good sir. Can I help you?
	Velim mālum.	I'd like an apple.
IV	Velīsne lūdum facere?	Would you like to play a game?
	Certē volō lūdum facere!	Sure, I want to play a game!
V	Silentium quaesō.	Silence, please.
	Aperīte librōs ad lectiōnem quīntam.	Open your books to the 5th lesson.
VI	Quid amās facere?	What do you like to do?
	Lūdōs facere amō.	I like to play games.

Colloquia

VII Quid est tibi? What's wrong with you?
Mē male habeō. I feel bad.

N.B.: Here are the names from book I and II, in both m. and f. forms (where possible):

Aemilius / Aemilia	Fābius / Fābia	Nicolaus, -ī, m.
Anna, -ae, f.	Flāvius / Flāvia	Petrus, -ī, m.
Antōnius / Antōnia	Gāius / Gāia	Porcius / Porcia
Aurēlius / Aurēlia	Horātius / Horātia	Publius / Publia
Brūtus / Brūta	Iēsus, Iēsū, m.	Quīntus / Quīnta
Caesar, Caesaris, m.	Iūlius / Iūlia	Scipiō, Scipiōnins, m.
Cāius / Cāia	Iūnius / Iūnia	Septimus / Septima
Cassius / Cassia	Livius / Livia	Sextus / Sexta
Catherīna, -ae, f.	Lūcius / Lūcia	Tarquinius / Tarquinia
Cato, Catōnis, m.	Lydia, -ae, f.	Tiberius / Tiberia
Cicero, Ciceronis, m.	Marcus / Marcia	Titus
Claudius / Claudia	Marius / Maria	Tullius / Tullia
Cornēlius / Cornēlia	Monica, -ae, f.	Valerius / Valeria

VIII Multum sternuō I am sneezing a lot
et caput mihi dolet. and my head hurts.
Gravedine labōrās! You have a cold!
Vīse medicum. Go see a doctor.

N.B.: Here are some other words for illnesses:

allergia, -ae, f	an allergy		pestilentiae, -ae, f.	plague
dēfectiō, -nis animī	a faint		vertigo, vertīginis, f.	dizziness
dolor, dolōris, m.	an ache		vulnus, vulneris, n.	a wound, a cut
eczēma, -ae, f.	a rash		tussis, tussis, f.	a cough
februs, febris, f.	a fever		umentēs narēs f. pl.	runny nose
fractūra, -ae, f.	broken bone			
gravedō, gravedinis, f.	a cold		sternuō, sternuere	to sneeze
horror, horrōris, m.	chills		tussiō, tussīre	to cough
luxatiō, luxātiōnis, f.	a sprain		vomitō, vomitāre	to vomit
nausea, -ae, f.	nausea		doleō, dolēre	to ache

IX Salvē, medice. Hello, doctor.
Salvē. Quid est? Hello. What's up?
Ego sum aeger! I am sick!
Manē in lectō trīs diēs. Stay in bed for three days.

X Quid velīs? What would you like?
Trāde mihi būtyrum, quaesō. Please pass me the butter.
Ecce. Here it is. (lit., Behold!)

XI Claudite librōs. Hōra est quaestiunculae. Close your books. It's time for a quiz.
Oieī! Ouch!

Colloquia

XII	Quota hōra est?	What time is it?
	Octāva hōra est.	It's eight o'clock.
XIII	Bla, bla, bla.	Blah, blah, blah.
	Silēte. Nunc attendite.	Be quiet. Now pay attention.
XIV	Converte hanc sententiam	Translate this sentence
	ex Anglicam in Latīnam: I prepare.	from English into Latin: I prepare
	Latīnē dīcimus: Parō.	In Latin we say: I prepare.
XV	Confēcistisne dēlāgātum vestrum?	Did you finish your assignment?
	Certē confēcimus!	Of course we finished!
XVI	Ubi sunt calceī meī?	Where are my shoes?
	Hīc sunt!	Here they are!
XVII	Quotum tempus annī tibi maximē placet?	Which season do you like most?
	Vēr mihi placet. Quotum	I like spring. Which
	tempus annī minimē placet?	season do you like least?
	Autumnus mihi nōn placet.	I don't like fall.
XVIII	Quō mense nātus es?	In which month were you born?
	Mense Augustō nātus sum.	I was born in the month of August.
	Quō mense nāta es tū?	In which month were you born?
	Mense Februāriō nāta sum.	I was born in the month of February
XIX	Manē dum, quaesō!	Wait a minute, please!
	Minimē! Festīnā!	No! Hurry up!
XX	Potesne venīre domum meam?	Can you come to my house?
	Certē! Quid possumus facere?	Sure! What can we do?
XXI	Quis rēsponsum scit?	Who knows the answer?
	Ō! Ego! Sciō! Ego!	Oh! Me! I know! Me!
	Attolite manūs.	Raise your hands.
XXII	Scīsne natāre?	Do you know how to swim?
	Ita, sciō natāre.	Yes, I know how to swim.
XXIII	Est frīgidum! (Decembre)	It's cold! (in December)
	Est calidum! (Augustō)	It's hot! (in August)
XXIV	Quotus diēs mensis est?	What day of the month is it?
	Vīcēsimus quartus diēs Iānuāriī est	It's the 24th of January.

Timeline

264-241 BC	**1st Punic War between Rome and Carthage**
218-201 BC	**2nd Punic War between Rome and Carthage**
149-146 BC	**3rd Punic War between Rome and Carthage**
133-121 BC	Land Reforms and the Gracchi
102-101 BC	Teutones and Cimbri invade Italy.
90-88 BC	The Social War between Rome and Italian allies
88 BC	Sulla elected consul; Marius exiled
83-82 BC	**Civil War between Marius and Sulla**
70 BC	Pompey elected consul
67 BC	Pompey defeats the pirates.
63 BC	Cicero consul; Cataline Conspiracy
63 BC	Pompey defeats Mithridates.
60 BC	**1st triumvirate between Caesar, Pompey, and Crassus**
58-51 BC	Caesar conquers Gaul and invades Britain.
49-48 BC	**Civil War between Caesar and Pompey**
47-44 BC	Caesar elected dictator; assassinated on the Ides of March
43 BC	**2nd triumvirate between Mark Antony, Lepidus, and Octavian**
31 BC	**End of the Republic; Battle of Actium**
23 BC	**Roman Empire: Julio-Claudian emperors**

- Octavian, Rome's 1st emperor (23 BC-14 AD) "Augustus"
- Tiberius (14-37 AD)
- Caligula (37-41 AD)
- Claudius (41-54 AD)
- Nero (54-68 AD)
- Military emperors Galba, Otho, Vitellius (68-69 AD)

69 AD	**Flavian and Antonine emperors**

- Vespasian (69-79 AD); eruption of Vesuvius (79 AD)
- Titus (79-81 AD); Jerusalem destroyed (70 AD)
- Domitian (81-96 AD)
- Nerva (96-98 AD)
- Trajan (98-117 AD)
- Hadrian (117-138 AD)
- Antoninus Pius (138-161 AD)
- Marcus Aurelius (161-180 AD) and Lucius Verus (to 169 AD)

180 AD	**Decline of the empire**
285 AD	**Reorganization of the empire**

- Diocletian (285-305 AD) reforms the government.
- Constantine (310-337 AD); Christianity sanctioned (313 AD)
- Valentinian I (364-375 AD)

476 AD	**Barbarian invasions; fall of the Western Roman Empire**
1453 AD	**Ottoman invasion; fall of the Eastern (Byzantine) Empire**

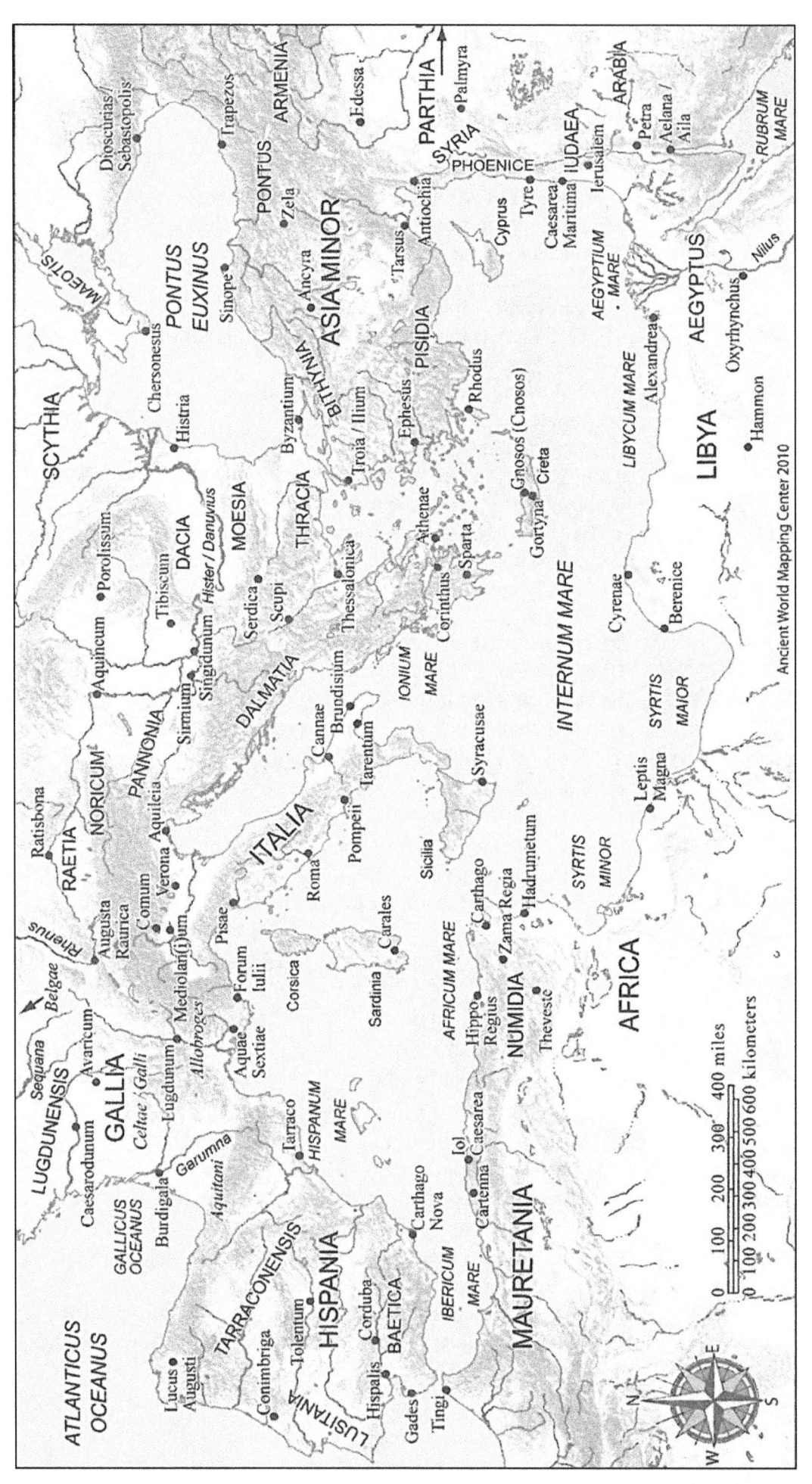

THE ROMAN EMPIRE
Used by permission of the Ancient World Mapping Center

Historia

Famous Men of Rome
by John H. Haaren and A. B. Poland
Revised by Thomas Caucutt and Ruth Baldwin

I – Prīma Lectiō: Regulus (*Famous Men of Rome* XIV.1-2)

The next great war the Romans engaged in was with Carthage. It was about the possession of the island of Sicily, in the Mediterranean Sea. It began not long after Pyrrhus left Italy and was the first of three wars called the Pu´nic Wars. Punic means Phoe-ni´ci-an, and the people who founded Carthage came from Phoe-ni´ci-a, so Carthage was called a Punic or Phoenician colony.

When the First Punic War began, both Rome and Carthage were very rich and powerful. Rome had great armies and great generals. Its common soldiers, too, were remarkably brave and patriotic. It was very successful in its wars. Before it began to fight Carthage, it had conquered nearly all Italy.

<small>264-241 BC
The First Punic War</small>

Carthage also had fine armies, but its greatest strength was in its navy. No other country in the world at that time had so many ships of war and trading ships. The ships of the Carthaginians went everywhere in the Mediterranean. Some of them even went past the Pillars of Hercules, as the rocky capes at the Strait of Gibraltar were then called, and sailed for some distance on the Atlantic Ocean.

The Carthaginian ships were small, but they were very strong. The warships were built to carry a good many soldiers, as well as sailors and oarsmen. They had great rounded iron prows, which could do much damage to an enemy's ships when run up against them. Each ship had a mast and large sail, but it was also rowed with oars by many oarsmen who sat on long benches, placed one above the other. With the sail and the oars, the ship could be made to go very fast through the water.

Carthage was in North Africa, in the country now called Tunis. It stood at the head of a beautiful bay of the Mediterranean. It was a large and handsome city and had a great commerce.

Many years before the beginning of the First Punic War, Carthage conquered a great part of Sicily and made it a Carthaginian colony. But the Romans wanted the island, and so under the pretense of protecting an Italian tribe that had settled there, they sent an army into Sicily. This was how the First Punic War began.

Both Rome and Carthage fought fiercely, and for a long time neither had much advantage over the other. At first the Romans had no warships. Up to that time they did not need any, for all their fighting was on land. But when they began war with the Carthaginians, they found that they must have ships to carry their soldiers to Sicily and to fight the Carthaginians at sea. So the Romans set to work to build ships and to train men to row them, and in a short time they had a great navy.

In the ninth year of the war the armies and fleets of Rome were put under the command of a general named Marcus A-ti´li-us Reg´u-lus. He was a great hero and patriot. He had been a general before the Punic War and had often led the Romans to victory. After years of good service, fighting, and winning battles for his country, he went to live on his little farm and, like Cincinnatus, he cultivated it with his own hands. A story is told of him which well illustrates ancient Roman honor and patriotism.

Until Regulus took command, the Punic War was carried on only in Sicily and on the Mediterranean. But he thought that Rome should fight the Carthaginians in their own country, and so he organized an immense army and navy to invade Carthage. He had 330 warships of the largest size and about 60,000 soldiers.

In those times, in fights at sea, they had an engine called a boarding bridge. One end of it was fixed to the deck of the ship. The other end, which was free, could be swung round and on to an enemy's ship, and it had a heavy iron spike underneath, so that when it fell on the deck, it would sink into it and thus hold the enemy's vessel for the attacking party to board it.

When everything was ready, Regulus set sail for Africa. Soon after starting, he met a large Carthaginian fleet, and in a short battle he destroyed it. Then he sailed on and, after landing in Africa, began a march toward Carthage. On his way he captured several towns, and he met and defeated a Carthaginian army. He then continued his march until he met another army of Carthaginians. This army was commanded by Xan-thip´pus, a famous general of Sparta in Greece, who happened to be in Carthage at that time. In the battle that followed, the Romans were defeated, and Regulus was made prisoner and taken off to Carthage.

But the Romans had other generals and other armies, and they carried on the war and defeated the Carthaginians in many battles.

At last the Carthaginians thought it better to try to make peace, and so they send ambassadors to Rome to propose that the war should be stopped on certain terms, which they were ready to offer. They sent Regulus with the ambassadors, but they made him swear that he would return to Carthage if the Roman Senate should refuse to agree to their terms. They thought that in order to gain his own freedom Regulus would try to get the Senate to accept their proposals. Regulus agreed to go and made the promise required.

"I give you my word of honor," said he, "that I will return if your terms are not accepted."

Then he set out for Rome with the ambassadors. As he approached the gates of the city, thousands of people came forth to welcome him and to escort him through the streets. But he refused to enter.

"I cannot enter Rome," said he. "I am no longer a Roman officer, but a prisoner of Carthage. Do not urge me to enter the gates. I am not even worth exchanging for a Carthaginian prisoner."

The people, however, insisted that he should enter the city, and so amid shouts and cheers, he was escorted to the Senate house.

In a little while the Carthaginian ambassadors presented their proposals, and the Senate began to consider them. After some discussions, Regulus was asked to give his opinion whether the terms ought to be accepted or not.

Regulus at first was unwilling to speak in the Senate. He said that by becoming a prisoner he had lost the honor of being a senator.

"I am no longer a Roman senator," said he. "I am a prisoner of Carthage."

The Senate, however, insisted that he should speak. Then Regulus said that the Senate ought not to accept the terms of peace offered by Carthage. He thought that they were not good terms for Rome, and he advised the Senate not to agree to them.

But the Senate was inclined to accept the terms for the sake of Regulus himself. If peace were not made, he would have to go back and remain a prisoner in Carthage or perhaps he would be put to death. Therefore the Senate was for agreeing to the Carthaginian terms. But Regulus again spoke strongly against them, and at last the Senate decided to reject the Carthaginian proposals.

Regulus now prepared to return to Carthage, but his family and friends clung to him saying: "You must not go! You must not go!"

To all their appeals he made but one answer: "I have given my word of honor to return, and I cannot break it."

So Regulus returned to Carthage with the ambassadors. When the people of that city heard that by his advice the terms had been rejected, they were very angry. They had wished very much to make peace with Rome, for the long war had cost them a great many lives and a great deal of money, and they wanted to stop it. Therefore, they were enraged against Regulus, and they put him to death in a very cruel way.

It is said that Regulus was shut into a chest into which nails had been driven so that, try as he might, he could never avoid their sharp points. Never able to rest or sleep, he finally died from exhaustion.

The war between Rome and Carthage continued for some years more, but at last the Carthaginians were defeated in a great sea battle near the coast of Sicily. They were then obliged to give up Sicily and pay a large sum of money to the Romans as a fine. This was the end of the First Punic War, in 241 BC.

II – Secunda Lectiō: Scipio Africanus (*Famous Men of Rome* XV.1-2)

But peace did not last long between Rome and Carthage. Some years after the end of the First Punic War, the Carthaginians attacked and took possession of a town in Spain, the people of which were friends and allies of Rome. This caused the Second Punic War, which began in 218 BC.

218-201 BC
The Second Punic War

One of the great soldiers of this war was Pu′bli-us Cornelius Sci′pi-o. In the latter part of his life he was called Scipio Af-ri-ca′nus, on account of the great victories which he won in Africa.

Scipio was a brave soldier from his youth. When only seventeen years old, he fought in a battle and saved his father's life. He was always gallant and heroic in war, so he soon became noted in the Roman army and rose to high rank. And although he was a member of a noble family, he was well liked by the plebeians, and they elected him ae′dile.

The aediles were magistrates, or judges. They were also superintendents of public buildings and of the games and shows of which the Roman people were so fond.

When Scipio was about 27 years of age, he was appointed to command the Roman army that was fighting the Carthaginians in Spain. Carthage had conquered some parts of Spain, and Rome had conquered other parts, and the two nations were often at war about places in that country.

When Scipio went to Spain, many of the people there were against him, but they soon became his friends. Whenever he took a city, he allowed the chiefs who were captured to go free, and he gave great presents to many of them. He always showed great respect to women and children who were taken prisoners. In those times it was the cruel custom to make slaves of women who were found in towns that had been taken in war. But Scipio never did this in Spain. He always let the women go free.

One day a beautiful Spanish girl who had been taken prisoner was brought before him. She seemed very much frightened, but Scipio spoke kindly to here and told her that no one should harm her. While speaking with her, he learned that a young man who was her lover had also been taken prisoner by the Roman soldiers. He sent for the young man and said to him: "Take your sweetheart and go. I set you both free. Go and be happy, and in future, be friends of Rome."

And so by many acts of kindness Scipio gained the friendship of the Spaniards. After a while they began to join the Romans and gave them great help in their war against the Carthaginians.

When his services were no longer needed in Spain, Scipio returned to Rome. He got a great reception in the city. There was a grand parade in his honor. He brought home an immense quantity of silver, which he obtained from the rich Spanish mines and from the cities he had taken. The silver was put into the Roman treasury to pay the expenses of the war.

Soon after he returned from Spain, Scipio was elected consul. The Carthaginian general, Han′ni-bal, was then in Italy with a large army. This Hannibal was one of the greatest generals of ancient times. When he was but nine years old, his father, who was also a great general, made him take an oath that he would hate Rome and the Romans forever. Then he took the boy with him to Spain and gave him a thorough training as a soldier.

When his father died, Hannibal became commander of the Carthaginian army in Spain. He was then little more that 21 years old. He fought well in Spain for some time and was well liked by his soldiers. Suddenly he resolved to make war on the Romans in their own country and to go by land to Italy. So he got ready an immense army and set out on his march. In passing through France he had to cross the broad River Rhone. This was not easy to do, for there was no bridge. He got his men over in boats, but he had a number of elephants in his army, and they were too big and heavy to be taken across in that way. The boats were small, and the elephants were afraid to go into them. Hannibal therefore got rafts or floats, made of trunks of trees tied together, and in these the elephants were carried over.

After crossing the Rhone, Hannibal marched over the Alps into Italy. He and his army suffered many hardships in making their way over those snow-covered mountains. He had often to fight fierce tribes that came to oppose him, but he defeated them all, and after being defeated, many of them joined his army and brought him provisions for his soldiers.

Very soon Roman armies were sent against Hannibal, but he defeated them in many battles. His army got into place near high hills where he could not march farther except through one narrow pass between the hills. The Roman general, Quintus Fabius, sent 4,000 of his troops to take possession of the pass, and he posted the rest of his army on hills close by.

Quintus Fabius

Hannibal saw that he was in a trap, but he found a way of escaping. He caused vine branches to be tied to the horns of a large number of the oxen that were with his army. Then he ordered his men to set the branches on fire in the middle of the night and to drive the oxen up the hills.

As soon as the animals felt the pain, they rushed madly about and set fire to the shrubs and bushes they met on the way. The Romans at the pass thought that the Carthaginians were escaping by torchlight. So they hastily quit their posts and hurried toward the hills to help their comrades. Then Hannibal, seeing the pass free, marched his army out and so escaped from the trap.

Quintus Fabius was very slow and cautious in his movements. The Romans had been defeated so often that he thought the best plan was to harass Hannibal in every possible way but not to venture to fight him in a great battle until he should be sure of winning. For this reason the Romans gave Fabius the name of *Cunc-ta'tor*, which means *delayer*, and so the plan of extreme delay or caution in any undertaking is often called a *Fabian* policy.

In spite of the caution of Fabius, Hannibal gained many great victories. His greatest victory was at the battle of Can'nae, in the south of Italy. Here he defeated and destroyed a Roman army of 70,000 men. And for several years after this battle, Hannibal remained in Italy doing the Romans all the harm he could.

At last Scipio thought it was time to follow the plan of Regulus. So he said to the Senate:

"We have acted too long as if we were afraid of Hannibal and Carthage. We defend ourselves bravely when we are attacked, and so far we have saved Rome from destruction; but we do not make any attacks on our enemies. We certainly ought to do this, for our armies are strong and fully ready to meet the Carthaginians."

Scipio then proposed that an army led by himself should go to Africa and carry on war there. He believed that if this were done, Hannibal would have to got to Africa to defend Carthage.

Perhaps on account of what had happened to Regulus, the Senate did not like Scipio's plan. Nevertheless, it gave him permission to go to Africa but would not give him an army. Scipio then raised a splendid army of volunteers and sailed across the Mediterranean Sea to Africa.

III – Tertia Lectiō: Scipio Africanus (*Famous Men of Rome* XV.3-4)

Scipio then tried for some time to obtain the aid of Sy´phax, a powerful king of Nu-mid´i-a, in Africa. But Syphax decided to join the Carthaginians. So Scipio found two great armies ready to fight him. One was the army of Carthage, with 33,000 men, commanded by Has´dru-bal Gis´co, and the other was the army of Numidia, with 60,000 men, commanded by King Syphax.

But Scipio found in Africa one strong friend, and that was a Numidian prince named Mas´i-nis´sa. This prince had a host of supporters among his countrymen and was therefore able to bring a large force of good soldiers to the aid of the Romans. He was of great service to Scipio in many ways.

When everything was ready, the Roman army, with Masinissa's force, encamped about six miles from the camps of the enemy. Scipio sent spies among the Carthaginians and the soldiers of King Syphax, and from them he learned that both armies were lodged in huts made of stakes and covered with reeds and dried leaves. He resolved to set those huts on fire.

So one very dark night the Roman army left its camp and marched silently to the plain occupied by the enemy. Then a division of the Romans went to the encampments of the Numidians, and a soldier crept cautiously from the Roman lines and set one of the huts on fire. The fire spread rapidly, and in a few minutes the whole camp was in flames.

The Numidian soldiers, suddenly awakened by the fire, fled from the burning huts without their weapons and made frantic efforts to escape from the camp. Hundreds of them were knocked down and trampled to death in the rush and confusion; hundreds more lost their lives in the fire. Those who got to the open country were attacked by the Romans and killed. The ground was covered with the bodies of the slain. King Syphax and a few horsemen managed to escape, but the rest of the vast Numidian army was destroyed.

In the meantime the Carthaginians had been aroused by the noise in the camp of the Numidians. They thought that the fire had been caused by an accident, and some of them ran forward to assist the Numidians. But the greater number stood in a confused throng, without their arms, outside their camp, looking at the fire with terror.

While they were in this helpless state, the Carthaginians were suddenly attacked by the Romans with Scipio at their head. Many were killed, and the others were driven back into their camp, which was immediately set on fire in a number of places. Then there was a frightful scene. Thousands of Carthaginians, struggling to escape the fire, were slain by the Romans while thousands more perished in the flames. Hasdrubal Gisco, the commander, and some of his officers escaped but only a few of the others. In less than an hour there was little left of the Carthaginian army.

Scipio now began to march toward the great, rich city of Carthage. He captured a number of towns and a great deal of treasure. In a few weeks, however, the Carthaginians were able to form another army of 30,000 men, and then they came boldly forth to meet Scipio.

A fierce battle followed. The Romans were driven back for a time, but with wonderful courage they charged the Carthaginians again and again and at last totally defeated them.

The Carthaginians now sent a message to Italy requesting Hannibal to come to the relief of his country. The renowned general did not want to leave Italy, for he hoped to be able to take Rome; but he thought it best to obey the call of Carthage, so he sailed for Africa with his army.

After arriving in Africa, Hannibal led his army to a wide plain near Za´ma, a town not far from Carthage. Here he awaited the Romans.

Hannibal had great admiration for Scipio, and he desired to see him before engaging in battle. So he sent a messenger to Scipio requesting an interview. The request was granted, and the two generals met.

They greeted each other cordially, and each complemented the other on his victories and greatness as a soldier. Then Hannibal proposed terms of peace to Scipio.

"We will give Spain and the islands of Sicily and Sardinia to Rome. Then we will divide the sea with you. What more would you have? Rome and Carthage would then be the two great nations of the world."

Scipio thought it was too late to make terms. "We must fight it out," said he, "until one side or the other is vanquished."

The generals then parted, and the next day the two armies were drawn up in battle array. On each side there were about 30,000 men, but Hannibal had a herd of fighting elephants.

The battle was long and severe. Both armies fought heroically, and there was terrible slaughter. But Hannibal's elephants were of little use to him, as the Romans frightened them by blowing trumpets and hurling balls of fire at them. At a moment when the lines of the Carthaginians were breaking, a strong force of Roman horsemen came up suddenly in the rear and overpowered all before it. This won the battle for the Romans. When Hannibal saw that the battle was lost, he fled from the field with a few friends (202 BC).

Scipio was now master of Carthage. He compelled the Carthaginians to pay him a vast amount in gold and silver and to give up some of their towns and lands. He also compelled them to destroy their great fleet of warships and to promise not to make war in future upon any people without the permission of the Romans.

When Scipio returned to Rome, he entered the city at the head of a grand procession. The greatest honors were paid to him, and he was called Scipio Africanus.

Some years afterward Scipio met Hannibal at the court of the king in Syria. The two generals had a friendly conversation and Scipio asked Hannibal who he thought was the greatest general who ever lived. Hannibal answered:

"Alexander the Great."

"Who was the second?" asked Scipio.

"Pyrrhus," replied Hannibal.

"Who was the third?"

"Myself," answered Hannibal.

"But what would you have said," asked Scipio, "if you had conquered me?"

"I should then have said," replied Hannibal, "that I was greater than Alexander, greater than Pyrrhus, and greater than all other generals."

IV – Quarta Lectiō: Cato the Censor (*Famous Men of Rome* XVI)

On a farm near Tusculum, a little town about 15 miles from Rome, there once lived a boy named Marcus Por´ci-us Ca´to. His father and his grandfather before him had been farmers, and he, too, expected to be one.

When he was about 17, Hannibal's army crossed the Alps into Italy, and young Cato became a Roman soldier. When the war ended, the country boy had become a man, stern and forceful. He attracted the attention of a neighbor, a rich man, who persuaded him to go to Rome and practice law.

In time he was elected to office, and he did his duty so well that he rose higher and higher, until he became one of the consuls. That same year a rebellion arose in Spain and Cato led an army against the Spaniards. It is said that in 400 days he captured 400 villages. On his return to Rome, he was honored with a triumph.

Shortly after this he was sent to Greece, where An-ti´o-chus was attacking Greek cities that were friendly to Rome. He defeated Antiochus in the Pass of Ther-mo´py-lae and won great fame as a soldier.

Cato was a very hard man: hard on himself; hard on his friends. And although he was rich and held office in a great city, he lived a hard life, taking no pleasures and saving his money. He ate the plainest food and drank the same cheap wine that he bought for his slaves.

Cato thought that the luxury and extravagance of the rich were taking away the strength of Rome. In order to put a stop to these things, Cato asked the people of Rome to elect him censor. The patricians opposed him bitterly, but he was elected by a large majority. One of the first things he did was to expel from the senate several senators who were leading improper lives. He had a heavy tax put on carriages so as to compel people to walk. He also placed a tax on jewels, handsome dresses, carpets, and fine furniture. So well did he do his work that he is always known in history as Cato the Censor, just as if he were the only man who ever held the office. A statue erected in his honor says nothing about his victories in Spain or at Thermopylae, but only that "When the Roman Republic was degenerating, Cato restored it by strict discipline."

In the later years of his life Cato was sent to Carthage to look into a certain matter for Rome. The trouble was this: you will remember that Carthage had agreed to make war upon no nation without the consent of the Roman Senate. A few years later, Masinissa, who was a friend of Rome, attacked the Carthaginians, and they appealed to Rome for protection. This was refused, and the people of Carthage took up arms to defend themselves against Masinissa.

Cato was sent to Carthage to find out who was to blame. When he arrived in the city, he was surprised to find it large and strong and flourishing. Only 26 years had passed since Scipio Africanus had conquered Carthage, and yet Cato saw crowds of young men on the street, stacks of arms in the arsenals, and a forest of masts in the harbor. The city itself was rich and prosperous.

Cato returned to Rome and warned his countrymen that Carthage must be destroyed. From that time forward, whenever he made a speech in the senate, no matter upon what subject, he always ended it by saying, "And my opinion is that Carthage must be destroyed." In time, the words of Cato had their effect, and war was declared against Carthage.

> Cato's words were: *Carthāgō dēlenda est!*

The troops had already embarked when envoys from Carthage reached Rome and offered to do whatever might be asked. The Roman Senate promised that the laws and liberties of Carthage should not be touched, but demanded hostages. So 300 children of the leading families of Carthage were sent to Rome. When the Roman army reached Carthage, the consuls insisted that the Carthaginians should give up their arms. This was done, and the Carthaginians asked if the Romans required anything more.

> 149-146 BC
> The Third Punic War

Then one of the consuls said, "Your city must be destroyed, and you must move ten miles inland from the sea." The Carthaginians now saw that they had been deceived. They closed their gates and determined to defend themselves to the last. They asked an armistice of 30 days, so that an embassy might go to Rome. It was granted, and thus a month of time was gained. During this time, men, women, and children went to work to make arms to defend their homes. The women even cut off their hair to furnish strings for the bows of the war machines with which stones were hurled at the enemy.

The embassy failed in its mission to Rome and the siege of Carthage began. It lasted three years.

The son of Paulus Ae-mil'i-us had been adopted by the son of Scipio Africanus and had taken the name Scipio. He was sent to Carthage and about a year after his arrival, forced an entrance into the city and captured it (146 BC). The walls were torn down and the buildings set on fire. Cato,

Historia

Scipio Africanus Minor (i.e., the younger) was the adopted grandson of Scipio Africanus Maior (i.e., the older). The grandfather had defeated Hannibal and had won the second Punic War for Rome. The grandson destroyed Carthage and won the third and final war with Carthage.

who was so largely responsible for the war, did not live to see its end. He died almost two years before the city was destroyed.

The Senate honored Scipio with the title of Africanus, which the older conqueror of Carthage had borne.

The young Scipio won fame not only in Africa but also in Spain, where he was sent against the Nu-man'ti-ans. These brave people had defeated two Roman armies, but Scipio soon succeeded in shutting them within the walls of Numantia. Around its walls he built walls of his own behind which his soldiers were safe from attack. Food soon became scarce in Nu-man'ti-a. At the end of 15 months the citizens were starving. They were willing to lose their lives, but Scipio stayed behind his own walls and refused to fight. Rather than trust to the mercy of Rome, the Numantians killed themselves.

In time all Spain was forced to submit and become a Roman province.

IV – Quīnta Lectiō: The Gracchi (*Famous Men of Rome* XVII)

The Gracchi brothers

Between the Second and Third Punic Wars there lived in Rome two brothers named Ti-be'ri-us and Caius Grac'chus, commonly called the Gracchi. They were very good men and great friends of the common people.

The mother of the Gracci was Cor-ne'li-a, a daughter of Scipio Africanus. She was an excellent woman, and she was very proud of her two sons. She taught them to be brave and manly and always to stand up for the people.

One day a rich lady, while on a visit to Cornelia, showed her some magnificent jewels. When they had looked them over, the lady said:

"These are my jewels; now let me see yours."

Just at that moment Tiberius and Caius, who were then boys, came into the room. As soon as she saw them, Cornelia called them to her and, putting her arms around them, said:

"These are my jewels."

When Tiberius and Caius grew up to be men, they took the side of the people in a quarrel that had been going on for a long time between the plebeians and the nobles. The quarrel was about land. Whenever the Romans conquered a country in war, they took possession of a portion of the land of the conquered country. Such land was called public land, and for many years after the founding of the city, the custom of dividing parts of the public lands among all the citizens was strictly observed.

But in later times this custom was changed. Instead of part of the public lands being divided among all the citizens, it was divided among only the nobles, and the plebeians got none at all. The lands were tilled by slaves, and all that was raised went to the nobles. So the poor soldiers who won the lands by hard fighting were without farms to till, and some of them were even without homes. They continually demanded that the old law, for a fair division of the lands among all the citizens, should be carried out. The nobles laughed at the demand.

But Tiberius Gracchus came forward boldly as the champion of the poor. He declared that the nobles should give up the lands they had unjustly taken and that the people should have their fair share. His words made the nobles very angry, and they became his bitter enemies.

But the people honored Tiberius and made him one of their tribunes. The tribunes were supposed to look after the people's interests, but sometimes they were not faithful to their duty. As we have already said, they had a great deal of power. They could sit at the door of the Roman Senate, and when a law was proposed that they did not like, they could say, "We veto it!" and the law could not be passed.

Whenever the tribunes wanted a law passed, they proposed it at the meeting of all the people in what was called the Assembly of Tribes. The common people had a great deal of power in this assembly, and any law proposed by the tribunes was generally passed. Then the tribunes had the power to compel the consuls to carry out the law.

Not long after Tiberius Gracchus became tribune, he proposed a law that each noble might have 500 acres of public land for his own use and 250 more for each son, and that the remainder of the lands should be equally divided among the poor citizens.

This law was passed, and then the nobles had to give up a large part of the lands they had seized. So the poor citizens got good farms.

About this time At´ta-lus, the king of Per´ga-mus, a country of Asia, died, leaving all his money to the Romans. The nobles tried to get this money for themselves, but Tiberius had it divided among the poor citizens.

Of course this made the nobles still more angry with Tiberius, and they resolved to get rid of him if they could. So on election day, when the people were voting to make Tiberius tribune for a second term, some nobles went to the voting place and raised a disturbance. But the friends of Tiberius drove them away. Then the nobles started a report that Tiberius was trying to induce the people to make him king.

Afterward they gathered their friends and slaves and began fighting with the people. No arms were used, but stones were thrown, and sticks, broken benches, and other things, hastily caught up, served as weapons. There was a dreadful tumult for a while, and many persons were killed.

Tiberius was in the midst of his friends bravely defending himself against an attack by a party of nobles when suddenly he stumbled and fell to the ground. In a moment the nobles rushed upon him. One of them struck him on the head with a piece of wood and killed him. Then they took his body and threw it into the Tiber.

Tiberius was now out of the way, and the nobles began to seize the lands that had been divided among the people. But Caius Gracchus suddenly appeared in Rome and declared that he had come to take his brother's place as the friend of the people. He had been with a Roman army in Spain when Tiberius was killed.

Tiberius Gracchus (circa 164-133 BC)

The verb *vetō, vetāre* means "to forbid." When the tribunes felt that a proposal was unfair to the common people, they had simply to declare: "Vetō!" (I forbid it!), and the proposal could not be made into law.

Historia

The people now elected him tribune, and he began to carry out his brothers plans. For this reason the nobles hated him as much as they hated his brother. They said that he was a dangerous man and was planning to make himself king. One day as he was passing through the Forum, a strange man said to him: "I hope you will spare the Republic!"

The friends of Caius were angry at these words, and they fell on the man and killed him.

Caius Gracchus (died 121 BC)

The nobles and their followers then armed themselves. The plebeians also gathered in great numbers, ready for a fight. Caius was asked to lead them, but refused. He did not want them to fight with the nobles. He knew that the nobles would be satisfied with his own death, so he ordered a slave to stab him to the heart. The order was obeyed, and thus perished the last of the Gracchi (121 BC).

VI – Sexta Lectiō: Marius (*Famous Men of Rome* XVIII.1-2)

Caius Marius (157-86 BC)

At the time of the death of Caius Gracchus, there was in Rome a great man named Caius Ma′ri-us. This man came forward and said to the people that if they would elect him tribune, he would get them their rights.

The people elected him tribune, and, true to his word, he did everything he could to improve their condition. He was afterward elected consul seven times, and for a long while he was the greatest man in Rome.

Marius was a tall and very powerful man and had a strong will. When he said he would do anything, he would do it in spite of all difficulties. He was a very great soldier. Many people thought him the best of the Roman generals.

He succeeded in a war against Ju-gur′tha, king of Numidia, after other generals had failed. He took many cities from Jugurtha and at last captured the king himself and all his treasure.

Jugurtha was brought to Rome and compelled to walk behind the chariot of Marius in a grand triumphal procession. He was afterward put into a foul dungeon and left there to die.

The nobles did not like Marius. He was the son of plebeian parents, and he had taken the side of the plebeians against the nobles. Therefore the nobles hated him, and they would have done anything they could against him, only that they needed his help to protect Rome from very dangerous enemies.

A host of barbarian people, called Cim′bri, Teu′to-nes, and Am-bro′nes, had left their homes on the shores of the Baltic Sea and invaded the southern lands. They were strong, fierce men, and they laid waste every country they passed through. They defeated several Roman armies that were sent against them. Some of the tribes of Hel-ve′ti-a (the country now called Switzerland) joined them and killed a Roman consul and made his army pass under the yoke.

The Romans were therefore very much frightened. They thought that the barbarians would soon be in Italy. So Marius was appointed to go against them with a great army. He crossed the Mediterranean into Gaul and met the Teutones and Ambrones near the city of Arles on the River Rhone. The Cimbri had already gone to Italy.

Marius first made a strong entrenched camp. He wanted to give his men time to get accustomed to the manners of the strange enemy before attempting to fight them. The Roman soldiers had shown fear at sight of the barbarians. They had never before seen such people.

The Teutones were like giants. They had large, wild, staring eyes and long hair, and they made terrible war cries. The Ambrones and the Cimbri were as savage in appearance. The king of the Teutones was very tall and so active that he could leap over six horses placed abreast.

When the barbarians saw that the Romans would not fight, they began to taunt and insult them. They walked up and down in front of the Roman camp day after day, calling the soldiers cowards.

"Why don't you come out and fight us like men?" they cried. "Are you afraid? Come out, come out; we are in a hurry! We are going to Rome after we kill you!"

Marius had hard work to keep his men from rushing out upon the barbarians. He did not yet want to fight, but he said to his soldiers:

"When the proper time comes, we will give these savages all the fighting they want."

One day a gigantic Teuton chief, with a long shield and spear, came up to the very entrance of the Roman camp and called loudly for Marius himself to come out and fight. The great general laughed heartily at the impudence of the barbarian, and he sent out a gladiator to fight with him in order to give sport to the Romans.

Gladiators were men who fought one another in the shows at Rome for the amusement of the people. They were usually slaves and were very strong, active, and well-trained fighters.

It did not take the gladiator long to defeat the Teuton. In a few minutes he laid the savage giant low, and the Romans shouted with joy at the sight.

After the Teuton was killed, the Romans still remained in their camp. Marius was not yet prepared to fight. At last the barbarians got tired of waiting, and they started off to march to Italy.

So great was the number of the barbarians that it took them six whole days to march past the Roman camp. When all had passed, Marius left his camp and followed them by slow marches. Before long, the two armies arrived at the city of Aix on the south coast of Gaul.

Marius now thought it was time to fight, so he led out his fine army against the Ambrones. They astonished the Romans with their war cry. They held their shields upright and at a little distance from their mouths and shouted: "Ambrones! Ambrones!" as if to terrify the Romans by letting them know who they were. Then they rushed furiously across the field.

The Romans met their charge with wonderful courage. Their lines were scarcely broken. Three times they drove back the enemy, and then they themselves moved steadily forward with their whole force. They cut down the Ambrones by thousands, took many prisoners, and sent others fleeing away in terror.

Next day there was another battle. The Teutones and Ambrones together attacked the Romans, but the Romans were again victorious. When the battle was over, it was found that more than 100,000 barbarians had been killed or taken prisoners.

Marius now turned his attention to the Cimbri, who had gone to Italy. They had encamped on a beautiful, fertile plain near the River Po and were enjoying the warm Italian sun and the sweet fruits of the country.

But Marius was not very long in reaching the same place with his victorious army. When the Cimbri saw the Romans marching on to the plain where they were encamped, they were astonished. To gain time they sent a messenger to Marius to ask him to give them lands to live on in Italy.

"Give us," said the messenger, "lands in Italy for ourselves and for our friends, the Teutones and Ambrones, and we will all live at peace."

"Never mind the Teutones and the Ambrones," said Marius, "They have lands already. We have given them some which they will keep forever. We will give you the same."

Then a battle began between the two great armies. The foot soldiers of the Cimbri were formed into an immense square, and the men in the front ranks were chained to one another by iron chains so that they could not run away. There were 15,000 horsemen, wearing on their helmets the heads of wild beasts.

The battle was a hard one for a while, but it did not continue long. Time after time, the Cimbri were driven back, and at last they were put to flight. Thousands of them were killed and thousands made prisoners.

When Marius and his soldiers returned to Rome, they got a splendid reception. There was a parade through the streets, and a great feast was given to the people. A large sum of money was divided among the soldiers to reward them for their brave conduct.

Marius was now in high favor at Rome. The nobles did not dare to speak a word against him. He was elected consul seven times, so that he was master of the Republic for a long time.

VII – Septima Lectiō: Marius (*Famous Men of Rome* XVIII.2)

> 90-88 BC
> The Social War
>
> Allies and peoples friendly to Rome were called *Socii*, and the war between these peoples and Rome is called the Social War.

In the sixth year that Marius was consul, the war called the Social War broke out. It lasted for three years. It was a war with some of the nations of Italy which Rome had formerly conquered. The people of those nations did not want to separate from Rome, but they wanted to have the right of voting as the Romans themselves had. Rome refused to give them this right, and at last they resolved to go to war.

All the greatest Roman generals of the time took part in this war. One of them was a young noble named Sul′la. He was a very successful soldier and won a number of great victories. The nations were defeated in the war, but Rome soon granted them most of the rights they had asked for.

Lucius Cornelius Sulla (138-78 BC)

The nobles gave great praise to Sulla for his victories in the Social War. They declared that he was a better general than Marius. So many fine things were said about the young noble that Marius became jealous and did a very foolish thing. He suddenly left his army in the field and came back to Rome. He complained that he was nervous and shut himself up in his house and refused to see any of his friends for weeks.

The nobles then started a story that Marius was getting silly and weak-minded from old age. He was about 70 at the time, and the nobles said that he ought to retire from the army. This made the old hero angry, and he declared that he was as strong in mind and body as any of the young Romans.

One morning he went to the place where the young men of Rome used to practice athletic sports, and for two or three hours he wrestled and ran and leaped with as much skill and strength as anyone. Some of the nobles who happened to pass by saw him and were very much amused.

About this time Sulla was elected consul on account of his victories in the Social War. Shortly afterward Rome declared war against Mith′ri-da′tes, King of Pontus in Asia Minor, who had cruelly put to death a number of the citizens of a Roman province in Asia.

The Senate appointed Sulla to command the Roman army in this war. But as soon as he left Rome with his army, one of the tribunes proposed that the command should be taken from him and given to Marius. The Assembly agreed to this, and Marius accepted the appointment. He sent word to the army, which was not far from Rome, that he would come in a short time to take command.

When Sulla heard this, he became very angry. He called his soldiers around him, told them what had been done, and asked them if they would submit to be the slaves of Marius and his party.

"No, no!" cried the soldiers, "We will not submit. We want you for our general."

"Then follow me to Rome," said Sulla. "We will teach Marius and his friends that they must not insult us."

So the soldiers marched quickly back to Rome with Sulla at their head. They declared that they would take the city out of the hands of rebels, as they called the friends of Marius. When they entered the city, they were met by Marius and his followers, and there was a battle, in which Marius was defeated. Then a law was passed declaring Marius a traitor and that he should be put to death.

88-82 BC
The Civil War

But Marius fled from Rome with some friends and went down the Tiber in a boat to the Mediterranean. He sailed along the coast and then he and his companions went ashore to seek for food. They wandered through the country for some time without seeing anyone. At last they met a farmer, who gave them something to eat. He told them that horsemen from Rome were riding through the place searching for Marius.

They were frightened at this, and they ran into a thick wood where they stopped all night. But while his companions were downcast, Marius was cheerful and hopeful.

"This bad state of things," he said, "will last only a short time. I know it, because the gods have revealed to me that I shall be once more consul of Rome!"

But next day Marius was taken by horsemen. he saw them coming and waded far into a great marsh and hid himself among some high, thick reeds. The horsemen rode into the marsh and found him, and they put a rope around his neck and dragged him to the shore. Then they shut him up in a hut and began to think what they should do with him.

At last they decided to put him to death at once. They thought this would please Sulla and that perhaps he would reward them for it. So they gave a sword to a slave and sent him to kill Marius. The slave entered the hut and stood for a few moments looking at the great general. Marius glared at him like a wild beast and said in a stern voice:

"Slave, will you dare to kill Caius Marius?"

The slave started back in terror and ran out of the hut. Then he threw down his sword at the feet of the soldiers and cried out that he could never have the courage to slay Marius.

It was now decided to send Marius out of the country. So he was taken to a ship and carried to Africa. After going ashore, he wandered through the country until he came to the place where Carthage once stood. Nothing now remained of the famous city but a mass of gloomy ruins, for the Romans had entirely destroyed it a few years before in the Third Punic War. In these ruins Marius lived for a short time. One day a soldier came to tell him that the governor of Africa wanted him to leave the country.

"Go to your governor," answered Marius, "and tell him that you saw Caius Marius sitting on the ruins of Carthage."

Not long afterward, when Sulla was away fighting king Mithridates, there was great trouble at Rome. One of the consuls, named Cin´na, aided by many of the plebeians, attempted to get control of public affairs but was defeated by the nobles. Then Cinna and his followers were forced to leave the city. They organized an army among the Italians who had been complaining of not getting their rights from Rome, and they sent to Africa for Marius to come and be their commander.

When Marius arrived, he made an attack on Rome and soon captured it. Then he marched in through the gates at the head of his army and took possession of the city. At the next election the people elected him consul.

Marius now resolved to have vengeance on the nobles who had driven him from Rome. For several days the old Roman, surrounded by a guard of freed slaves, went through the city seeking the nobles in their houses, in the temples, in the Forum, and everywhere that they could be found, and killing them without mercy.

These were dreadful days. Some of the noblest men of Rome were put to death. None of Sulla's friends was spared. Even his wife and children were harshly treated and forced to leave the city.

Marius did not stop the bloody work until he had killed all his enemies that he could find. But his triumph was short. He died in a little more than two weeks after he had become consul for the seventh time.

VIII – Octāva Lectiō: Sulla (*Famous Men of Rome* XIX)

We have said something of Sulla, but there is much more to be told about him, for he was a very remarkable man, and he did remarkable things in Rome. His full name was Lu'ci-us Cornelius Sulla. He belonged to a very noble family. When he was a young man, he was very fond of study and became an excellent scholar. He was also a good speaker and often made eloquent speeches in the Forum on public affairs.

He was a large, strong man, with red hair and a ruddy face. He was a very great soldier and one of the greatest of Roman generals. They called him "the Lion." He was so successful in war that he also got the name of *Felix*, a Latin word which means *happy* or *fortunate*.

One of the greatest wars that Sulla was in was a war against the Greeks. Rome had conquered Greece some time before, and the governors of many of the Greek cities were Romans. These governors were very cruel to the Greeks; therefore, the people hated them. Mithridates, King of Pontus, knew this, and he offered to send armies to Greece to help to drive the Romans out of the country. The Greeks were very glad of this, and they prepared for war against the Romans.

Sulla arrived in Greece with a strong army and began a march through the country. He captured several of the cities and compelled them to submit to the Roman governors. Then he marched on to Athens, the capital city of Greece. But he found that it was occupied by Ar-che-la'us, one of the generals of King Mithridates, who had brought from Asia Minor an army to help the Greeks.

Athens at this time was one of the most strongly fortified cities in the world. Its walls were 70 feet high, and they were made of huge, thick blocks of hard, smooth stone. It took thousands of men many years to build these massive walls. The city was also well supplied with food, so that it could hold out against a siege for a long time.

For several weeks Sulla attacked Athens furiously day by day, but it was all in vain. He could not take the city. His soldiers tried many times to mount the high walls, but they could not do it.

At last Sulla had battering rams made. These were engines for breaking down the walls of towns. They were long, heavy beams of wood, with iron at one end, formed like the head of a ram. This was why they were called battering rams. At first they were worked by men with their hands and bodily strength. In later times they were hung from a cross beam, so as to swing back and forward, and the iron end was made to strike against the wall with great force.

When a number of battering rams were ready, Sulla began another attack on Athens. But at dead of night, a party of Athenians came out of the city and burned all the battering rams. Sulla quickly had new ones made, and after months of hard labor, the Romans at last succeeded in breaking down the walls and taking Athens. They plundered the beautiful city and destroyed many fine works of art. It is said that they carried off more than 600 pounds of gold and silver.

Sulla remained in Athens only long enough to establish Roman authority there once more. Then he departed with his army and marched to Chaer´o-ni-a, another town of Greece, where there was a force of 120,000 men, which King Mithridates had sent to help the Greeks.

The Romans numbered only about 40,000 men, but Sulla was not afraid to fight the immense army of Mithridates. By placing his troops in good positions at the beginning of the battle, and afterward by moving them skillfully from one point to another, he was able to win a great victory.

This was a remarkable battle in one respect. Although there were furious charges and hand-to-hand combats, in which thousands upon thousands of the soldiers of Mithridates were slain, the Romans lost only a few men. We are told that, when the roll-call of the Roman army took place after the battle, only 12 men failed to answer their names! The army of Mithridates had lost 110,000 men; the Romans only 12!

But perhaps we ought not to believe that so very few Romans were killed, for it seems hardly possible that it could have been so. It is certain, however, that Sulla gained a great victory. He also defeated another army sent by Mithridates soon afterward.

Then Archelaus, the general of the army of Mithridates, begged for peace. Sulla made terms that were very good for Rome, and Archelaus and Mithridates had to accept them. Mithridates had to give the Romans a large sum of money and 70 ships of war and to promise to be the friend of Rome in future. Thus the war with Greece ended.

Sulla now prepared to return to Italy. He had heard how his friends in Rome and his wife and children had been treated by Marius. He was greatly enraged, and in his letter to the Senate, telling them of his victories in Greece, he said:

"In return for my services, which have brought honor and glory to Rome, my wife and children have been driven from their home, my house has been burned, and my friends have been put to death. I am now going back to punish those who did these things."

When the letter was read to the senators, they were very much alarmed, for they knew that if Sulla did as he threatened, it would cause a dreadful civil war in Rome. In reply to Sulla, they begged him not to make war on his own countrymen, and they promised to do their best to bring about a friendly understanding between him and the followers of Marius.

Sulla answered that he did not want any understanding with them.

"I want no friendship with my enemies," he said. "I am able to take care of myself. It will be well for them if they can take care of themselves."

Soon afterward he set out for Italy with his army. Rome was then under the power of the Marian party. This party was led by Cinna and by Marius the Younger, the son of the great Marius. When they heard that Sulla was coming, they raised an army and went forth to drive him back. Young Marius said:

"Now it will be decided who shall be the master of Rome!"

A battle was fought between the two armies. It was long and severe, and for a time it seemed as if the Marians would win. Even Sulla himself had no hope of victory. But soon very bad blunders made by the Marians turned the tide of battle in his favor, and he was victorious. He took six thousand prisoners.

Sulla now entered Rome as its master, and cruel master he proved to be. He first got himself appointed dictator for as long a time as he wished to hold the office. Then he commanded that all the followers of Marius should be slain. So they were hunted out of their hiding places and all put to death without mercy.

When every person who was known to have been connected with the Marian party was killed, the people thought Sulla would cease his murderous work, but he did not. He went on killing this and that one – now a poor man and then a rich man – until at last the Romans became dreadfully frightened. "When will he stop?" they said to one another in trembling tones.

One day a senator had the courage to ask Sulla if he would please say whom he intended to spare from death. Sulla coolly answered:

"I have not yet made up my mind, but if it is the wish of the Senate, I will shortly make out a list of persons who must die!"

And Sulla really did make out a list of persons he intended to kill. It was called a *proscription list* and was hung up in the Forum. Oh, how anxiously the poor, terror-stricken Romans went to that list to read the names! And if a man saw that his name was not there, he went away with joy in his heart. But if his name was there, he covered his face with his toga and ran off to hide himself.

The next day another and longer list of proscribed persons was hung up, and the day after still another list. Anyone who killed a proscribed person got a large reward in money, but if anybody helped a proscribed person to escape, he was punished by death. This dreadful work was continued until many thousands of people in Rome and throughout Italy were slain.

Then Sulla had his Triumph in the streets of Rome. It was the most magnificent procession that had yet been seen in the city. There were hundreds of beautiful horses drawing bright, golden chariots; there were long lines of soldiers in glittering armor; there were wagons containing gold and silver and other precious things, which Sulla had gotten in Greece after his victories over Mithridates. The dictator himself rode in the most splendid chariot of all. He seemed like a king, and indeed was a king in power, though not in name. This was what was called a Triumph.

Sulla, for his own protection, had a bodyguard formed of slaves who had belonged to the people he had proscribed and put to death. This bodyguard is said to have numbered 10,000 men, and they were called Cornelii, after Sulla's family name.

Under the rule of Sulla, his own will was law. He could do whatever he pleased. But he did not remain dictator a long time. In about a year after his Triumph, he seemed to have gotten tired of ruling and resigned the office. Then he left Rome and went to reside in his country house on the beautiful Bay of Naples. Here he spent the rest of his life, passing his time partly in feasting and merriment and partly in study. He died in 78 BC.

IX – Nōna Lectiō: Pompey the Great (*Famous Men of Rome* XX)

Not long after the death of Sulla, a new enemy to Rome appeared upon the Mediterranean Sea. A large number of people who lived on the coasts of Asia Minor built and armed fleets of ships, sailed along the shores of Italy, and attacked and plundered Roman vessels.

The searovers, or pirates, as the Romans called them, had more than a thousand well-built, fast-sailing ships. Many of them were adorned with richly gilded bows and sterns, purple sails, and silver mounted oars. They seized trading vessels, robbed them, and killed every person on board.

Often, too, the pirates committed robberies on land. A boat's crew from a pirate ship would go ashore, put to death all the farmers in the neighborhood, and lay waste their farms. So in a short time, the pirates made themselves masters of the Italian coasts and kept the people in constant excitement and terror.

But at last the Romans resolved to make war upon the robbers and selected a very popular young man named Cne´i-us Pom´pey to be the general. The people had great confidence in Pompey. They said that he was the only one who could put down the Mediterranean pirates and demanded that he should be sent to do the work.

Pompey was a fine-looking man, with very pleasant manners. He had made himself famous as a soldier by brave deeds in wars in Spain and Africa and was generally called Pompey the Great. His father had been a great commander, and the boy had lived in camps and taken part in wars almost from childhood. He had had many adventures during his army life and had always shown the qualities of a hero. He fought on the side of Sulla in many battles against the Marians, and he was thought to be one of Sulla's greatest generals.

The Roman Senate therefore, yielded to the demand of the people and appointed Pompey to go forth against the pirates. He accepted the

Pompey the Great
(106-48 BC)

command and promptly set to work to carry out the important undertaking.

He gathered 14 powerful fleets. He kept one for himself and put the others under the command of good officers. Then he divided the Mediterranean into 13 districts, and sent a fleet to each district to hunt the pirates.

With his own fleet he sailed as far as the Strait of Gibraltar and then turned back toward Italy. On the way he chased the pirate vessels before him as he met them, until they were stopped and seized by some of the 13 fleets stationed here and there all over the Mediterranean. The pirates were thus caught in a trap. Thousands of them were killed in battles with the different fleets, and their vessels were burned. The remainder soon surrendered to the Romans, and in three months the sea was cleared of pirates.

Pompey was much praised for this great work, and the people said he was just the man to take charge of the war against Mithridates. This king had again attacked a Roman province in Asia, and the Romans resolved to punish him. But Mithridates was a very powerful man. He had great armies; he was a skillful general, and he defeated the Romans in many battles. The Roman people therefore resolved to send Pompey against him. Pompey was much pleased to be placed in command of a great army, and he proudly started off with his soldiers for the eastern lands.

Pompey remained in Asia several years and won many great victories. He conquered a number of countries and put Roman governors over them. Then he came back to Rome, bringing kings and princes as prisoner and an enormous amount of gold and silver and other valuable things to enrich the republic and himself. He was welcomed in a magnificent manner and he had a Triumph such as was given to great and victorious generals.

But Pompey now began to think of making himself master of Rome during his life time. He had greatly pleased the people by his victories in war, and they were praising him on every side. How to keep their favor, and by it to get power, was what now occupied his mind. He had been consul before, but he was now elected again; then he set about providing various sorts of amusements for the people. He believed that if the people were amused, they would be less likely to object to his taking the powers of the government entirely into his own hands.

He built a theatre large enough to seat 40,000 persons. This was the first great theatre erected in Rome. It was of stone and very strongly made. It had no roof, and the rows of seats rose one above another in a half circle. At one end there was an immense stage on which all the performances took place.

In this grand theatre Pompey gave some very wonderful exhibitions from time to time. He had lions, elephants, and other wild animals brought from Asia and Africa at great expense. These animals were let loose upon the stage, and gladiators fought them in full view of the people in the theatre.

There were also thrilling combats in the theatre between the gladiators themselves. They fought each other savagely until one was wounded and fell upon the stage. Then the victor would turn toward the audience to find whether they wished him to kill the wounded man. If the people wanted this, they would stretch out their hands with their thumbs down; if they did not want him killed, they would hold their thumbs upward. If he had shown skill and courage and fought well, they would give the sign to let him live, but if he had not made a brave fight, they would turn down their thumbs, and the unfortunate man would be instantly killed.

Slaves and prisoners taken in war were taught to be gladiators in schools established for the purpose. There were hundreds of these trained fighters always ready for the combats. The Romans were very fond of such amusements, and great crowds of men, and women too, attended the theatre whenever there was a fight of gladiators.

By giving the people a great deal of amusement of this kind on a grand scale, Pompey became the great popular favorite in Rome, and while the people were entertained at his theatre, he managed the government to suit himself.

At this time the Romans ruled a vast territory, which included not only all Italy, but Greece, Spain, Syria, Egypt, Turkey, Switzerland, and parts of France and Germany. Country after country had been conquered during a long series of years, and millions of people of different races and languages were subjects of Rome.

Rome itself was a city with a population of about half a million. It covered a very large area, including the famous seven hills. Its streets were narrow and crooked but well-paved and clean. In the center of the city were a number of large squares in which there were handsome buildings. There were magnificent temples and baths, and the houses of the nobles and wealthy plebeians were very large and splendid. Many of the fine houses were built of marble, with great pillars in front. Elegant furniture and handsome carpets and rugs filled the rooms.

There were many rich men in Rome at this time. Most of them had obtained the greater part of their wealth by plundering the conquered countries. They lived in a very magnificent manner, gave splendid dinners and entertainments, and had hundreds of slaves to attend upon them.

The slaves were a large class who were brought to Rome from many nations conquered in war. Many of them belonged to high families in their own country and were well educated. Some of them were physicians, and others were good scholars and could read and write for their masters. The best cooks, builders, tailors, and farmers were slaves. In fact, it was by slaves that nearly all the skilled work in Rome was done.

There were markets in Rome where slaves were sold. The slaves to be sold were placed on a platform. Labels hung from their necks, showing their age and what they were able to do.

The Roman children were taught to read and write Latin, which was their own language. They were also taught arithmetic and history. Most of the teachers were well-educated slaves.

Rome, then, was very rich and very powerful in the time of Pompey, and for many years Pompey was very popular. At one time he became dangerously ill while visiting Naples. Then the people showed their great love for him in many ways, and when he recovered, there were public thanksgivings throughout Italy. On his journey home, great crowds came out to greet him as he passed through the towns, and when he arrived at Rome, he was received with unbounded joy.

Pompey had now a very strong hold on the affections of the people, so he cared little for the efforts made by a very ambitious Roman named Ju´li-us Cae´sar to win public favor. But Caesar was a man of strong will and great energy. He had resolved to be the ruler of Rome, and he spared no labor to accomplish his purpose. Pompey at last became alarmed by Caesar's efforts, but it was then too late. He was defeated by Caesar in a great battle and soon after lost his life. How these things came about we shall learn in the next story.

X – Decima Lectiō: Julius Caesar (*Famous Men of Rome* XXI.1)

Of all the Roman heroes, the greatest was Caius Julius Caesar. He was a very remarkable man in many ways. He was remarkable as a soldier, statesman, scholar, and as an orator. He wrote a history of his own wars which is one of the best ancient histories that have come down to us. It is called *Caesar's Commentaries*, and it is used as a textbook in all schools where Latin is taught.

Julius Caesar (100-44 BC)

This famous Roman was tall, handsome, agreeable in his manners, and of a lively disposition. He liked songs and stories, and even when he was a great general, he often was as merry and frolicsome as a boy. Sometimes however he was stern and cruel instead of kind and forgiving.

Caesar was a member of the Julian family, which was one of the first families in Rome. Four Caesars of this family had been consuls of Rome in one century.

The aunt of Julius Caesar was the wife of the great leader Marius. Naturally, Sulla was Caesar's bitter enemy and did all he could against him. "In that young man there is many a Marius," Sulla is reported to have said. However, by keeping out of Rome, Caesar was able to escape the traps laid for him at Sulla's orders. As soon as Sulla died, Caesar returned to Rome.

Although he was a rich noble, Caesar became a friend of the plebeians and always supported their cause. He spoke a great deal in the Forum upon political questions, and the people looked upon him as their champion. They elected him to several public offices, one after the other, and thus his influence and power were much increased. At last he was appointed governor of Spain, which was then ruled by the Romans.

On his way to Spain, he stopped for a night at a little village among the mountains. One of his companions remarked that perhaps in that small place the people had their contests and their jealousies, just as people in large cities.

"Poor as this village is, I would rather be first here than second in Rome!" said Caesar.

Caesar was very successful in Spain, and the Romans were so pleased with his conduct that when he came home, they made him consul. During his consulship he had many good laws passed. When about 40 years old, he was given command of an army, and for some years he followed the life of a soldier with wonderful success.

The Roman armies were formed of regiments called *legions*. Each legion contained over 3,000 men, who were sometimes called legionaries. The weapons of the legionary were a short sword and a long spear called a *pilum*.

Besides spears and swords, the Roman soldiers used slings for hurling stones against the enemy. They also had a machine called a *ballista* for throwing stones too heavy for handslings.

The military standard of the Romans was a figure of an eagle borne on the top of a pole. Each legion had one of these, and the soldier who carried it was called the *eagle-bearer*. Other standards also were used by the *cohorts* or companies into which the legions were divided.

58-51 BC
The Gallic War

Caesar's first great battles were in Gaul. The Romans called all the inhabitants of that country Gauls, although they were of many nations and spoke different languages. The Gauls were brave, but Caesar proved to be a great general, and in a few years he conquered all Gaul.

The Roman soldiers had great confidence in Caesar. When he led them, they believed victory was certain. He was strict in his discipline, but very friendly and pleasant with the men, and often gave them praise. He himself shared in their hardships. Day after day he marched on foot at their head through heat and rain and snow and fought with them in the front ranks.

On one occasion Caesar built a very remarkable bridge. He wanted to get across the River Rhine with his army to punish some German tribes who were in the habit of attacking the friends of Rome in Gaul. There was no bridge. The Germans used to get over in small parties by swimming or in small boats. But a large army could not cross in this way without a great deal of trouble and loss of time, so Caesar resolved to build a bridge. He quickly set his men to work, and they finished the bridge in ten days, though all the wood had to be cut down in the forests and carried to the riverside.

One of Caesar's greatest victories in Gaul was the taking of the town of A-le´si-a. This town had very strong walls all round it, and it was defended by a great army of Gauls commanded by a brave chief named Ver-cin-get´o-rix. Caesar surrounded the town with his army and prevented food from being sent in to the inhabitants. He also defeated an army that came from other parts of Gaul to help the Alesians.

Vercingetorix then had to come out from the town and give himself up to Caesar.

After many conquests in Gaul, Caesar sailed over with an army to the island of Britain, now called Great Britain. The natives were a wild, fierce people, and they fought bravely against Caesar and his army. But the Romans were victorious, and they took possession of Britain, and for over 400 years the island was a part of the Roman empire.

55-54 BC
Invasion of Britain

XI – Ūndecima Lectiō: Julius Caesar (*Famous Men of Rome* XXI.2)

Caesar was engaged eight years in his wars in Gaul and Britain. It is said that during these years he conquered 300 tribes or nations, took 800 cities, fought battles with 3,000,000 men and made 1,000,000 prisoners. He obtained immense quantities of treasure in the conquered lands, and he himself, as commander of the victorious armies, kept a large part of it as his own share, so that he became very rich.

Caesar's wonderful victories made him a great man in Rome. The plebeians rejoiced at the success of their leader and favorite and were ready to welcome him with the highest honors whenever he should return to the city.

But Caesar had now made up his mind to become the master of Rome. So he began to plan and to work to destroy the power of Pompey, who at that time ruled public affairs in Rome almost completely.

In order to gain still greater favor, Caesar sent a number of his friends to Rome to spend immense sums of money in various ways to please the people. They got up splendid games and feasts; they divided large quantities of corn among the poor; and they paid the debts of hundreds of men who had influence among the plebeians. The people knew that all this was done at Caesar's expense, and they praised and loved him for his generosity.

Pompey, with a great show of authority, now ordered Caesar to disband his army and send the soldiers to their homes, for he said that Caesar had no need of an army any longer, as he had finished his work in Gaul. But Pompey, too, had an army at this time in Spain, and Caesar said to him:

"If you will disband your army, I will disband mine."

This made Pompey very angry, and he got the Senate to pass a law declaring that Caesar was a public enemy and must be put down. One senator asked Pompey what he should do if Caesar should come to Rome with his army.

"What should I do?" cried Pompey, in a tone of contempt. "Why, I have only to stamp my foot and thousands of men will spring up to march under my orders."

At this time Caesar was with his army in the northern part of Italy. When he heard what the Senate had done, he called his soldiers together and made an eloquent speech. He told them of the injustice that Pompey and the Senate had done to him, and he concluded by saying:

"This is my reward for all that I have done for my country. But I shall go to Rome and establish an honest government of the people, if you, my brave soldiers, will be faithful to me."

The soldiers answered with a loud shout, saying:

"We shall be faithful to you. We will stand by you to the last."

Caesar then started with his army and marched rapidly through northern Italy until he came to the banks of a little river, at that time called the Ru´bi-con and known as the southern boundary of Gaul. What river this was no one can now exactly tell, but it is supposed that it was one of several small rivers which flow into the Adriatic Sea south of the River Po.

Caesar halted his army at the Rubicon and forbade anyone to cross it until he gave the order. He stood for some time on the banks in deep thought, as if trying to decide whether he should cross the river and proceed or give up his dangerous undertaking. He was still within his own territory as commander of Gaul; if he should cross the Rubicon, he would be on territory directly under the government of the officers at Rome. By law it was made an act of treason, to be punished with death, for any Roman general to enter this territory with an army without permission of the Senate.

"We can retreat now," said Caesar to some of his officers who stood near him, "but once across the Rubicon it will be too late to draw back."

While Caesar was talking, a shepherd came along from a field close by, playing lively music on a reed pipe. The soldiers gathered around him to listen to the music, and some of them began to dance. One of Caesar's trumpeters stood among the soldiers with his trumpet in his hand. The shepherd saw the trumpet, suddenly seized it, and waded to the bridge over the Rubicon, which was but a few steps off. Then he put the trumpet to his lips, sounded the stirring notes for an advance of the troops, and began to march across the bridge.

"A sign from the gods!" shouted Caesar. "Let us go where we are thus called. The die is cast!"

So saying, he turned his horse right into the stream and rode across the Rubicon, followed by his army. It was a daring thing to do, and the phrases "he has crossed the Rubicon" and "the die is cast" are now often used to mean that a bold or dangerous step has been taken from which there is no drawing back.

There was no one to oppose Caesar as he marched through Italy. On the contrary, city after city surrendered to him. There was very little fighting. In most places the people seemed glad to have him as their ruler, and gave him a warm welcome and feasted his soldiers. He had only words of kindness for everyone, even for those who were against him, and he won hosts of friends and supporters all along the route.

There was great alarm at Rome when it was learned that Caesar was advancing toward the city. The supporters of Pompey became terrified,

---

49 BC
Caesar crossed the Rubicon and began a civil war.

The Rubicon was the boundary between the province of Gaul and the land of Italy. Caesar had authority to command an army only in Gaul, and to cross the Rubicon with his army was illegal and an act of war against his own country.

and the rich nobles gathered up their money and other valuables and fled. Pompey could do nothing to defend the city against Caesar, and at last he too ran away. He went to Greece to raise an army to fight Caesar.

When Caesar arrived at Rome he met with no opposition. He entered the city amid shouts of welcome from the people. He harmed no one, but he set up a new government and organized a new Senate. He was now the master spirit of the republic.

After arranging everything to his satisfaction in Rome, Caesar went to Spain and defeated Pompey's generals there. Then he came back and turned his attention to Pompey himself.

In the meantime, Pompey had been very busy gathering an army in the eastern countries controlled by Rome. In one way or another, he collected 50,000 men. They were stationed on the coasts of Macedonia and Greece. There they waited for Caesar and his army to cross the Adriatic Sea to give them battle.

Caesar had a great deal of trouble getting across the stormy sea with his army of 40,000 soldiers, but at last a landing was made in Greece. Then the two armies had some skirmishing but no great battle.

This continued for months. Pompey at one time would gain the advantage, and Caesar at another time. But it was evident that neither of the great rivals was in any hurry to risk the chance of defeat in a general battle. They know well that such a defeat would entirely ruin the one who was defeated.

But at last the two armies met for battle on the plain of Phar-sa´li-a, in Thessaly, a district of Greece. The soldiers on both sides were armed with spears and broadswords. Some carried slings to hurl large stones, and others had bows and arrows. The greater part of the fighting however was done with swords. *[48 BC Battle of Pharsalia]*

80,000 men were engaged in the battle, about 40,000 on each side. It was a brave heroic struggle and lasted for hours. Both armies fought splendidly, but in the end Pompey's army was forced back to its camp after dreadful slaughter. For a few minutes the camp was bravely defended against the attacks of Caesar's soldiers and then had to be abandoned. The battle did not last long after this. Pompey's great army was utterly beaten.

Pompey himself, with a few followers, fled to the seashore and sailed across the Mediterranean to Egypt. There he was treacherously murdered by order of Ptolemy, the Egyptian king.

XII – Duodecima Lectiō: Julius Caesar (*Famous Men of Rome* XXI.2)

Caesar gained a splendid victory at Pharsalia, but he was not yet master of the Roman Empire. The rich nobles and senators formed armies to fight him in Asia Minor, Africa, and Spain. Caesar went with an army to Asia Minor, attacked his enemies, and won a great battle at a place called Ze´la. This victory was so quickly gained that in sending news of it to *[47 BC Battle of Zela]*

Rome Caesar wrote the famous dispatch, "*Vēnī, vīdī, vīcī,*" which is, in English, "I came, I saw, I conquered."

He had equal success in Africa and Spain. In a very short time he destroyed the armies opposed to him. Then he returned to Rome and had the grandest Triumph ever seen in the city.

The celebration lasted four days, and during that time Rome was in a high state of pleasant excitement. Thousands of persons from the surrounding country came to the city to witness the magnificent show.

On each day there were splendid processions, in which there were great numbers of gorgeous chariots, drawn by beautiful horses and filled with Caesar's principal officers. Behind them marched hundreds of soldiers bearing banners on which were pictured scenes from Caesar's important battles. Herds of elephants and camels from Asia and Africa appeared in the procession, and there were also long lines of prisoners carrying valuable articles obtained by Caesar in the lands he had conquered.

In addition to the processions, many kinds of entertainments were provided for the people, such as plays, circus exhibitions, combats between gladiators, wild-beast hunts, and chariot races. There were also feasts served to all the people of the city. It was a time of unbounded enjoyment and delighted the Romans so much that they became very devoted to Caesar.

There was now no opposition to him. Both the nobles and the plebeians were willing, and even glad, to have him as their ruler. He was chosen dictator for life and put in command of all the armies of the Empire. He was called *imperātor*, which means *emperor*.

The people gave him the title of *Father of his Country*. Statues of him were erected in the public buildings and squares. A grand chair, made somewhat like a throne, was placed in the Senate chamber, and whenever he came to listen to the debates, he sat in this chair as if he were king.

Caesar now had laws passed making many improvements in the government. He also carried out a number of plans to make Rome of more importance as a commercial city. He erected magnificent buildings, made aqueducts to bring plenty of water to the city, established a great library, and did many other things which were of much benefit to the people.

One of the most useful things he did was to make a new calendar. Before his time the Romans had not a very clear knowledge as to the length of a year. At one time they had only ten months in their year. Afterward they had twelve, but they only counted 365 days in every year. They did not know or they did not give attention to the fact that the real length of a year is 365 days, 5 hours, 48 minutes, 50 seconds. They did not reckon the extra hours, minutes, and seconds, and so their calendar got quite wrong in the course of a number of years. Caesar corrected the error by making one year in every four have 366 days, and the calendar thus corrected was called the *Julian Calendar*.

Caesar now possessed all the glory and power of a king, and it began to be believed that he wanted to be a king in reality. The Romans had not had a king for 500 years and would not have one. Their feeling against kings was so strong that none of the men who had ruled Rome, at times with almost kingly power, had ever dared to call himself king.

One day an intimate friend of Caesar saluted him in public as king. Caesar replied: "I am not king, but only Caesar."

Some of the nobles however felt certain that he meant to make himself king, and they formed a plot to kill him in the Senate house on the Ides of March, that is, on the fifteenth of March. The Romans had certain days in their months which they called Kalends, Nones, and Ides.

One of the persons who made the plot against Caesar was Junius Brutus, a highly respected Roman. It is said that he was a descendant of the Junius Brutus who, five centuries before, had helped to overthrow the tyrant King Tarquin. Brutus was an intimate friend of Caesar, but he thought that Caesar intended to destroy the Republic by making himself king, and therefore he joined the plot against him.

As the Ides of March drew near, the plan for putting Caesar to death was carefully arranged and settled. An augur, or fortune teller, one day stopped Caesar in the street and said to him, "Beware the Ides of March!" but the great conqueror laughed at the warning.

Mar. 15, 44 BC the death of Caesar

On the day appointed, the plotters met in the senate chamber, ready to do the wicked deed they had planned. When Caesar entered the chamber, all present rose to greet him. He bowed and smiled pleasantly to the people and took his usual seat. Now was the fatal moment.

As had been arranged, one of the plotters went up to him with a request for the pardon of a prisoner. Then the rest crowded around his chair as if to urge him to grant the request. Caesar seemed somewhat alarmed at the crowd and rose from his chair. At this moment, he was stabbed in the side with a sword. Then there were loud outcries in the chamber, and all was excitement and confusion.

Caesar used his stylus to defend himself. The stylus was an instrument made of iron, with a sharp point on one end for writing on wax tablets, and with the other end smooth, for rubbing out a word when necessary. For writing on parchment or paper, a pen made of reed was used. Educated Romans carried their stylus and tablet in their pockets. From the name of the instrument, the word *style* is now used to mean a particular manner of writing.

Caesar had nothing but his stylus with which to defend himself. He fought bravely until he saw his friend Brutus coming to strike him. Then he cried out, "You, too, Brutus!" and made no further resistance.

They stabbed him until he fell dead. Then they went out of the Senate and through the streets of Rome with Brutus at their head. They told the people what they had done and rejoiced at the deed. They said the death of Caesar saved the Roman Republic.

The famous English author William Shakespeare wrote a play named Julius Caesar. In the play Caesar fights off the assassins for a while, but when he sees Brutus among them, he asks "Et tū, Brūte?" which means "And you too, Brutus?" But the historian Plutarch says that Caesar's last words were Greek: "kai su teknon?", which means "And you too, my child?"

But the people were very angry and threatened to put to death those who had killed Caesar. They would have done this, only that Brutus and his friends fled from the city.

There was a grand funeral service in honor of Caesar. The body was laid in the Forum, and a famous Roman named Mark Antony made an eloquent funeral speech over it. He praised Caesar and spoke so bitterly against Brutus and his party that the people were now more angry than ever. This Mark Antony was afterward a very powerful man in Rome.

Caesar died 44 years before Christ was born. Of course his death did not save the Roman Republic. It had, indeed, already ceased to exist in all but the name. Rome was no longer a republic, but an empire, and as we shall see, the family of Caesar gave it its first emperor. All the emperors adopted the name of Caesar as part of their title.

XIII – Tertia Decima Lectiō: Cicero (*Famous Men of Rome* XXII)

> Cicero (106 – 43 BC) was one of Rome's greatest authors, orators, and statesmen. He was just a few years older than Caesar.

Marcus Tul´li-us Cic´e-ro was a prominent man at Rome for some time in the latter years of the Republic. He was a great orator – one of the greatest the world has ever known. His principal speeches have been preserved and are read and studied at the present day.

He often spoke in the Forum before large audiences, and by his wonderful eloquence, he delighted all who heard him. Both the nobles and plebeians admired him for his learning, his oratory, and his manly qualities.

Cicero was a tall, graceful man, with an intellectual and rather handsome face and very bright black eyes. He was so great a favorite that he was chosen to fill several public offices and at last was elected consul.

> 63 BC
> the Catiline Conspiracy

In the early part of his year as consul, there was a mysterious plot formed in Rome by some nobles of bad character, old soldiers, and others ready for any mischief. What their real object was no one seemed to know. But it was said that the conspirators wanted to overthrow the government and set up a new one of their own.

There was a senator named Ser´gi-us Cat´i-line, and many believed that he was at the head of the plot. He had a bad reputation, and for some time, the other senators had looked upon him with suspicion. There was no proof however that he was engaged in any unlawful proceedings, so no charge could be made against him.

But one day a young woman named Ful´vi-a came to Cicero and gave him some important information about the plot and Catiline's part in it. She said that she had a lover who was one of the plotters and that he had told her some of their secrets. She was greatly frightened, for she thought that there might be bloodshed in Rome if the plot went on, and she felt it her duty to tell Cicero about it.

Cicero immediately went to the Senate and made a powerful speech. He charged Catiline with being the leading person in a plot to overthrow the government. There was great excitement at his words. Catiline was present, and he boldly denied the charge and defied Cicero to prove it.

"If Consul Cicero is afraid of my doing harm in Rome," said he, "I am willing to place myself as a prisoner in the hands of any senator."

"I do not think it is safe to have you in the city," replied Cicero, "and do you expect anyone to take you into his house?"

After a great deal of exciting talk, the Senate laid aside the charge against Catiline for a while.

A few weeks later, in a city near Rome, there was an uprising of the people against the public officers. This caused a great deal of alarm, and Cicero said it was the beginning of the plot that he had charged Catiline with forming.

Then Cicero hurried to the Senate, where Catiline was, and made a great speech against him. He called him a traitor to his country. Catiline turned pale and began to tremble. He attempted to speak, but the senators shouted and hooted and hissed him. Those who sat near him got up in disgust and took seats in another part of the chamber, leaving the conspirator sitting by himself. At last Catiline ran out of the Senate, furious with anger and threatening revenge. Then he mounted a horse and rode quickly out of the city.

Shortly afterward Cicero learned the names of nine Roman citizens who were leaders in the plot, and he had them arrested. He declared in the senate that they had planned to murder the senators and the high officers and to burn Rome. The senators declared at once that the nine must die, and so Cicero had them put to death.

Catiline now fled to the mountains called the Apennines and there raised a force of 20,000 men. Two armies were sent against him from Rome. A battle took place, in which Catiline's army was defeated and he himself killed.

Thus ended what was known as the Catiline Conspiracy. Cicero's action in helping to destroy it greatly pleased the Romans. In the Senate he received much praise and honor. It was even declared that he was the "Father of His Country."

Antony did not like Cicero, and when the Triumvirate was formed, the great orator was put to death by Antony's order.

> Five years later, in 58 BC, Cicero was exiled because he approved the execution of these nine conspirators. Cicero's enemies argued that he had illegally put citizens to death without a fair trial – a right guaranteed to citizens by Roman law. A year later, Cicero was acquitted and allowed to return to Rome.

XIV – Quarta Decima Lectiō: Augustus (*Famous Men of Rome* XXIII)

The first of the long line of Roman emperors was Oc-ta'vi-us, called in history Au-gus'tus. He was the grandnephew of Julius Caesar. Although he was scarcely 20 years old when Caesar died, he was very ambitious. He often said that he should one day be at the head of the Roman Empire.

"I shall rule Rome like Caesar," he would say to his companions. "You may laugh at me now, but the time will come when I shall be master of the Romans."

Shortly after Caesar's death, Octavius began to take an active part in political affairs. At this time, Mark Antony was in control of Rome and was managing everything to suit himself. He had been an intimate friend of Caesar and had commanded one of his armies. He obtained a great deal of power, but he was not liked very much either by the nobles or the plebeians. He was a bad ruler, and nobody trusted him.

Once Antony tried to prevent Octavius from being elected a tribune of the people. "I will be a tribune in spite of you," Octavius said, and he set to work with all his energy to get the office. There was a severe struggle on election day, but the boy was successful.

After this Octavius hated Antony and planned in secret to bring about his downfall. And he succeeded in all he attempted to do. From a tribune he advanced steadily, step by step, to more important offices. At last he obtained command of an army and marched his soldiers to northern Italy, where a war was going on. While in this region, he met Antony with his army. The two began to quarrel and at last came to blows. Then the army of Octavius fought the army of Antony, and the northern plains were reddened with the blood of the soldiers.

When the fighting had gone on for some time, Octavius sent to Antony and asked him to stop it. He pretended that he was very sorry he had begun to fight with Antony and asked for his friendship. "Let us be friends and work together," he said to Antony. "By joining our armies we shall be able to do some good."

The fighting was then stopped, and the two generals had a meeting. They agreed to unite their armies, and to invite another Roman general, named Lep´i-dus, who had a large army, to join them. Lepidus accepted the invitation and came to have a talk with Antony and Octavius. They agreed to a plan by which they themselves were to rule Rome together. This rule, or government, was called a *triumvirate*, and Octavius, Antony, and Lepidus were called *triumvirs*, a word which means *three men*.

After making all their arrangements, Antony, Octavius, and Lepidus started for Rome with their armies and took possession of the city. Then they began to kill those whom they thought were their enemies. More than 2,000 Romans were slain. They would have killed Brutus, only that he was then in Greece, where he had gone after Caesar's death to raise an army to fight Antony and his friends. Antony and Octavius now went with an army to Greece to fight Brutus. Both armies met at Philippi, in Macedonia, and then there was a battle in which the army of Brutus was defeated. After the battle, Brutus requested one of his slaves to kill him. The slave refused, but when Brutus still pressed him to do it, he held out his sword, and Brutus killed himself by falling upon it.

It is told that some time before the battle of Philippi, as Brutus was sitting one night in his tent, a vision or spectre appeared to him and said, "I am thy evil genius, Brutus; we shall meet again at Philippi." It is also said that the spectre again appeared to Brutus on the night before the battle of Philippi and told him that his death was at hand.

There was no one now to interfere with Antony, Octavius, and Lepidus, and they managed everything in Rome as they liked. They pretended all the time to have great respect for the Senate and officers of government who had been elected by the people.

---

43 BC
The second triumvirate was formed by Mark Antony, Lepidus, and Octavius, who agreed take control of the government at Rome and share their power with each other.

NB – The first triumvirate had been formed by Julius Caesar and his allies in 60 BC.

42 BC
The Battle of Philippi

After a short time, Antony went to some of the Eastern countries that were a part of the Roman Empire, and Lepidus went to Africa. Octavius was left in Rome to attend to its affairs. He then began to plan to get rid of Antony and Lepidus, so that he might rule Rome himself. With this object, he raised a great army and determined to make war on his rivals.

Sextus Pompey, a son of Pompey the Great, was at this time in control of the island of Sicily. He was always making trouble for Octavius, and he was aided by Lepidus, who had come from Africa to Sicily with his army. One day Octavius sailed over the Mediterranean Sea to Sicily with thousands of soldiers, destroyed the army of Sextus, and induced the army of Lepidus to leave him. Lepidus was then taken prisoner.

"Now to put an end to the power of Antony!" said Octavius to himself, when he returned to Rome from Sicily. So he went to the Senate and accused Antony of treason in Asia and Africa and asked that war be declared against him. The Senate declared war, and Octavius began to make great preparations for it.

Antony was in Egypt when he heard of the declaration of war. He laughed scornfully at the idea of Octavius being able to beat him. Then he gathered an army of more than 100,000 men and a fleet of several hundred warships and set out to meet Octavius. He had with him Cle-o-pa´tra, the beautiful queen of Egypt, whom he had married, and she had a fleet of her own, numbering 60 ships.

Octavius had about as many soldiers and ships as Antony. The two fleets met near a place called Ac´ti-um, on the coast of Greece, and fought a battle. For several hours the fight went on bravely, but neither side gained any great advantage. Suddenly Cleopatra sailed away with her fleet, and Antony quickly followed her with a few ships. Thus he deserted his men while they were fighting.

31 BC
The Battle of Actium. The end of the Roman Republic and the beginning of the Roman Empire.

The sailors and soldiers of the deserted fleet kept on fighting for a short time and then surrendered to Octavius. A few days later, a part of Antony's army, which was encamped on the shore near Actium, also surrendered.

Antony went back to Egypt with Cleopatra. His friends and supporters then left him, and his power was gone. Soon after, he stabbed himself and so died. It is said that Cleopatra died from the bite of a poisonous serpent called an asp, which she placed on her arm on purpose to kill herself.

Octavius continued to fight in different parts of the Empire until he defeated everyone who dared oppose him. Then he went back to Rome with a great deal of glory and riches and let it be known at once that he intended to be the master of the government. Although he pretended to protect the rights of the people, he made himself consul and also assumed other high offices, which greatly added to his power. Thousands of soldiers were at his call, and finally he became very much like a king.

Historia

27 BC
Octavius granted the title "Augustus."
The end of the Roman Republic and the beginning of the Roman Empire.

"The accumulation of all powers, legislative, executive, and judiciary, in the same hands . . . may justly be pronounced the very definition of tyranny."

James Madison, *Federalist* 47, 1788.

The Senate asked him if he would wish to be appointed dictator for life, but he thought it wise to refuse this office. The Senate then gave him the name of Augustus, which meant that he was worthy of respect. The word *augustus* in the Latin language means *sacred*. He called himself emperor, and, as Emperor Caesar Augustus, he ruled the Romans all the rest of his life, a period of about 27 years. And when Augustus became emperor, the Republic of Rome was no longer in existence.

What were known as the Prae-to´ri-an Guards were organized by Augustus to protect himself and uphold his authority as emperor. These guards were about 10,000 in number, and they were composed of the most trusty soldiers of the Empire. Each soldier had high rank and large pay and had to serve for many years. Whenever Augustus appeared in public, he was attended by some of the Praetorian guards, and they looked very imposing with their handsome uniforms and glittering swords and spears.

Augustus made many good changes in the government. He very much improved the condition of the plebeians. His principal ministers were two able men named A-grip´pa and Mae-ce´nas, who gave him very valuable assistance.

Whenever these wise men saw that the Romans were getting uneasy and beginning to grumble, they would advise the emperor to distribute corn or money to the poor or to give the people grand exhibitions to amuse them. Augustus would follow the advice and by so doing, made himself very popular.

During his long reign, Augustus had many splendid palaces, temples, and other buildings erected in Rome, and they made the city very beautiful. Augustus also founded cities in various parts of the empire. He encouraged literature and art and was himself an author. In his time, the famous Roman poets Hor´ace, Ver´gil, Va´ri-us, and O´vid lived, and also the great historian Li´vy, who wrote the history of Rome from the earliest period down to his own time. Vergil was the author of a celebrated poem called *The Ae-ne´id*, which tells of the wanderings and adventures of the Trojan hero Aeneas, whom the Caesars said was their ancestor.

Circa 1 AD
The birth of Jesus

It was in the reign of Augustus that Jesus Christ was born in Bethlehem, a town of Palestine, or Judea, in southwest Asia. Judea was then part of the Roman Empire.

14 AD
Emperor Tiberius

XV – Quīnta Decima Lectiō: Tiberius, Caligula, Claudius, Nero
(*Famous Men of Rome* XXIV.1-2)

Circa 33 AD
Crucifixion, death, and resurrection of Jesus Christ

On the death of Augustus, in the year 14 AD, his stepson Ti-be´ri-us became emperor. He was a cruel tyrant. He put to death a great many people only because he thought they were his enemies. A Roman emperor could put to death anyone he pleased. If he did not like a person, he would charge him with some crime and order his soldiers to kill him. Tiberius had many people killed in this way, but he was himself killed by the commander or general of the Praetorian Guard.

The next two emperors were Ca-lig´u-la and Clau´di-us. They also were tyrants and put many people to death without just cause. It is said that Caligula once wished that all the Roman people together had but one head so that he might cut it off with one blow.

But the next emperor was a still greater tyrant. His name was Nero. He became emperor in the year 54 AD. He was the son of a wicked woman named Ag-rip-pi´na. This woman married Claudius and got him to appoint her own son, Nero, his successor, instead of his own little son Bri-tan´ni-cus. Then she killed Claudius by poison, and Nero became emperor.

Nero was a tall, strong, good-looking, bright youth. He was fond of games, and could play several musical instruments. When he first became emperor, he seemed to be affectionate and kind-hearted, and he did a number of good things. Once, when he was asked to sign a warrant for the execution of a man condemned to death, he exclaimed:

"I wish I had never learned to write, for then I shouldn't have to sign away men's lives!"

Then the people around him cried:

"What a noble young man our emperor is! What a good heart he has!"

But in a very short time it was found that Nero was not at all kind or merciful, but that he was a cruel and wicked man.

Nero's mother, Agrippina, expected that when her son was emperor, she herself would be the real mistress and would rule the Roman Empire as she pleased. Nero was only a boy, she thought, and he would not want to take upon himself the cares and burdens of government.

And for a while Agrippina did rule Rome. She had a woman she hated put to death, and she punished several other persons who had offended her. She made some of the richest Romans pay her large sums of money. But Nero soon put an end to his mother's power. One day he said to her:

"I, not you, am the ruler of the Empire. You have no right to take any power upon yourself, and you must not do so again. Whenever you want anything done, you must ask me to do it for you."

"Ask you?" cried Agrippina in a rage. "How dare you talk this way to me, who made you emperor? You the emperor! You are not the rightful emperor. The true heir to the Empire is your stepbrother, young Britannicus, the son of Claudius!"

Then there was a fierce quarrel between Nero and his mother, and at last he turned her out of his palace and ordered her never to appear there again.

But what she had said alarmed him very much. He feared that Britannicus might be made emperor, and therefore he determined to get him out of the way as soon as possible.

At this time there was in Rome a dreadful woman named Lo-cus´ta, who made poisons and sold them secretly to anyone who wanted them. Nero went one night to this woman and said:

37 AD
Emperor Caligula

41 AD
Emperor Claudius

54 AD
Emperor Nero

> "Make me a strong poison – so strong that it will kill a person like a flash of lightning!"

Locusta made the poison and gave it to him. He tried it on a pig, and it killed the animal in a few moments.

"Ha!" said he, "this will do the work."

Now Britannicus lived in the palace with his stepbrother and next day, when dinner was served, Nero put some of the poison into a cup of wine which he knew the boy was to drink. The moment Britannicus drank it, he fell to the floor dead. Then Nero said to the guests who were at the table:

NB – Nero's guests might have been deceived by his lie because the effects of the poison would have appeared very similar to an epilectic seizure or "fit."

"Do not be alarmed. It is nothing. My poor stepbrother always was subject to fits."

The attendants carried the body of Britannicus out of the room, and the dinner went on gaily.

A little while after he had poisoned his stepbrother, Nero made up his mind to get rid of his mother also. He was afraid that as long as she lived, he would not be safe as emperor. She might stir up the people against him any day. So he went to see her and pretended that he was sorry he had ill-treated her. He kissed and caressed her so affectionately that she was entirely deceived.

Then the cruel son made a plan to drown his mother. He had a ship so built that by pulling out certain bolts and pins, it would suddenly fall to pieces and sink. He then hired a wicked captain and crew to do his bidding and got his mother to take a sail in the ship down the Tiber.

Agrippina took a maid with her and went aboard. She was in a happy humor, because her son, as she thought, was so kind to her. When the ship came to a certain place in the river where the water was very deep, the sailors pulled out the bolts and pins. Then the ship began to fall apart and to sink.

The sailors sprang into the river to swim to the shore, and Agrippina and her maid jumped overboard. The maid was killed by a sailor, but Agrippina was picked up by the crew of a fishing boat.

*59 BC
Agrippina murdered*

Nero was greatly troubled by his mother's escape. He believed that now she would certainly try to have him removed from the throne. So he sent some men to kill her in her house, and they did so in a most cruel manner.

XVI – Sexta Decima Lectiō: Nero (*Famous Men of Rome* XXIV.3-4)

None of the emperors before Nero lived so grandly as he did. He had a splendid marble palace at Rome, containing immense quantities of beautiful furniture, gold and silver ornaments, and works of art of the finest kind. On the pleasant shores of the Mediterranean Sea, he had several houses where he lived in the summer and autumn months. Wherever he went, he had, as his court or companions, three or four hundred richly dressed men and women, with many slaves to wait upon them. They traveled in chariots covered with ivory and gold and drawn by beautiful horses.

Nero was famous for the splendid dinners he gave in his palace. The rarest and most costly food and wines were spread upon the tables in great plenty, and when the feasting was over, troops of actors and dancers would give performances which lasted until late at night.

Sometimes at these dinners, Nero would play the harp or flute. Sometimes he would act portions of plays or recite poems which he himself had composed. He was a very clever musician and actor, and he wrote very good poetry.

One evening a fire broke out in Rome and raged furiously for a week. Half the city was burned, and hundreds of people lost their lives. Some of the Romans said that Nero had started the fire and had prevented it from being put out. Most of the six days during which the fire lasted, he spent in a high tower, enjoying the sight. He played on his harp, sang merry songs, and recited verses about the burning of the ancient city of Troy.

64 AD
Rome burned; Nero blamed the Christians.

After the fire was put out, Nero said that it had been caused by the believers in the religion of Christ. At this time, there was a very large number of Christians in Rome. But most of the Romans still worshipped their old pagan gods, and they hated and ill-treated the Christians.

When Nero declared that the Christians had caused the great fire, the people began to persecute them in a dreadful manner. Many of the Christians were hanged, some were covered with pitch and burned, and others were hunted to death by savage dogs. During the time of this persecution, the Apostle Paul was beheaded, and the Apostle Peter was crucified, as Christ had been crucified 31 years before.

63 AD
St. Peter and St. Paul martyred at Rome.

After a short time, Rome was rebuilt in greater magnificence than before. Nero built for himself an immense and splendid palace on the famous Palatine Hill. This palace contained so many ornaments of gold that it was called the Golden House.

In governing the Empire, Nero was very harsh and cruel. He often put innocent men and women, and even his own friends, to death. He killed his wife in a fit of passion. He did so many wicked things that at last the Romans got tired of having such a tyrant to rule them, and they formed a plot to dethrone him and make someone else their emperor.

But the plot came to nothing, because a slave who had heard of it went to Nero and told him all about it. The Praetorian Guards seized the leading plotters and put them to death. Nero then became more wicked than he had been before. He even accused his old tutor, Se´ne-ca, and the famous poet Lu´can, of taking part in the plot against him, and he sent them an order to put themselves to death. Seneca was a very good man and a great writer. When he received the cruel order from Nero, he knew that if he did not obey it, the tyrant would send someone to kill him, so he had the veins of his arms cut open, and he died after much suffering. Lucan also obeyed the tyrant's order. While dying, he repeated lines from one of his own poems.

65 AD
Seneca and Lucan die by Nero's orders.

This wicked emperor had reigned for 14 years. But at last there was a rebellion against him, and the soldiers elected Gal´ba, the Roman governor of Spain, to be the new emperor.

Then Nero acted like a miserable coward. He was afraid to stay any longer in Rome, for most of the people hated him and favored Galba. So he mounted a horse and rode out of the city to the home of a trusty slave. But while he was there, he received word that the Senate had condemned him to death and that horsemen had been sent out to capture him. "Now dig a grave for me," he said to the slave, "and I will kill myself!" At this moment the galloping of horses was heard.

"Hark! They are coming to kill you," cried the slave. "Use the dagger while it is time and save yourself from disgrace!"

With trembling hand, Nero placed his dagger at this throat but did not have the courage to use it. The slave then seized it and plunged it into the emperor's throat, and the wicked Nero fell dead.

XVII – Septima Decima Lectiō: Galba, Otho, Vitellius, Vespasian, Titus (*Famous Men of Rome* XXV)

69 AD
The year of the four emperors: Galba, Otho, Vitellius, and Vespasian

69 AD
Emperor Vespasian

66-63
The Jewish Revolt

70 AD
Jerusalem and the temple destroyed, fulfilling the prophecy in Matthew 24:2 "Jesus said unto them, See ye not all these things? verily I say unto you, There shall not be left here one stone upon another, that shall not be thrown down."

79 AD
Emperor Titus

During the two years that followed the death of Nero, there were three emperors: Gal´ba, Ot´ho, and Vi-tel´li-us. They were generals of Roman armies and were made emperors by their soldiers. But they reigned only a few months each, and they did nothing of importance.

Vitellius was a glutton. He took pleasure only in eating and drinking. He would often visit the houses of rich Romans without invitation and take breakfast with one, dinner with another, and supper with another. After breakfast he thought only about dinner; and when dinner was over, he began to think of what he would have for supper.

The next emperor was Titus Fla´vi-us Ves-pa´si-an, commonly called Vespasian. He also was an army general. When he was made emperor by his soldiers, he was in Palestine. He had been sent there by Nero with an army to punish the Jews who had rebelled against Rome. As soon as he was declared emperor, he returned to Italy and left his son Titus Flavius, called in history simply Titus, to carry on the war against the Jews.

Titus captured Jerusalem after a siege of six months, and his soldiers took possession of all the valuable things they could find. Then they burned the city to the ground. The famous temple was also destroyed and thus was fulfilled the prophecy of Christ that not one stone of the building should be left upon another. When Titus returned to Rome, he had a grand Triumph, and a beautiful arch was built in his honor. This arch is still in existence.

Vespasian died in 79 AD, and then Titus became emperor. One of the remarkable things Titus did during his reign was to finish the Colosseum, which had been begun by his father. The Colosseum was the largest theatre in the world. It had seats for over 80,000 people. It was first called the Flavian Amphitheatre, from the family name of the emperors who built it. Inside, it had seats all round the ring or arena, and as the word *amphi* means *around,* they called the great building an amphitheatre. In later times, it got the name of Colosseum. The Greeks used the word *colossus* as a name for any very large statue, and because the Flavian Amphitheatre was so large, it was called the Colosseum. In our own language, we use the word *colossal* to describe anything of immense size.

In the Colosseum they had many kinds of amusements. When it first opened, the shows and games lasted for 100 days, and 5,000 wild beasts were killed in the arena by gladiators. The arena was a vast space fenced round about with a strong wall, and around it were circular tiers or rows of seats, one behind the other, like steps of stairs. Sometimes the arena was turned into a lake by letting water flow into it from pipes. Then they put ships upon it and had sham fights in imitation of a battle at sea. This sort of show was called a *naumachia*, which means a fight with ships. It was first introduced into Rome by Julius Caesar, who had a lake dug for the purpose in the Campus Martius.

The Colosseum is still in existence, but it is partly in ruins. Yet from its ruins we can still form an idea of how grand a building it once was.

Besides finishing the Colosseum, the Emperor Titus also built splendid baths. They were called the Baths of Titus. The Romans were very fond of baths. Wealthy citizens used to bathe several times every day, and often they spent the greater part of the day at the baths, where there were finely furnished rooms.

It was in the reign of Titus that the cities of Pom-pei´i and Her-cu-la´ne-um, in the south of Italy, were destroyed by an eruption of Mount Vesuvius. A famous Roman author, Pliny the Younger, saw the eruption from a distance and wrote a description of it. He tells that a fiery cloud of cinders, stones, and ashes burst from the top of the mountain and rained down upon the country all round, destroying towns and villages and people. The ruins of Herculaneum were accidentally discovered by workmen in 1709, and the ruins of Pompeii were discovered some years later.

Titus was a very good emperor. He always did everything he could for the welfare and happiness of the people, and he was so much liked by everybody that he was called the "Delight of Mankind." It is said that one night he thought he had done nothing during that day for the good of any person, and that he cried out, "I have lost a day."

XVIII – Duodēvīcēsima Lectiō: Domitian, Nerva, Trajan (*Famous Men of Rome* XXVI)

On the death of Titus, his brother Do-mi´ti-an became emperor. He was a very bad man and took pleasure only in doing cruel and wicked things. It is said that one of his amusements was catching flies and sticking them with pins. Once when a visitor called and inquired whether

---

80 AD
Colosseum completed

NB –Nero had once erected an enormous bronze colossus, or statue, portraying him as the sun god Helios. This colossus stood next to the site where Vespasian and Titus later built their amphitheatre. The statue was still standing until Medieval times. For this reason, we now call the amphitheatre built by the Flavians the "Colosseum."

79 AD
Eruption of Vesuvius

81 AD
Emperor Domitian

there was anyone with the emperor, the servant answered:

"No, not even a fly."

It is not to be supposed that such an emperor could have been liked by the people. Even his soldiers hated him, and at last they formed a plot against his life and killed him in his own palace.

Ner´va, who had been a favorite of Nero, was the next emperor, but he was an old man and died after a reign of two years. He was succeeded by his adopted son, Trajan, who became emperor in 98 AD and reigned for 19 years.

Trajan was a good man and a brave soldier. At the time he became emperor, he was governor of one of the Roman territories or provinces in Germany along the banks of the Rhine and he resided at Colonia, now called Cologne.

Not long after his return to Rome, Trajan was engaged in a war with the King of Da´ci-a. This was the name of the country lying north of the Danube River. The greater part of it is now called Hungary. The Dacian king, whose name was De-ceb´a-lus, had frequently made raids into neighboring countries which belonged to Rome and had robbed and killed many of the people. Trajan resolved to punish Decebalus, and so he set out with a large army and marched into Dacia. The war continued three years, for the Dacians were brave and skillful fighters; but at last Decebalus was defeated in a great battle, and he had to come to Trajan and humbly beg for peace. He agreed to be a vassal of Rome, that is, to hold his kingdom subject to the control of the Roman emperors.

But in less than a year, Decebalus again attacked his Roman neighbors, and Trajan had again to march against him with an army. The Dacians were once more defeated in a great battle, and Decebalus, after failing in an attempt to escape, put an end to his own life. Dacia was then made a Roman province. During this year, Trajan built a remarkable bridge across the Danube. Before that time, bridges were built of wood, but in the bridge over the Danube, Trajan used stone for the piers, which were of great size. The bridge had 22 arches, and its ruins, which are still to be seen, show what a wonderful work it was.

When Trajan returned to Rome after his victory over Decebalus, he had a grand Triumph, and there were games and shows in his honor which lasted 120 days. It is told that during these celebrations 10,000 gladiators fought in the amphitheatre, and 11,000 wild animals were killed in the arena.

A marble column was erected in honor of Trajan's victories in Dacia. This monument is still standing in Rome. It is called Trajan's Column. Many scenes showing battles and other events in the Dacian war are engraved upon it from the base to the top.

Trajan also had wars in Asia, and he won many victories. He conquered Armenia and Mesopotamia and added them to the empire. But he did not live to return to Rome. He died in a town in Asia Minor, which, in honor of him, was afterward called Trajanopolis.

Margin notes:
96 AD Emperor Nerva

98 AD Emperor Trajan

101-106 AD Dacian Wars

The Romans were much grieved at the death of Trajan, for he had been a good emperor and had done much to benefit the people. He built fine roads and canals and bridges in Italy and the provinces. He greatly improved and beautified the Circus Maximus. This was the place in which the Romans had their horse races and chariot races. It was built in the hollow between the Palatine and Aventine hills, and it had seats for 250,000 people.

Trajan also made a forum in Rome, which was called, after his name, the Trajan Forum. In the center of this forum Trajan's Column was built, and around it were temples and libraries established by the good emperor. For a long time after Trajan's death, the people of Rome, whenever they got a new emperor, used to wish that he would be "as great as Augustus and as good as Trajan."

Some great writers lived in Rome in the time of Trajan. One of them was Plu'tarch, who wrote the famous book called *Plutarch's Lives*. This book, which you will perhaps someday read, contains an account of the lives of many great men of Greece and Rome. The historian Ta'ci-tus, the poet Ju've-nal, and Pliny the Younger, already mentioned, also lived in the time of Trajan.

Pliny the Younger was so called to distinguish him from his uncle, Pliny the Elder, who lived in the time of Nero and was the author of a celebrated work on natural history.

XIX – Ūndēvīcēsima Lectiō: Hadrian, Antoninus Pius, Verus, Marcus Aurelius (*Famous Men of Rome* XXVII.1)

The next emperor was Trajan's cousin Ha'dri-an. He was a good ruler and did a great deal to improve the city of Rome. He traveled through many parts of the empire to see that the people were justly governed and that the public officials were doing their duty. He visited Britain, which was then a Roman province, and he caused a strong wall to be built from sea to sea across the country near Scotland, to prevent the fierce tribes of the north from making raids upon the Roman settlements in the south. Some remains of this wall can still be seen.

117 AD
Emperor Hadrian

Hadrian also built a great tomb in Rome, which was called Hadrian's Mole. He and many other Roman emperors were buried in this tomb. It is now known as the Castle of St. Angelo.

When Hadrian died, a very good man named An-to-ni'nus was made emperor. He showed so much filial regard for Hadrian by building a temple in his honor, that he was called Antoninus Pi'us. Under the emperors who ruled before his time, the Christians were very cruelly treated. They were not allowed to have churches or places of worship, and numbers of them were put to death in the most shocking manner. Often Christians were thrown into the arena in the Amphitheatre and devoured by wild beasts.

138 AD
Emperor Antoninus

NB – The adjective *pius, -a, -um* means *loyal, faithful,* or *reverent.*

In those times the Christians of Rome held their religious meetings in passages dug under the city for burying places. These Catacombs, as they were called, extended under all the Seven Hills of Rome, and were hundreds of miles in length. Along both sides of the tunnels were openings, one above another, in which the dead were buried. Many of the Catacombs have been explored in recent times. They are among the sights which visitors to Rome are always eager to see.

Antoninus Pius was very friendly to the Christians. He gave orders that they should be allowed to practice their religion and that anyone who interfered with them should be punished.

161 AD
Co-emperors
Marcus Aurelius and
Lucius Verus

The next emperor of Rome was a very remarkable and a very good man. His name was Marcus Au-re′li-us. He governed the empire justly and well for nearly 20 years. He began to reign in the year 161 AD. He was the adopted son of the good emperor Antoninus. For some time before the death of Antoninus, he held a high office and helped to govern the empire.

As soon as he became emperor Aurelius invited a young man named Ve′rus to share the throne with him. Verus had also been adopted by Antoninus. The generous act of Aurelius surprised everybody. Never before was there a Roman emperor who wanted to give half of his power to another person, and it seemed strange to the people that Aurelius should do so. But Aurelius said:

"I think my adopted brother has a right to be emperor with me."

And so Verus was made emperor with Aurelius, and for the first time Rome was ruled by two emperors. Verus had great respect for Aurelius. He seldom attempted to do anything in matters of government without asking his advice. But he did not have much to do with public affairs. He cared very little about being emperor and generally spent his time amusing himself. He was not a good young man, and his conduct gave Aurelius a great deal of sorrow. After nine years, Verus died, and Aurelius was the sole ruler during the rest of his life. In his youth Aurelius studied under the best teachers in the empire and so had an excellent education. He always had an eager desire for knowledge and was constantly learning. Even in war times, when he was fighting in the field, he carried a library with him and could often be seen in his tent engaged in study. He was one of the most learned of the Roman emperors, and his intimate friends were scholars and authors.

169 AD
Emperor M. Aurelius

When a boy of only 12 years Aurelius joined the Sto′ics. These were followers of a famous wise man or philosopher of Greece called Ze′no. This man taught that the people should act according to reason and virtue and should keep an even temper and a brave heart under all circumstances. He also taught that men should show neither joy nor sorrow but control their feelings and passions and submit without complaint to what could not be prevented.

The followers of Zeno were called Stoics, from the Greek word *stoa*, which means a roofed colonnade or porch. It was in a roofed porch at Athens that Zeno taught his doctrine.

The Emperor Aurelius was one of the best and most earnest of the Stoics. He carefully trained himself to control his feelings at all times and to do his duty honestly and faithfully. The Romans never had a purer or nobler emperor or one more respected and beloved. His style of living was very simple. He had no idle courtiers at his house, and he kept only a few servants. He gave no costly dinners and entertainments. He spent much of his salary to improve the condition of the poor and to provide good schools for their children.

Aurelius used to walk through the streets of Rome in plain clothing, attended only by a favorite slave. He returned the greetings of the people with bows and pleasant smiles. Anyone could go to him and talk freely, and he encouraged the people to tell him about their troubles so that he might understand how to help them.

Aurelius gave the Senate a great deal of power which he thought it ought to have, and gave back to the people many rights and privileges which former emperors had taken away from them. No wonder the Romans loved him and called him a good man.

XX – Vīcēsima Lectiō: Marcus Aurelius (*Famous Men of Rome* XXVII.2-3)

But the reign of Aurelius was full of troubles. Early in his reign, the Tiber overflowed its banks, and the waters swept away a large portion of Rome, destroying many lives. After this, there were dreadful earthquakes, very destructive fires, and other serious misfortunes.

There were also many wars. There was a war with the Parthians, a brave, warlike nation in Asia, that destroyed a Roman army and then invaded Syria. Large armies were sent against them, and they were soon conquered and forced to pay homage to Aurelius.

The Parthian horsemen had a strange way of fighting. They were armed with bows and arrows and small spears called javelins and were mounted on very swift horses. They would make attacks on the rear lines of the Romans, and when the Romans turned to attack them, they would lash their horses and ride off as fast as the wind. And while their horses were going at full speed, they would turn in their saddles and cast their javelins or shoot their arrows with wonderfully accurate aim.

After the Parthian War, there were wars with a number of wild tribes living in the countries now called Austria and Hungary. The tribes there rebelled against their Roman governors, and Aurelius had years of hard fighting before he could subdue them. He was himself a remarkably brave and able general and gained many splendid victories. So at last he taught the barbarians to respect and obey the Romans who governed them.

Once, when Aurelius was fighting a tribe called the Qua´di, his soldiers were hemmed in by the enemy in a small rocky valley and suffered greatly from thirst. Suddenly the sky darkened, and rain fell in torrents. The thirsty soldiers collected the water in their helmets and drank it eagerly.

While the soldiers were drinking and their lines were in confusion, the Quadi suddenly attacked them in large numbers. The Romans would have been cut to pieces, but there came a violent hailstorm, with lightning and thunder, which stopped the battle. When the storm had ceased, the Romans, much refreshed by the rainfall, boldly fought the Quadi and won a great victory.

Some of the Romans believed that the sudden storm which relieved them so much was caused by the magical power of an African wizard who was with the army at the time. But there was also with the army a legion of soldiers, some 3,000 in number, who were Christians. The Christians had prayed for rain, and they believed that the rain came in answer to their prayers. They said that it was a miracle sent by God to prove the truth of Christianity.

Now Aurelius was a pagan. Some of his Christian soldiers had tried to convert him to their faith, but they had not succeeded. He lived and died a believer in the pagan gods and goddesses. After the strange storm, however, he seemed to have a greater respect for Christianity, and he named his Christian legion of soldiers the "Thundering Legion."

Once the commander of the Roman armies in Asia, a man named A-vi´di-us Cas´si-us, planned a rebellion against Aurelius. When everything was ready, Cassius declared himself emperor and started with his army to Rome to take possession of the city. Aurelius collected his troops and went to meet Cassius, but no meeting took place, for Cassius was killed by own soldiers, and the rebellion quickly came to an end.

Those who had aided Cassius were brought before Aurelius for punishment. But the emperor would not punish them.

"No, I will not punish them," he said. "I think I have governed the empire too faithfully and liberally to fear plots. I can afford to forgive traitors. Let all the friends of Cassius go free; they are to be pitied rather than punished."

Aurelius was always very industrious and would never waste any of his time. It was a part of his duty as emperor to attend the games and sports in the Colosseum and Circus. Aurelius cared nothing for such sports, and whenever he attended them, he always spent his time at some useful occupation while sitting in the splendid chair of state provided for him. Sometimes he would study his favorite books and make notes from them, and sometimes he would dictate letters and government orders to a secretary. Thousands of excited Romans around him would be shouting their delight at the sports in the ring, but Aurelius would go on calmly with the work he had in hand.

"I do not like to waste my time by sitting here doing nothing," he would say. "To waste time is one of the greatest of crimes."

And so by never allowing himself to be idle, Aurelius was able to do many useful things. He established good schools and hospitals in Rome and other cities of Italy. He introduced new trades so that the poor people could get a much better living than before.

Aurelius always gave great encouragement to art and literature. He welcomed authors and artists to Rome and was always their friend. He established libraries and halls of paintings and statuary. He himself wrote several books.

It is said that with all his virtue, the life of Aurelius was not a happy one. He had serious troubles at times in governing the empire, and the cares of a ruler often weighed heavily upon him. His wife, whom he dearly loved, behaved very badly and caused him much anxiety, and his only son was a very bad young man. So in the later years of his life, Aurelius always appeared melancholy. A smile was seldom seen upon his face. He died at the city now called Vienna, in Austria, in 180 AD.

XXI – Vīcēsima Prīma Lectiō: Diocletian (*Famous Men of Rome* XXVIII)

After the death of Marcus Aurelius in 180 AD, there was a long, dreadful period in Rome's history. For 100 years there was great confusion. Emperors came and went almost every year. They were very weak and selfish, and other government officials often refused to do what the emperors ordered (because the emperor who gave the order might not be emperor for very long).

180-285 AD
Military Anarchy

The army placed most of the emperors in power. If the emperor did anything that displeased the soldiers, or if the emperor could not give them enough money or land (which happened frequently), the army named a new emperor. For this reason, the period from 180-285 AD is often called the "Military Anarchy."

As you might expect, the empire did not prosper during the period when it was ruled by the army and weak emperors. Many of the governors, mayors, judges, tax collectors, and other government officials became quite corrupt and wouldn't do their jobs unless given large bribes.

The emperors and governors kept raising taxes, which became more and more difficult for ordinary people to pay. To make matters worse, prices for everything went up rapidly every year. Many of the old sturdy Roman middle class of farmers and tradesmen lost everything they had and became poor.

For the first time in a long while, it was no longer safe to travel from city to city in the Empire. Pirates attacked ships in the Mediterranean, and thieves robbed travelers on the roads between cities.

The wild German tribes in the north and the fierce Parthians in the east attacked more and more frequently and seized large parts of some Roman provinces.

Di′o Cas′si-us, a Roman historian who wrote during the Military Anarchy, described it like this:

"Our history and the affairs of the Romans descend from an age of gold to one of iron and rust."

Historia

285 AD
Emperor Diocletian

In 285 AD, the soldiers named yet another of their generals, Di-o-cle´ti-an, as emperor, but Diocletian was different from the many other men the soldiers had made emperor in the previous 100 years. He vowed not to let the soldiers remove him from office once he took over. He was descended from Roman nobility. He had been born in the Roman province of Illyria. He had been a successful general, leading his troops against invading tribes in the north. And he knew something about organizing and leading people.

293 AD
The Tetrarchy

NB – *Tetrarchy* is a Greek word that means "a government with four leaders."

Diocletian was convinced that the empire was too large for one man to govern, so he divided it into two parts, the Eastern Roman Empire, with a capital at Ni-co-me-di´a, which he ruled himself, and the Western Roman Empire, with its capital at Mi-lan´. He named another general, Max-i´mi-an, as co-emperor, to rule the Western Roman Empire. To prepare for a peaceful succession (not one dictated by the army), each co-emperor named a vice emperor. The co-emperors planned to resign eventually and to be succeeded by their vice emperors. The new emperors would then name new vice-emperors, thus solving the problem of succession and keeping the army from interfering.

The great armies of many legions were broken up into smaller units so that they would be less able to threaten the emperor. The commanders of these armies had been powerful generals. Diocletian hoped that with fewer men under the command of each general, the armies would no longer be able to remove the emperor if they did not like what he was doing.

Diocletian is best known for his reform and reorganization of the Roman government. Because he thought the Empire had become too large, he divided almost every province and every office between two officials so that each would be responsible for a smaller area. Diocletian hoped that this would result in better government with less corruption. With each new official having less power, he hoped that it would make them more willing to obey the emperor. In some cases the reforms worked, but in many cases, they did not. The new officials usually obeyed the emperor, but they were often just as corrupt as the old ones.

Finally, Diocletian created a new branch of the government called the inspectorate, which was supposed to inspect local officials and catch those who were stealing or taking bribes. Unfortunately, the inspectorate soon became corrupt itself, and the inspectors began using their powers to demand bribes from the officials they were supposed to be investigating.

303 AD
Christians persecuted

Diocletian is also remembered as the last emperor under whom there was widespread persecution of Christians. Diocletian himself did not seem to have ordered the persecution or to have had any special hatred for Christians. Many of his new officials, however, did not like Christians and thought their religion was somehow not Roman. In many provinces, Christians were imprisoned and sometimes executed because they would not worship the official Roman gods. If Diocletian was not responsible for ordering the persecution of Christians, it is also true that he did nothing to stop it.

Diocletian did try to do something about the economic hardships suffered by the Roman people, especially the farmers, tradesmen, and middle class. He was troubled by the yearly increases in the price of food, houses, land, and everything else. In 301 AD, he issued an Edict of Prices, which fixed uniform prices for nearly everything. No one was supposed to charge any more than the official price in the edict, but Diocletian found that one couldn't give orders to merchants and traders the same way he could to soldiers. Almost everybody ignored the edict, and prices continued to go up.

Diocletian managed to control the army and make some progress in stopping the corruption of government officials. However, the vice-emperors he and Maximian had named were not as capable as they were, and so his reforms did not endure. It seems as though Diocletian may have been right when he said, "The Empire is too large to be ruled by one man."

Diocletian's plan for selecting new emperors when the old emperor died or resigned sounded good, but it never really worked. It was a new idea with no tradition or authority behind it, and the vice-emperors were not as strong and able as Diocletian. In 305 AD, after ruling as co-emperors for 20 years, Diocletian and his co-emperor Maximian resigned and were succeeded by their vice-emperors. Within five years, there was a civil war between five men, each claiming the title of emperor. One of the men was Maximian's son. Another was a general named Constantine, who was in charge of the legions in Britain and Gaul.

305 AD
Abdication of Diocletian and Maximian

XXII – Vīcēsima Secunda Lectiō: Constantine (*Famous Men of Rome* XXIX.1)

For more than 100 years after the time of Marcus Aurelius, none of the Roman emperors did anything great or remarkable. They were nearly all bad men, and many of them were put to death for their evil deeds.

In the year 307 AD, the empire had been divided up through many quarrels and wars between generals of armies. Often an army would declare its commander an emperor, and he would set himself up as a ruler of part of the empire. So in this way there came at last to be six persons who claimed to be emperors.

None of these three emperors was in any way remarkable except the emperor Con´stan-tine, called Constantine the Great. He was the son of a former emperor named Con-stan´ti-us. When Constantius, died the army chose Constantine to be emperor. But he did not go to Rome to be crowned. He remained in Gaul, for he learned that five others had taken the title of emperor in different parts of the empire.

After a while, however, Constantine got messages from people in Rome, begging him to come and relieve them from the cruel government of Max-en´ti-us, who was acting as emperor there. But Constantine was

Historia

NB – Maxentius had tried to provoke a fight many times before, but Constantine did not respond. Then Maxentius sent an unsealed letter. The message (and its insult) public for anyone to read. Constantine could no longer overlook the insults and attacked.

312 AD
Battle of the Milvian Bridge

313 AD
The Edict of Milan permits Christians to worship openly.

a wise man. He thought it would not be good for him to leave Gaul and enter into a fight with Maxentius, so he paid no attention to the messages.

At last Maxentius openly insulted Constantine and threatened to kill him. Then Constantine was aroused to anger, so he gathered a great army of good soldiers and set out for Rome. He marched over the Alps and in a short time was fighting the army of Maxentius on the plains of Italy.

The first battle took place near Turin. The soldiers of Maxentius were clad in steel armor, but Constantine's men fought so fiercely that their armor was of little use to them, and they were speedily defeated. There was another battle at Verona, where Constantine was again the victor.

The third battle took place on the banks of the Tiber, near Rome. Maxentius led more soldiers than Constantine, but he was not a good general, so he was easily beaten. He himself was drowned while fleeing across the Tiber.

After the battle, Constantine entered Rome amidst the cheers of the people. A little while afterward, he told an interesting story to a Christian bishop named Eu-se′bi-us. He said that while he was marching through northern Italy, on the way to Rome, he was constantly thinking about the Christian religion. It had been spreading in every civilized country for more than two centuries, and Constantine thought that he too should become a Christian and no longer worship pagan gods. But he could not make up his mind to do so.

One day while Constantine was in front of his tent, with his officers and troops around him, there appeared in the heavens an enormous cross of fire. A little on one side of the cross were these words in the Greek language, "By this, conquer." The words are sometimes given in the Latin form, *In hōc signō vincēs*, the translation of which is, "Through this sign thou shalt conquer."

Constantine was astonished at the wonderful vision, and he gazed at it until it faded away. He could not understand what it meant and was greatly troubled. But that night, he dreamed that Christ appeared to him in robes of dazzling white, bearing a cross in His hands, and that He promised him victory over his enemies if he would make the cross his standard.

Constantine now declared himself a Christian and had a standard made in the form of a cross, with a banner attached to it bearing the initial letters of the name of Christ. This banner was called the *Lab′a-rum*, and it was afterward the standard of the Roman emperors.

When Constantine became a Christian himself, he began to take Christians into his favor. He made some of them high officers of the government; he built Christian churches and destroyed the pagan temples. He also made the Christian religion the religion of the empire, and he had the sign of a cross painted on the shield and banners of the Roman armies.

Thus after many, many years of terrible persecution, the Christians were befriended by the Roman emperor, and soon they became very powerful. Thousands of Romans were converted to Christianity, and the churches were crowded with worshippers.

XXIII – Vīcēsima Tertia Lectiō: Constantine (*Famous Men of Rome* XXIX.2)

Constantine also very much improved the Roman laws and system of government. He put a stop to the dishonest practices of the officers and established just methods of carrying on public affairs. He disbanded the famous Praetorian Guards, which had been an evil power in Rome for centuries. Many other reforms were carried out by Constantine, who seemed anxious to do what was right and what was for the best interests of the people.

Under Constantine's rule, therefore, Rome was happy and prosperous. To show their gratitude to him for his noble deeds, the people erected in his honor a grand marble arch in the central square of the city and inscribed on it:

"To the founder of our peace."

Four of the six emperors who had at one time ruled the empire were now dead. But in the east, there was one emperor named Li-ci′ni-us. Constantine attacked him, scattered his armies, and took away from him the greater part of his territory.

The two emperors then became friends, but after some time, they had a quarrel and went to war again. Each had a large army and a fleet of warships. Two great battles were fought, and Constantine won both. Licinius soon afterward died.

Now for the first time Constantine was sole emperor, and for more than 14 years he ruled the immense Roman Empire. He built the most magnificent palace Rome had ever seen. He surrounded himself with hundreds of courtiers and lived in great splendor.

324 AD
Emperor Constantine

After a time, Constantine resolved to move the capital of the Empire to a more central place than Rome. He selected Byzantium, an ancient city of Thrace, at the entrance to the Black Sea. To this city Constantine sent numbers of workmen to make alterations and improvements, and he changed its name to Constantinople, which means "City of Constantine." He spent vast sums of money erecting gorgeous buildings, making aqueducts, constructing streets and public squares, and doing the many many other things proper to be done in a capital of a great empire. The finest statues and other works of art that could be obtained in Greece, Italy, and the countries of Asia were brought to make Constantinople beautiful.

330 AD
Constantine made Byzantium capital of the empire but named it Constantinople.

When everything was ready, Constantine, with the officers of his government removed to Constantinople. He lived for about seven years afterward. There were no more wars, except for a slight conflict with a tribe called the Goths, and the people of the empire were contented and prosperous.

Historia

Constantine died in Constantinople at the age of 63, after a reign of nearly 31 years. He was the first Christian emperor of Rome.

XXIV – Vīcēsima Quarta Lectiō: The End of the Western Empire
(*Famous Men of Rome* XXX)

Most of the Roman emperors after Constantine were either cruel tyrants or very worthless persons, who spent their time in idle pleasure and neglected their duties to the people. A few, however, did some remarkable things and therefore deserve to be mentioned among the Famous Men.

One emperor, whose name was Ju'li-an, is called in history Julian the Apostate, because he gave up the Christian religion and tried to establish the worship of the pagan gods again in Rome. Julian also attempted to rebuild the Temple of Jerusalem which, as we have seen, was destroyed by Titus. There was a Christian prophecy that it would never be restored, and Julian thought of rebuilding it to prove the theory false.

*360 AD
Emperor Julian "the Apostate" attempted to revive pagan religion*

A story is told that as soon as the men began the work, balls of fire burst from the ground close by them, and they had to stop. They tried again and again, and the same thing happened, and at last they had to give up the work altogether.

Not long after he became emperor, Julian set out with a large army to conquer Persia. For a while he was very successful and defeated the Persian king in many battles. But one day he was shot in the breast by an arrow, and he died soon after. It is said that while he lay wounded, he cast a handful of his blood toward heaven, crying out, "Thou hast conquered, O Galilean." By Galilean he meant Christ, who is sometimes called the Galilean because He was brought up in Galilee.

*364 AD
Emperor Valentinian divided the Empire. He ruled the west and Valens ruled the east.*

Not long after the reign of Julian, there was an emperor named Val-en-tin'i-an. He made his brother Va'lens emperor of the eastern part of the empire while he himself ruled over the western part. And for many years afterward the empire was ruled in this way by two emperors, one called the Emperor of the East, and the other the Emperor of the West.

*392 AD
Emperor Theodosius*

On the death of Valentinian, his son Gra'ti-an became Emperor of the West, and a talented soldier named The-o-do'si-us became Emperor of the East on the death of Valens. Gratian was weak and unfit to rule, and he was killed by a Spaniard named Max'i-mus, who made himself Emperor of the West.

Theodosius fought Maximus and defeated him and afterward had him put to death. Then he made a son of Valentinian Emperor of the West as Valentinian II and gave him, as his advisor, a chief named Ar-bo-gas'tes. But Arbogastes was soon the real master of the Western Empire. One day Valentinian was found dead in his bed, and Arbogastes then made Eu-ge'ni-us, a teacher, the emperor. Theodosius, who well knew that Valentinian II had been murdered, made war on Eugenius and Arbogastes and defeated them, and until his death a few months afterward,

Historia

Theodosius was emperor of both east and west.

Theodosius had been a wise ruler, but he did one very bad thing. The people of Thes-sa-lo-ni´ca, a city of Macedonia, a country north of Greece, had killed their governor because he had put one of their favorite circus riders in prison. When Theodosius heard of this, he was very angry, and he gave orders that they should be invited to a show in the circus and there be put to death. This cruel order was carried out. The citizens of Thessalonica were invited to come one day to the circus to see a grand show. Thousands came, and as soon as they had taken their seats, a troop of soldiers under the command of one of Theodosius' generals entered the building and massacred them all without mercy. More than 6,000 men, women, and children died.

Theodosius resided in Milan, a city in northern Italy. A bishop named Am´brose, a good and holy man, also lived in Milan. When Ambrose learned of the massacres at Thessalonica, he was shocked. He severely reprimanded Theodosius and would not permit him to enter the doors of the church until he had done penance for the sin he had committed in so cruelly killing thousands of innocent people.

Theodosius' successor as Emperor of the West was his son Ho-no´ri-us, who reigned for 29 years. However, the actual ruler during all that time was a soldier named Sti´li-cho, the emperor's guardian. Honorius was a simpleton and had no desire or ability to attend to the affairs of the government.

395 AD
Emperor Honorius

The Goths and Vandals and other barbarous tribes from the north and east of Europe began to overrun the Western empire and to threaten Rome itself. Twice the great city was actually captured and plundered, the first time by the Goths under Al´ar-ic, and next by the Vandals under a bold warrior named Gen´ser-ic.

410 AD
Goths sack Rome.

455 AD
Vandals sack Rome

To defend the seat of their Empire against the attacks of its enemies, the Romans were obliged to withdraw their forces from several outlying provinces, including Britain, which was then left to its native inhabitants. For more than 50 years, a number of men who had little ability took part in ruling what was left of the once mighty Empire. One of these had the high-sounding name of Romulus Au-gus´tu-lus. He was the son of O-res´tes, the general of the army of Italy, and had been made emperor by his father. He was the last of the Western emperors.

476 AD
The last emperor,
Romulus Augustulus

Among the Italian soldiers there was a huge, half-savage man named O-do-ac´er, who belonged to a wild northern tribe. He was a favorite of the army because of his courage and strength. He resolved to be the ruler of Italy, so with the army supporting him, he put Orestes to death, took Romulus Augustulus prisoner, and forced him to give up the title of emperor. Then Odoacer became king of Italy in the year 476 AD.

By this time the world had nearly entered that period which is known as the Middle Ages, and many of the other countries which had been parts

476 AD
Fall of the Western Roman Empire

1453 AD
The Byzantine Empire fell with the capture of Constantinople.

NB – After the fall of the Ottoman Empire, Constantinople was renamed Istanbul in 1933.

of the Roman Empire were either ruling themselves or defending themselves against new invaders. Gaul was invaded and conquered by the German tribes called Franks, from whom the country subsequently got the name of France. Britain, abandoned by the Romans, was soon after conquered by other German tribes. And so at last the great Roman Empire had crumbled to pieces, and Rome, so long the Mistress of the World, as she was called, had fallen from her proud position of grandeur and power to that of a second- or third-rate city.

But the empire of the East continued to exist for centuries afterward, with Constantinople as its capital. It included many of the countries of Asia, Africa, and Eastern Europe which had formerly belonged to the undivided Empire. In course of time, the power of the Greeks, aided by the influences of the Greek division of the Church, became supreme at Constantinople, and so the Empire was also called the Greek Empire, and sometimes the Byzantine Empire, from the ancient name of the capital.

In the fourteenth century, the Turks, or Mohammedans, then very powerful in southwestern Asia, began to make inroads on the empire. They conquered and took possession of several of its provinces, and in 1453 they captured Constantinople, which has since been the capital of the Turkish, or Ottoman, Empire.

www.ingramcontent.com/pod-product-compliance
Lightning Source LLC
Chambersburg PA
CBHW080912170426
43201CB00017B/2299